Heidegger & the Political

"I find this book exceptional and unique in the way it poses and develops its topic within the 'setting' of Heidegger's thought. de Beistegui shows on the one hand that many efforts to derive Heidegger's nationalistic politics from his philosophical 'position' have been truncated and ill-conceived with regard to his philosophy and his problematic of the political. On the other hand, he shows the way in which Heidegger's thought fails from within in confrontation with fascism and the Holocaust. It is a subtle and finely conceived study. Most of the work on Heidegger and political questions remains on the outside of his thought and lacks both the understanding and nuance one finds in this book."

Charles Scott, *Pennsylvania State University*

Recent studies of Heidegger's involvement with National Socialism have often presented Heidegger's philosophy as a forerunner to his political involvement, his thought being read in search of pro-Nazi sentiment in order to explain his personal political involvement. This has occurred often to the detriment of the highly complex nature of Heidegger's relation to the political. *Heidegger & the Political* redresses this imbalance and is one of the first books to assess critically Heidegger's relation to politics and his conception of the political.

Miguel de Beistegui shows how we must question why the political is so often displaced in Heidegger's writings rather than read the political into Heidegger. Exploring Heidegger's ontology where politics takes place after a forgetting of *Being* and his wish to think a site more originary and primordial than politics, *Heidegger & the Political* considers what some of Heidegger's key motifs – his emphasis on lost origins, his discussions of Hölderlin's poetry, his writing on technology and the ancient Greek *polis* – may tell us about Heidegger's relation to the political. Miguel de Beistegui also engages with the very risks implicit in Heidegger's denial of the political and how this opens up the question of the risk of thinking itself.

Heidegger & the Political is essential reading for students of philosophy and politics and all those interested in the question of the political today.

Miguel de Beistegui is a Lecturer in Philosophy at the University of Warwick.

Thinking the Political

General editors:
Keith Ansell-Pearson, *University of Warwick*
Simon Critchley, *University of Essex*

Recent decades have seen the emergence of a distinct and challenging body of work by a number of Continental thinkers that has fundamentally altered the way in which philosophical questions are conceived and discussed. This work poses a major challenge to anyone wishing to define the essentially contestable concept of 'the political' and to think anew the political import and application of philosophy. How does recent thinking on time, history, language, humanity, alterity, desire, sexuality, gender and culture open up the possibility of thinking the political anew? What are the implications of such thinking for our understanding of and relation to the leading ideologies of the modern world, such as liberalism, socialism and Marxism? What are the political responsibilities of philosophy in the face of the new world (dis)order?

This new series is designed to present the work of the major Continental thinkers of our time, and the political debates their work has generated, to a wider audience in philosophy and in political, social and cultural theory. The aim is neither to dissolve the specificity of the 'philosophical' into the 'political' nor evade the challenge that 'the political' poses the 'philosophical'; rather, each volume in the series will try to show it is only in the relation between the two that the new possibilities of thought and politics can be activated.

Volumes already published in the series are:
• *Foucault & the Political* by Jon Simons
• *Derrida & the Political* by Richard Beardsworth
• *Nietzsche & the Political* by Daniel W. Conway

Heidegger & the Political

Dystopias

———

Miguel de Beistegui

London and New York

First published 1998
by Routledge
11 New Fetter Lane, London EC4P 4EE

Simultaneously published in the USA and Canada
by Routledge
29 West 35th Street, New York, NY 10001

Typeset in Sabon by Florencetype Ltd, Stoodleigh, Devon

Printed and bound in Great Britain by TJ International Ltd,
Padstow, Cornwall

British Library Cataloguing in Publication Data
A catalogue record for this book is available from the British Library

Library of Congress Cataloging in Publication Data
Beistegui, Miguel de
    Heidegger & the Political / Miguel de Beistegui.
    p. cm. – (Thinking the political.)
    Includes bibliographical references and index.
    1. Heidegger, Martin. 1889–1976–Political and social views.
    2. National socialism. I. Title. II. Series.
    B3279.H49B43 1997
    320'.092–dc21   96–48677

ISBN   0–415–13063–8 (hbk)
        0–415–13064–6 (pbk)

For John Sallis

"Prior to the question that alone always seems to be the most immediate and urgent, What is to be done? we must ponder this: *How must we think?* Thinking is indeed the proper acting insofar as to act means to comply with the essential unfolding of being."

Martin Heidegger, *Die Technik und die Kehre*

"It would be best to talk about a revolution of the locality of thinking [*der Ortschaft des Denkens*]. Rather than revolution, even, we would simply need to hear *displacement* [Ortsverlegung]."

Martin Heidegger, *Vier Seminare*

Contents

Preface

There will come a day, perhaps, when philosophers will no longer feel the need to write about Heidegger's politics. There will come a day when, everything said and done, every single aspect of Heidegger's life, every single detail of his work having come under the inquisitive and scrupulous gaze of those doctors with an eye for Heidegger-the-Nazi, the age of a freer and more fruitful relation to the Heideggerian heritage will finally emerge. In the meantime, everything happens as if the deluge of monographs devoted to a (more or less sincere) understanding of Heidegger's relation to Nazism and to politics were not about to come to an end. Given the popularity of the topic in academia, one might even wonder whether there is a better way of securing for oneself access to the temple of academic respectability than through writing a book with "Heidegger" and "politics" on the cover. This inflation is certainly largely due to the fact that, for too long, and under the influence of many "Heideggerians," most commentators remained remarkably silent on this issue. After this all too suspicious silence came the no less suspicious cacophony which today surrounds us, and in the midst of which the average reader finds himself or herself utterly bewildered, wanting to flee the Heideggerian premises at once, if not to sacrifice the *Gesamtausgabe* to the altar of Western good conscience.

Why, then, a further book on Heidegger's relation to National Socialism?

Is it to throw yet another stone at his *corpus*, another way to make sure that he will remain forever buried? Or is it to keep his memory alive, to bring yet another stone, yet another inscription to his mausoleum? Or is it a matter of yet a third? A matter of keeping the matter of thinking alive, simply by reading Heidegger? And why read, if not because Heidegger's text calls for thinking, provokes thinking, begs and cries out for thinking? So, in a way, yes, it will be a matter of salvaging Heidegger, his texts, that is, a matter of not letting the closure of thinking silently take place. Salvaging from what? From that simple equation which, willy-nilly, is slowly being accepted, an equation so simple and so convenient that it has become almost irresistible: Heidegger was a Nazi, Nazi from the start, Nazi till the end. To this equation, it is not a question of opposing a counter-proposition, the revisionist version of the first equation: Heidegger was not a Nazi, he never was. This, too, is impossible: the evidence is too massive, too brutal: devastating. Heidegger's involvement was, at least for a few months, total and unconditional.

Given the inflation in publications devoted to the question of Heidegger's politics, the reader will possibly wonder how this book differs from all the other books on that question and what, if any, original insights it might contain. As for the latter, only the reading of the analyses will tell. As for the former, that is for the specific approach that is privileged in this book, I have tried to outline it in the Introduction. When, as a doctoral student, I embarked on a project aimed at retrieving the political dimension and implications of Heidegger's thought in 1988, in the first after-shock of "l'affaire Heidegger" (which, at the time, was restricted to the French intellectual scene, Victor Farias' *Heidegger et le Nazisme*[1] having been accepted for publication only in France), I had little awareness of how central to the academic debate the topic would become. I was then convinced – as I am now – that the proper response to this question is not scandal-mongering, but philosophical. In that respect, my own research was inspired more by the work of those readers of the Heideggerian text who had always been attentive to its highly complex political dimension than by those who, for reasons that may vary, wished to categorize Heidegger as a Nazi thinker.[2]

Is it a coincidence if, in disappointing contradistinction to the philosophical nature of some of the work that originated in France and Germany, the majority of the Anglo-American response concerning Heidegger's relation to politics has kept itself safe from the questioning dimension of Heidegger's own thought?[3] The arguments and the stakes behind the idiosyncratic reception of the Heidegger affair in the United States would itself require a lengthy study, one that I am neither willing nor capable of carrying out here. Suffice it to say that this reception is largely dependent, amongst many other conditions, upon the place of the university in American intellectual life, the place of so-called Continental Philosophy within the discipline as a whole, the political situation (and its ethical and often religious overdetermination) of the United States, and the country's relation to the history of the twentieth century. In the end, the reception of the Heidegger "scandal" in the United States often reveals more about the situation of the country and of its intellectuals than it does about Heidegger's thought. Such is the reason why, ultimately, the overwhelming production that continues to come from the United States has only had a limited impact on the elaboration of this book.

The first element that convinced me to undertake this project, then, was the lack of personal satisfaction with respect to the literature produced in North America. To this purely personal impression was added the fact that, thanks to the generosity of its editors, this book is published in a series devoted to political philosophy: it therefore suggests that Heidegger's own thought, no matter how problematic, or even perhaps because of its very problematicity, deserves a place in a series that attempts to think and problematize the fate of the political in the twentieth century. The very series of which this book is only a moment should indicate that Heidegger's own thought and texts will be given the utmost seriousness. Finally, this book is the first of its kind to be published in the United Kingdom, often renowned for its hostility toward Contemporary European Philosophy, to say nothing of its opinion regarding thinkers who once held a card of the Nazi Party. To be the first of its kind does not make this book necessarily good. It only makes it overdue.

Acknowledgments

I owe my thanks to many people who, in varied ways, encouraged and assisted me with this book over the years. I wish to thank Simon Critchley and Keith Ansell Pearson for having asked me to write this book; John Sallis, Thomas Sheehan, Robert Bernasconi, Françoise Dastur, Michel Haar, Andrew Benjamin and Christine Battersby for their unfailing support; and John Protevi, Peter Poellner and Peter Osborne for their scholarly and critical advice. But most of all, I would like to express my deepest gratitude to Simon Sparks for his invaluable editorial and translating skills, his philosophical insights and ingeniosity, as well as his unlimited generosity.

List of Abbreviations

References to Heidegger's works will use the following abbreviations. All references will include a cross-reference to the English translation, where such exists. Thus (SZ 83/114) indicates that I am quoting from p. 83 of *Sein und Zeit*, a translation of which is found on p. 114 of the English edition listed in the *Sein und Zeit* entry found below. Occasionally, the translations are my own, though I have sometimes used (and frequently modified) existing translations.

I begin the listings with volumes from Heidegger's *Gesamtausgabe (Collected Works)*, all of which are published by Vittorio Klostermann, Frankfurt am Main. In the case of some books which are published in editions outside the *Gesamtausgabe* and in the *Gesamtausgabe* as well – especially *Sein und Zeit*, *Holzwege*, *Wegmarken*, *Vorträge und Aufsätze*, *Erläuterungen zu Hölderlins Dichtung*, and *Unterwegs zur Sprache* – I have cited the non-*Gesamtausgabe* editions, since they are more generally available.

Gesamtausgabe

GA 1   *Frühe Schriften*, ed. Friedrich-Wilhelm von Herrmann (1978).
GA 2   *Sein und Zeit*, ed. Friedrich-Wilhelm von Herrmann (1977).
GA 29/30 *Die Grundbegriffe der Metaphysik: Welt–Endlichkeit–Einsamkeit* (Winter Semester, 1929/30), ed. Friedrich-Wilhelm von Herrmann (1983).
GA 34   *Vom Wesen der Menschlichen Freiheit* (Winter Semester, 1931/2), ed. Herrmann Mörchen (1988).
GA 39   *Hölderlins Hymnen "Germanien" und "Der Rhein"* (Winter Semester, 1934/5), ed. Suzanne Ziegler (1980).
GA 43   *Nietzsche: der Wille zur Macht als Kunst* (Winter Semester, 1936/7), ed. Bernd Heimbüchel.

GA 45   *Grundfragen der Philosophie: Ausgewählte "Probleme" der "Logik"* (Winter Semester, 1937/8), ed. Friedrich-Wilhelm von Herrmann.

GA 48   *Nietzsche: Der europäische Nihilismus* (Second Freiburg Trimester, 1940), ed. Petra Jaeger (1986).

GA 50   (1) *Nietzsches Metaphysik;* (2) *Einleitung in die Philosophie. Denken und Dichten* (Winter Semester, 1941/2, announced, but not held), ed. Petra Jaeger (1990).

GA 51   *Grundbegriffe* (Summer Semester, 1941), ed. Petra Jaeger (1981).
         Basic Concepts, trans. Gary E. Aylesworth. Bloomington: Indiana University Press, 1993.

GA 52   *Hölderlins Hymne "Andenken"* (Winter Semester, 1941/2), ed. Curt Ochwadt (1982).

GA 53   *Hölderlins Hymne "Der Ister"* (Summer Semester, 1942), ed. Walter Biemel (1984).

GA 54   *Parmenides* (Winter Semester, 1942/3), ed. Manfred S. Frings (1982).
         Parmenides, trans. André Schuwer and Richard Rojcewicz. Bloomington: Indiana University Press, 1992.

GA 55   *Heraklit.* (1) *Der Anfang des abendlandischen Denkens (Heraklit)* (Summer Semester, 1943); (2) *Logik. Heraklits Lehre vom Logos* (Summer Semester, 1944), ed. Manfred S. Frings (1979).

GA 56/57 *Zur Bestimmung der Philosophie* (1) *Die Idee der Philosophie und das Weltanschauungsproblem* (War Emergency Semester, 1919); (2) *Phänomenologie und transzendentale Wertphilosophie* (Summer Semester, 1919), ed. Bernd Heimbüchel (1987).

GA 61   *Phänomenologische Interpretationen zu Aristoteles. Einführung in die phänomenologische Forschung* (Winter Semester, 1921/2), ed. Walter Bröcker and Kate Bröcker-Oltmanns (1985).

GA 63   *Ontologie. Hermeneutik der Faktizität* (Summer Semester, 1923), ed. Kate Bröcker-Oltmanns (1988).

GA 65   *Beiträge zur Philosophie (Vom Ereignis)*, ed. Friedrich-Wilhelm von Herrmann (1989).

Other Works by Heidegger

DR   *Das Rektorat 1933/34. Tatsachen und Gedanken*, ed. Hermann Heidegger. Frankfurt am Main: Vittorio Klostermann, 1983.
         'The Rectorate 1933/34: Facts and Thoughts," trans. Karsten Harries, in *Martin Heidegger and National Socialism, Questions and Answers*, ed. Günther Neske and Emil Kettering. New York: Paragon House, 1990.

EHD   *Erläuterungen zu Hölderlins Dichtung.* 5th edn. Frankfurt am Main: Vittorio Klostermann, 1981.
pp. 9–30: "Remembrance of the Poet," trans. Douglas Scott, in *Existence and Being*, ed. Werner Brock. Chicago: Henry Regnery Co., 1949.
pp. 31–45: "Hölderlin and the Essence of Poetry," trans. Douglas Scott, in *Existence and Being.*

EM   *Einführung in die Metaphysik.* Tübingen: Max Niemeyer Verlag, 1953.
An Introduction to Metaphysics, trans. Ralph Manheim. New Haven: Yale University Press, 1959.

G   *Gelassenheit.* 10th edn. Pfullingen: Günther Neske, 1992.
Discourse on Thinking, trans. John M. Anderson and E. Hans Freund. New York: Harper & Row, 1966.

Hw   *Holzwege.* 5th edn. Frankfurt am Main: Vittorio Klostermann, 1972.
pp. 7–68: "The Origin of the Work of Art," in *Poetry, Language, Thought*, trans. Albert Hofstadter. New York: Harper & Row, 1971.
pp. 248–95: "What are Poets For?" in *Poetry, Language, Thought.*

N I   *Nietzsche*, Volume One. 2nd edn. Pfullingen: Günther Neske, 1961.
pp. 1–220: *Nietzsche*, Vol. I, *The Will to Power as Art*, trans. David Farrell Krell. San Francisco: HarperCollins, 1991.
pp. 1–233: *Nietzsche*, Vol. II, *The Eternal Recurrence of the Same*, trans. David Farrell Krell. San Francisco: HarperCollins, 1991.
pp. 1–158: *Nietzsche*, Vol. III, *The Will to Power as Knowledge and as Metaphysics*, "The Will to Power as Knowledge," trans. Joan Stambaugh, David Farrell Krell and Frank A. Capuzzi. San Francisco: HarperCollins, 1991.

N II   *Nietzsche*, Volume Two. 2nd edn. Pfullingen: Günther Neske, 1961.
pp. 159–83: *Nietzsche*, Vol. III, *The Will to Power as Knowledge and as Metaphysics*, "The Eternal Recurrence of the Same and the Will to Power."
pp. 1–196: *Nietzsche*, Vol. IV, *Nihilism*, "European Nihilism", trans. Frank Capuzzi, ed. David Farrell Krell. San Francisco: HarperCollins, 1991.
pp. 185–250: *Nietzsche*, Vol. III, *The Will to Power as Knowledge and as Metaphysics*, "Nietzsche's Metaphysics."
pp. 197–250: *Nietzsche*, Vol. IV, *Nihilism*, "Nihilism as Determined by the History of Being."

SA   *Schellings Abhandlung über das Wesen der Menschlichen Freiheit (1809).* Tübingen: Max Niemeyer, 1971.

SDU   *Die Selbstbehauptung der deutschen Universität*, ed. Hermann Heidegger. Frankfurt am Main: Vittorio Klostermann, 1983.

'The Self-Assertion of the German University," trans. William S. Lewis, in *The Heidegger Controversy*, ed. Richard Wolin. Cambridge: The MIT Press, 1993.

Sp   "Nur noch ein Gott kann uns retten." *Spiegel*-Gespräch mit Martin Heidegger am 23 September, 1966. *Der Spiegel*, 26, 31 May 1976, pp. 193–219.

"Only a God Can Save Us: *Der Spiegel*'s Interview with Martin Heidegger," trans. Maria P. Alter and John D. Caputo, in *The Heidegger Controversy*.

SZ   *Sein und Zeit*. 16th edn. Tübingen: Max Niemeyer, 1986.

Being and Time, trans. John Macquarrie and Edward Robinson. New York: Harper & Row, 1962.

TK   *Die Technik und die Kehre*. Pfullingen: Günther Neske, 1962.

pp. 1–36: "The Question Concerning Technology," trans. William Lovitt, in *Martin Heidegger: Basic Writings*, ed. David Farrell Krell. New York: Harper & Row, 1977.

pp. 37–47: "The Turning," in *The Question Concerning Technology*, trans. William Lovitt. New York: Harper & Row, 1977.

US   *Unterwegs zur Sprache*. 3rd edn. Pfullingen: Günther Neske, 1965.

pp. 9–33: "Language," in *Poetry, Language, Thought*.

pp. 35–end: *On the Way to Language*, trans. Peter D. Hertz. New York: Harper & Row, 1971.

VA   *Vorträge und Aufsätze*. 2nd edn. Pfullingen: Günther Neske, 1967.

pp. 13–44: "The Question Concerning Technology," trans. William Lovitt, in *Basic Writings*.

pp. 71–99: "Overcoming Metaphysics," trans. Joan Stambaugh, in *The Heidegger Controversy*.

pp. 187–204: ". . . Poetically Man Dwells . . .," in *Poetry, Language, Thought*.

WHD   *Was Heisst Denken?* Tübingen: Max Niemeyer, 1954.

What is Called Thinking? trans. Fred D. Wieck and J. Glenn Gray. New York: Harper & Row, 1972.

Wm   *Wegmarken*. 2nd edn., revized and expanded. Frankfurt am Main: Vittorio Klostermann, 1967.

pp. 1–44: "Anmerkungen zu Karl Jaspers "Psychologie der Weltanschauung (1919/21)."

pp. 73–98: "On the Essence of Truth," trans. John Sallis, in *Basic Writings*.

pp. 103–21: "What is Metaphysics?" trans. David Farrell Krell, in *Basic Writings*.

pp. 145–94: "Letter on Humanism," trans. Frank A. Capuzzi, with J. Glenn Gray and David Farrell Krell, in *Basic Writings*.

pp. 213–53: *The Question of Being*, trans. Jean T. Wilde and William Kluback. New Haven: College and University Press, 1958.

Introduction

Behold the good and the just! Whom do they hate most? Him who smashes their tables of values,the breaker, the law-breaker – but he is the creator.

Friedrich Nietzsche, Thus Spoke Zarathustra

Heidegger is essentially a writer, and therefore also responsible for a writing that is compromised (this is even one of the measures of his political responsibility).

Maurice Blanchot, The Infinite Conversation

To think is to risk. Every thinking thought is a thought that risks the entirety of thinking. It is a thought that departs from thinking but that, at a decisive moment, ventures into the void, broaches an abyss and reveals the groundlessness of true thinking. Thinking is essentially transgressive, intrinsically dangerous. In this movement of transgression, thinking opens onto itself, in such a way that this opening will always exceed any closure and any totalizing. As an opening, thinking clears a space, yet a space that is not easily delineated: not an enclosed space, but a horizon, an unfolding. Thinking, in that respect, is a clearing, one that allows for a new light to shine. Whenever thinking happens, beings come to shine anew. This clearing, of course, also presupposes a certain relation to time, and particularly to the present, which is not left untouched by thinking. For thinking opens onto the future, which is the future of thinking. It is not as if some future awaited thinking, secured in some present to come. Rather, thinking is itself futural: it is a leap ahead, a transgression that opens onto another present, another historical possibility, a "dangerous perhaps" (Nietzsche). Is it time itself, then, that thinks in thinking? Thinking is at once closest to history, essentially historical, and farthest from history, beyond history. Thinking is essentially a departure: de-parting from the present, thinking ventures into the promise of another time, of another configuration. Its sacrificial gesture is its very venture, one that opens onto pure possibility. Its ground is its own ability to broach the actualization of its very nothingness. It is an ad-venture, that is, a venture that allows for a happening – an event. This is a solitary venture, even when it takes the form, as it always does, more or less explicitly, of a confrontation with the history of thinking. The history of thinking (of philosophy) is the history of that risk: from Plato to Descartes, from Heraclitus to Heidegger, thinking unfolds as a series of transgressions, each representing a moment of rupture. Every voice that speaks the risk, that opens the today onto the abyss of its own nothingness and pierces through the present is historical in the most concrete sense. Speaking the risk is risking to speak. For speech does not leave the world untouched. In the silent undoing of its word lies its danger. From the very start, speech upsets and undoes the order of things, leaving it adrift, yet open to the possibility of its own future. Every thinking thought is a thought for the future, but for the future that only such thought broaches. It is not *l'air du temps*, this cheap perfume, that thinking invites us to breathe; rather, it is the air of the open sea and of great heights, it is fresh air. He who has not felt the silence and the trembling at the origin of thinking cannot understand the stake of its history. He who has not experienced the risk inherent to thinking remains sealed from the essence of thinking. Were it not for those moments, necessarily rare, there would be no philosophy, but simply the ordering and the formalization of diffuse opinion.

To annul or reduce the risk of thinking is to put thinking at risk. Thinking is most at risk when not confronting the risk, when, holding back from the risk, it indulges in the stillness of the present and embraces the shared evidence of "facts." Thinking is most threatened when its threatening power is silenced. When things (beings as a whole) are in the hands of the *doxa*. When thinking is no longer in a position to oppose the dominating discourse, when the weight of the ortho-doxy is such that the voice of the para-dox can no longer speak, then history ceases to be. When speech is turned into doxology, when thinking falls under the yoke of the proper and the correct (the *orthos*), when philosophy puts on the robe of values and the crown of reason, then the risk is immense. Such a risk one cannot help but see at work today. Haunted by the destructive power of its ideologies and by the deceptive mystique of its narratives, the West has sunk into absolute fixation. Because it can no longer relate to the future in the way of a promise (there is no hope for hope), because it is not able to invent another concept of the future, another meaning of the promise, the future itself has become altogether impossible. The today is time thus suspended, time closed off from the very possibility of a future, awaiting its final undoing. Under the guise of thought, a state of facts is today condoned, the obvious is held for the true and the good, a status quo is all that is hoped for. Our epoch has become that of reaction and conservation, of good conscience and of moral order. Thinking itself has become suspicious, whenever it does not respond to the sole exigency of a vague and complacent thematization of opinion, or to the demands of performance.

The Heidegger "affair" can be perceived as the effect of such a historical situation. The stakes behind it are high: the nature, the task and the danger inherent to thinking are all at issue. Why, after all, is there such an affair? Why has the polemic come to focus on Heidegger? Why not on intellectuals such as Schmitt or Hartmann, or on ideologues such as Rosenberg and Bauemler? Why is the scandal not that of a whole generation of German intellectuals and academics, to which we should immediately add the names of certain European writers (Céline, Brasillach, Pound, Lewis) who were amongst the most zealous supporters of fascism? The uneasiness, the sense of embarrassment, deception and perhaps outrage that one feels in the case of Heidegger exceeds by far his mere academic and administrative responsibilities as well as the most despiteful of his actions: it is not only, perhaps not at all, as professor, or even as professor-rector that Heidegger bears a political responsibility. The scandal is not primarily biographical. And such is the reason why biographies, however faithful, correct and illuminating they may be, will never exhaust or even touch upon the heart of the matter. No, the responsibility and the uneasiness lie elsewhere: in the fact that Heidegger was a thinker, in the fact that thinking is what is at issue, from the start and throughout, even in the darkest hours of his political misadventure. The fault is that of thinking; the uneasiness and sense of loss involves the essence of writing. Not every academic is a writer, not every philosopher a thinker. If there is a Heidegger "scandal," it is essentially because we are confronted with a thinker, in the sense that I have tried to articulate, because his mistake, some wish to say his fault, which was immense, was not such *despite* his thought, but *because* of it. Does this mean, as Heidegger himself claimed, that the error was great because the thought behind it was great too? Whatever the objections and the reservations, whatever the power of the critique and the extent of the rejection – all of this is possible only because, from the very start, there is the recognition that what we are faced with is a moment of thinking, that Heidegger himself was a writer. If there is a fault, if there is an erring, it is because, from the start, there is thinking. Such is the fact we are forced to confront: how thinking can fall prey to the most absolute of all derelictions. This is what we are forced to accept: that thinking itself can embrace the event of this century which has become synonymous with the death of time and of thinking, and yet remain thought-provoking throughout, that this thinking calls for thinking in the very moment in which it lets its name be associated with the most disastrous episode in the history of the West. We must learn to live with this uneasiness, if we are to continue to read Heidegger. Such is perhaps the most difficult task: to accept that a thinker, or a writer, be great, ground-breaking, abyssal *and* Nazi, if not, at times, despicable.

Or is there, after all, something unquestioned and perhaps illegitimate in the assumption that thinking would open the way to the "right" choice? Is there not something wrong in seeing thinking as this practical guide through history? If thinking is, as we have suggested, essentially risky, if it consists in broaching possibilities so far unimaginable, must it not assume the potential consequences of such a risk? There is something suspicious in the way in which philosophers are asked to illuminate every single event, to project themselves into the future, not as creators, but as future-tellers, as if there still was something of a priest in them. We want our philosophers to be priests: we want them to guide us, to show us the way. But this is not what thinking is about. True, philosophy is, to a large extent, responsible for this opinion. It itself emerged out of priest-hood, it itself often has claims over the good, the beautiful, the true. But philosophy is not the guardian of a moral order, it is not there to justify and legitimize a given situation. This is not to exonerate philosophy, to wrest from its responsibility; its responsibility simply does not lie in making the right choices: it lies in questioning what right is, in not allowing the space of questioning to be closed off in the name of a right and a good or a true. Paradoxically, there was a bit of a priest in Heidegger, something of a *Führer*: there was a temptation to seal off the space of questioning, or the temptation to see the possibility of ques-tioning outside of the space of writing, in politics. If philosophy is the question, if the question takes place in writing, the answer is not in poli-tics. Or rather, there is, in philosophy, in writing, something that always exceeds the answer that is given in politics: in every question, there is something that cannot be captured in an answer. It is this impossibility to which philosophy must devote itself. Its place is writing. Not the insti-tution, not the nation or the people. The time has come to no longer ask of philosophers that they show the way, that they be spiritual leaders and illuminate the masses with their wisdom. The time has come to acknowl-edge the fragility of thinking, this perilous exercise.

What is most uncanny and most bewildering about Heidegger's case is that we cannot simply rank him amongst Nazi ideologues, and that his writings cannot simply be made to exemplify this ideology. There is almost always something in Heidegger that escapes such a possibility, not in such a way that it would save or preserve some part of pure thought, untouched and uncontaminated by the necessity of the political choice, but precisely in such a way that this line of flight, ever so thin, ever so tentative, signals the site of Heidegger's own choice. It is only by following such lines, that is, by tracing the contours and the detours of Heidegger's own thought, that we can be in a position to sketch the meaning and the stake of his relation to National Socialism. Heidegger's thought brings National

Socialism under a new light, the light of light, or of being. Any confrontation with Heidegger's relation to National Socialism is, at bottom, a confrontation with the thought of being. It is in the name of this question that Heidegger embraced the "movement," in the name of this same question that he subsequently engaged in a long and convoluted *Auseinandersetzung* with the movement, as well as with the historical situation and the future of the West. It is this very relation this book wishes to thematize.

The hypothesis that governs this book is that the relation in question begins to articulate itself long before 1933, in those sections of *Being and Time* devoted to the historicity of Dasein. This is not to say that, to use Adorno's own words, Heidegger's thought is "fascist in its most intimate components."[1] I would even wish to suggest that Heidegger's early thought is not fascistic at all, but that it puts a number of motifs into place that will be mobilized in 1933 in order to welcome and legitimate the coming into power of Nazism, thus exemplifying an ontic realisation of those ontological structures laid out in 1927. I wish to suggest also that this relation cannot be limited to the period of the rectorate, and that the majority of the lecture courses and the writings from 1934 to 1945, particularly those devoted to Nietzsche and Hölderlin, are an attempt to come to grips with the reality of National Socialism, with the historical and political situation of the West, as well as with the present and future of Germany in the age of global technology.

Yet before I begin to show in detail how and where this relation takes place, a few words regarding the title of this book might seem appropriate. Hopefully, they will throw some light on the project as a whole. On the one hand, everything happens as if Heidegger had very carefully avoided, if not politics itself, at least a philosophical discourse on the political. In other words, everything happens as if the political had been set aside by Heidegger, cast out onto the periphery of genuine thinking. This, I wish to suggest, is both correct and incorrect. Correct, in the sense that there is no apparent political concern in Heidegger's thought, and certainly no explicit political philosophy. Incorrect, however, insofar as the space of the political is not simply set aside by Heidegger, but taken up in a way that he believes to be more originary and historically more decisive. In other words, in place of the political, Heidegger thinks a number of originary *topoi* to which the political remains ultimately subordinated. This means that "in place of" should be understood in a twofold sense: indeed as "instead of," but precisely insofar as that which is thought instead of the political is actually thought in the very place or space occupied by the political, as the place that is proper to the political. This does not mean that the political is without a place, that there is no space for politics in thinking and in history. Rather, it means that the political is without a *proper* place: the space that it occupies is a site opened up by the unfolding of an event (not a "fact," but a certain configuration of presence) which surpasses it. The political only takes place and establishes itself on the basis of a sending which precedes and exceeds it at the same time. The political does indeed constitute a mode of organization of beings, a way in which words, things and actions come together, but this gathering happens on the basis of a historical-destinal constellation of which the political is only one crystallization. To bring the political back to its proper place is thus to wrest it from politics so as to give it back to history conceived in a destinal or aletheiological sense. To think the political is thus to place it anew in the very site of its essence, and to thus displace it. If Heidegger indeed replaces the space of politics by that of *topoi* that we shall have to identify, it is by way of an operation that consists in re-placing that which the space of politics would have covered up in the very movement of its happening and unfolding. As a result, the space of politics is dis-located, dis-placed, yet in such a way that this dis-placement simply consists in bringing the political back into the proximity of its own essence. It is this movement of dis-placement/re-placement that I wish to evoke in mobilizing the term "dystopia." In place of politics, in that very place that metaphysics has ascribed to politics, Heidegger has always thought something other and destinally more decisive, something more fundamentally attuned to the historical unfolding of Being. Even when, as in 1933–4, Heidegger succumbs to the most disastrous politics, he does so, paradoxically perhaps, in the name of something that will have from the start called into question the very legitimacy of politics as an autonomous and ultimately decisive space. In other words, his political action intersected with a concrete space across which it cut, thus revealing it in its originary dys-topia. Heidegger's politics consisted in wanting to bring politics back to the site of its own essence which, in itself, is nothing political. Thus, if there once was a coincidence and correspondence between the political space and the space of Heidegger's own thinking, and even his own praxis, that coincidence, though perfectly real, was nothing but an attempt at re-placing or re-situating politics. This does not excuse Heidegger. On the contrary, we must raise the question of what allowed for this re-placing of politics to take place in the very movement that has become synonymous with the all-pervasiveness and absolute presence of the political (with totalitarianism in the form of fascism). We must raise the question of the failure of thinking, of that thinking which constitutes one of the most decisive philosophical events of this century.

What about these *topoi* that would mark the place proper to the political? What can we say about them? First, that they are many, essentially plural. This is not due to some insufficiency or deficiency on the part of Heidegger's thought. Rather, it is the very nature of the *Sache* of thinking that is itself topical and multiple: being, or presence, takes place in different ways and at different times, and it is the task of the thinker to identify those points at which presence is gathered most intensely. The places (*Örter*) of being are to be understood as points of intensification, in which presence itself has for a time come to crystallize. As Heidegger himself suggests, the word *Ort* originally means the extremity of the knife edge where everything is brought together, concentrated.[2] Second, and as a direct consequence of the plural nature of the topology of being, if the site of the political is located outside of politics, in a *topos* that would be more originary, the origin itself serves neither as a ground nor as an absolute point of departure. For how grounding is a ground that is multiple? How absolute is an origin that is plural? The ineliminable plurality of the originary suggests that the political cannot simply be derived from a metaphysical *archè*, but that it must be thought on the basis of points of intensity in which presence bespeaks itself more essentially.[3] The first five chapters of this book aim to locate and thematize the various *topoi* which can be seen to dis- and re-place the political, those very *topoi* that think the place of politics more originarily. In every chapter, then, this place will undergo a certain dis-location, one that will enable us to consider the political under a new light. The political as such will, therefore, never be at the very forefront of the discussion, but always, structurally as it were, in its margins or at the periphery, if not in the background. This specific situation of the political suggests that it can never be confronted directly, that, if we are interested in thinking its ultimate stakes as well as its essence, then this can itself only be done by way of an essential and originary dis-placement in which the political as such comes to be revealed in its truth. Whether the *topos* be that of destiny, as in *Being and Time*, whether it be that of Science, of technology, of poetry or of the Greek *polis*, as in the 1930s and 40s, it is always a question of locating that which, in the very place of politics, speaks more originarily. As for the last chapter, which deals with the question concerning Heidegger's silence in the face of the Holocaust, silence there speaks not as the site in which the political would have withdrawn, not as the sole *topos* left intact in the face of horror, but as the painful echo that shatters Heidegger's own dystopian thought.

1
Bordering on Politics

Dasein's ways of behaviour, its capacities, powers, possibilities, and vicissitudes, have been studied with varying extent in philosophical psychology, in anthropology, ethics, "politics". ... But the question remains whether these interpretations of Dasein have been carried through with an originary existentiality comparable to whatever existentiell originarity they may have possessed.

Martin Heidegger, *Being and Time*

A certain suspicion will perhaps never cease to haunt Heidegger's 1927 *magnum opus*: given the philosopher's enthusiastic embracing of National Socialism in 1933, is it not appropriate to look at his earlier thought, and particularly at *Being and Time*, to find the grounds for his disastrous politics? This suspicion never ceased to taint the otherwise much praised achievement of 1927.[1] More recently, though, and increasingly, *Being and Time* finds itself under severe attack:[2] on the European continent as well as in the United States, Heidegger's text is being submitted to a political "reading" which serves to present his early project as the antechamber of his later massive support for the Third Reich. Rather than attempt to provide such a reading myself, and to trace the "fascistic" elements of Heidegger's thought in *Being and Time*, rather than try to decipher a hidden political project or philosophy behind the apparently purely descriptive ontology that this text carries out, I shall try to pay specific attention to some Heideggerian motifs so as to let them resonate within the context of Heidegger's later works, specifically those works that coincide with his political misadventure. I shall treat *Being and Time* not as the antechamber that opens onto the unrestricted glorification of Nazism, but as a resonance chamber, where motifs, certainly of a very specific kind, are introduced in a way that is not devoid of political vibrations.

The philosophical project of fundamental ontology that was to culminate in the publication of *Sein und Zeit* in 1927 was to remain devoid of worldviews, metaphysical constructions and anthropological considerations. As such, it was still indebted to the Husserlian demand that a phenomenon be isolated and decribed in its "essence," and that means regardless of the way in which it is ordinarily viewed by the "natural attitude." The project of fundamental ontology was to attend solely to the question of what it means to be; it was to address the question of the meaning of the being of all beings and sketch its *formal* structure. As *fundamental* ontology, it was also to be sharply distinguished from what Heidegger calls *regional* ontologies. Such ontologies are characterized by the fact that they investigate a specific kind of beings, or, to be more precise, that they question beings from a pre-given perspective. Thus, biology will have as its field of investigation those beings that can be understood on the basis of a certain concept of *bios* or life. Similarly, psychology will consider certain beings, most likely human beings, from the perspective of their *psychè*. Likewise, then, a politology will consider those beings to whom belong the character of living in a self-organized community or *polis* (or however one might decide to characterize such a community). All regional ontologies presuppose a certain concept of being (being in the sense of life, being in the sense of nature, being in the sense of *polis*, etc.) in order to operate and be successful. Yet none of them can address the concrete question of what it means to be for all beings. None of them are in a position to address the question of the meaning of the being of *all* beings, even though each and everyone of them presupposes it. This task can only be reserved for a fundamental ontology, which, for Heidegger, is philosophy proper. In the process of its fragmentation into various fields (ontology, theology, epistemology, psychology, ethics ...), philosophy became unable to think the ground common to all such sciences and thus became estranged from its own essence. Specifically, the fragmentation of philosophy into a manifold of sciences and the consequent absorption of philosophy into such sciences, or, to put it yet differently, the becoming-science of philosophy, is due to philosophy's failure to raise the question of the meaning of being adequately, that is, with time properly understood as its guiding thread. Part I of *Being and Time* was to raise such a question adequately: it was to show that "the central problematic of *all* ontology is rooted in the phenomenon of time, if rightly seen and rightly explained."[3]

From the perspective of the project of fundamental ontology, it is thus easy to understand that philosophy is not to exhibit views concerning the world, that it is not to engage in either judgments or evaluations. It is only to lay out the fundamental structures of being, and specifically of that being's being which Heidegger calls Dasein. Philosophy as fundamental ontology ought not be a platform for discussing political issues, for such issues presuppose a certain understanding of the *meaning* of the being of man, which the "analytic" of Dasein is precisely to examine. One needs to go even further and add that if the project of questioning the meaning of existence in its being is to be successful, then the overall unquestioned definition of man as "the political animal by nature"[4] is to be suspended, insofar as this definition is indeed such that it only serves to obstruct and impede the investigation by providing an all too hasty answer to a question inadequately raised. The word "politics" itself needs to be altogether avoided, for its use only leads to a concealment of the *Sache des Denkens* and to the constitution of an anthropology. Like names such as "man" (*anthropos*), "ethics" and "physics," "politics" would be in need of its own *Destruktion*.[5] Philosophy properly understood should *above all* not be political in its approach. Thus *Being and Time* would be *radically* apolitical: the very project of fundamental ontology would be such that it suspends the privilege traditionally granted to the "political nature" of "man."

And yet. As *fundamental* ontology, it is also to lay the ground for the possibility of any such discourse. In other words, it is not simply *indifferent* to politics, since it precedes it ontologically. The ontological precedence of philosophy over politics, the order of grounding that exists between the two, is perhaps what lies at the very source of Heidegger's essentially ambiguous and even duplicitous politics. Given the *grounding* priority of philosophy over politics that is established in the 1920s, and which will only be confirmed by the introduction of the *Seinsgeschichte* in the 1930s, the way in which the discourse on being will come to be construed will itself become decisive for the way in which Heidegger will analyze and react to the political situation of his time. To put it in yet another way: if we are even to begin to understand the motivations behind Heidegger's politically most decisive gestures, we shall have to constantly bear in mind the way in which Heidegger never ceased to subordinate the political to the metaphysical. It is the specific way in which the relation of precedence and priority of the philosophical over the political was established and reformulated, but never called into question, that made Heidegger's support for Nazism possible and, at once and simultaneously, irreducible to it. Because of his philosophical presuppositions, Heidegger was able to see in Nazism a historical mission that was never there (a historico-political response to the essence of our time as dominated by planetary technology) and was never able to see, even after the war, what was really there (a form of terror and a power of destruction hitherto unknown). Not only did Heidegger's political involvement constitute the "greatest stupidity" (*die grösste Dummheit*) of his life;[6] it also and primarily revealed a certain blindness of his thought.

To write the story of this blindness, then, is to follow Heidegger's own path of thinking. Specifically, it is to go along with the priority in the order of grounding that Heidegger establishes between the philosophical and the political. For if there is to be a *radical* critique of Heidegger, it can only stem from an engagement with the very philosophical presuppositions upon which his thought rests. The difficulty, then, lies in the necessity to reach the very heart of Heidegger's thinking without simply reinscribing the philosophical gesture that allowed for Heidegger's own political blindness. If this angle excludes the possibility of ultimately understanding Heidegger with Heidegger and on the basis of Heidegger, a possibility which can easily evolve into the temptation to understand Heidegger's Nazism, if not Nazism itself, on the basis of yet another rethinking of history as the history of being, it also refuses to envisage Heidegger's idiom and politics as the sole symptoms of a reactionary ideology (although it will occasionally point to what it takes to be irreducibly reactionary motifs). If the former approach serves to highlight the specificity of Heidegger's Nazism, it does so only at the cost of remaining caught within its metaphysical presuppositions; as for the latter approach, it simply misses the specificity of the Heidegger case, which ultimately cannot simply be viewed as a philosophical variation on an essentially ideological theme.

Thus the seeming apoliticality of the project of fundamental ontology cannot be settled so easily. If *Being and Time* is indeed apparently devoid of political views and opinions, if it displaces the terrain of the philosophical investigation in the direction of an analysis of being, or of the way in which things come to be present for Dasein on the basis of the way in which they are granted with meaning, it also acknowledges the essentially collective and historical dimension of human existence, prior to questions concerning the modes of organization of this being-in-common. In that respect, *Being and Time* can be said to be pre-political, where the "pre" would need to be thought as the onto-chronological condition of possibility of the political sphere in general. Yet the way in which the collective dimension of human existence comes to be determined in *Being and Time* provides a specific and decisive orientation towards a possible thematization of the political. Is it this very delimitation of the political on the basis of an ontological thematization of existence that allowed for Heidegger's own politics in the 1930s?[7] If so, where is such a delimitation most rigorously articulated?

Karl Löwith recalls how, as he and his former professor met for the last time in Rome in 1936, he suggested to Heidegger that his involvement with Nazism stemmed from the very essence of his philosophy; "Heidegger agreed with me without reservations and spelled out that his concept of 'historicity' was the basis for his political engagement."[8] One could immediately be surprised by Heidegger's response, insofar as another, perhaps more directly and obviously political place to look at in the overall economy of *Being and Time* would be the sections devoted to the being-with of Dasein. Yet the discussion concerning the historicity of Dasein (Division Two, Chapter V) is the one that provokes the most burning questions and calls for the most vigilant reading.

To treat the sections on historicity as marking an opening onto the political is of course a delicate operation, one which requires the greatest care.[9] Far from assuming that the historical is *de facto* translatable in political terms, I wish to explore the various ways in which such a translation is suggested by Heidegger. In other words, it is the very bordering of the historical on the political to which I want to pay particular attention. Specifically, I want to mark the passages and emphasize some of the motifs that seem to provoke an irreversible slippage into specific ways of framing the political.

The analysis of history (*Geschichte*) in *Being and Time* arises from a difficulty concerning the meaning of Dasein's being as care (*Sorge*). Having identified the being of Dasein as care in the last chapter of the preparatory analysis of Dasein, and having then revealed the meaning of care as temporality in section 65, Heidegger proceeds to show how temporality is necessarily presupposed in what Division One revealed as Dasein's foremost way of being, namely, everydayness. At the end of Division Two Chapter IV, ("Temporality and Everydayness"), then, one would expect the second division of the treatise to reach a conclusion. Was the goal of this division not precisely the "Interpretation of Dasein in terms of Temporality"? Was that goal not achieved in section 65, and made explicit in Chapter IV, through a renewed analysis of everydayness?

Without calling into question either the interpretation of Dasein's being as care or the meaning of this being as temporality (*Zeitlichkeit*), Heidegger points to a difficulty regarding such interpretation, only to reaffirm it and consolidate it in the end. The difficulty has to do with the way in which Dasein's temporality was made manifest, and specifically with an unquestioned orientation with respect to this temporality. Indeed, Dasein's possibility of being-a-whole, that is, the possibility of grasping Dasein in the totality of its being, was revealed in Dasein's basic way of being ahead of itself towards the end, or being-towards-death. Insofar as Dasein has the character of being-towards-the-end, the ontological question concerning its totality seems to have found its answer. But is death the *only* "end" Dasein is confronted with, or are there other ends besides death? What about "birth"? As the "beginning," is it not also the other end to which Dasein necessarily comports itself? Is the answer of Dasein's totality not contained in the life that stretches between birth and death?[10]

If the task becomes to analyze ontologically the meaning of the being of Dasein as the stretching between two ends, then the analysis does not cease to be temporal. On the contrary: temporality remains what needs to be thought, but in a way that now includes such stretching along as constitutive of Dasein's being. How are we to understand the birth/death connectedness? Is Heidegger simply suggesting that Dasein is contained within two boundaries, that it enters time, fills up a stretch of life with its experiences, and then steps out of time? Or are we to consider the "between" which relates birth to death in a more originary way, as an ontological-existential structure? Heidegger's answer is quite clear:

> Dasein stretches itself along [erstreckt sich selbst] in such a way that its own being is constituted in advance as a stretching along. The "between" which relates to birth and death already lies *in the being* of Dasein. ... Understood existentially, birth is not and never is something past in the sense of something no longer present-at-hand. ... Factical Dasein exists as born; and as born, it is already dying, in the sense of being-towards-death.
>
> (SZ 374/426)

As soon as Dasein is born, it is old enough to die, for it is, from the start, towards its own death. But Dasein is not born just once: understood existentially, birth is facticity, which means that Dasein never ceases to be thrown into the world and into a life which it has to live. As born, Dasein must *be*, and such being involves being-towards-death. Death and birth are connected in care: "As care, Dasein *is* the 'between'."[11]

The question of how such a "between" unfolds becomes all the more urgent. What must be Dasein's temporal constitution so as to allow for Dasein's stretching-along (*Erstreckung*)? This question is precisely the way into the question of history:

> The specific movement in which Dasein *is stretched along and stretches itself along* [*Die spezifische Bewegtheit* des erstreckten Sicherstreckens], we call its "*historical happening*" [Geschehen].[12] The question of Dasein's "connectedness" is the ontological problem of Dasein's historical happening. To lay bare the *structure of historical happening*, and the existential-temporal conditions of its possibility, signifies that one has achieved an ontological understanding of *historicity* [Geschichtlichkeit].
>
> (SZ 375/427)

What is now required from the analysis is an exposition of Dasein's historical character and of its temporal conditions of possibility. The historicity presupposed in Dasein's being as care is now to become an object of investigation. This is not to say that the analysis needs to become historiographic. Rather, it must remain ontological through and through, so as to reveal the basic phenomenon of History (*Geschichte*) necessarily presupposed in Dasein's ordinary understanding of history as well as in the science (*Historie*) that is based on this ordinary understanding.[13] In fact, the existential-ontological interpretation of History must be grasped in spite of and almost against the way Dasein's historical happening is ordinarily interpreted. Why does Dasein's ordinary historical self-interpretation serve to cover up its fundamental historicity? If Dasein's historicity is rooted in the meaning of care as ecstatic temporality (as the temporalizing of temporality) as established in section 65, then how is it that by "History" Dasein usually understands something that belongs to the past? Why is the dimension of the past privileged in the concept of History (a dimension which would reveal itself in ordinary language when, referring to a particular event, or a particular person, we say that "It/He/She is now *history*)? Why, if not because Dasein, proximally and for the most part, understands itself not from itself but from the beings present-at-hand in the world and in time? Why, if not because for Dasein time is a space within which things happen and pass, thereby allowing for a concept of "History" that serves to define that which has passed and which is no longer?

If the ordinary conception of History described in sections 73 and 75 is based on Dasein's fallen interpretation of its own historicity, does it not become necessary to outline *the basic constitution of historicity on the basis of Dasein's own way of being*? This is the task ascribed to section 74. Heidegger takes up the basic structure of care once again, but this time with a view to answering the question concerning Dasein's historicity: To what extent does the temporality revealed in authentic existence as anticipatory resoluteness imply an authentic historical happening of Dasein? It is in the wake of this question and in the analyses attached to it that a discreet yet decisive shift takes place.

Section 74 starts off by stating that if Dasein has a history, a personal history, as it were, it is because Dasein is essentially historical. Historicity belongs to the very being of Dasein: it is an existential. Hence the *problem* of history is primarily an ontological one. Since the being of Dasein as care is grounded in temporality, the nature of Dasein's historicity is to be sought in temporality itself as it has been so far interpreted. Needless to say, then, the question of the historical happening of Dasein is in perfect accord with the overall project of clarifying the meaning of Dasein's being as time. It is a further step in the elaboration of such meaning. Or, as Heidegger puts it, "the interpretation of Dasein's historicity will prove to be, at bottom, just a more concrete working out of temporality."[14]

In order to address the question of Dasein's *Geschehen*, Heidegger suggests that we look further into the constitution of temporality as it is revealed in the authentic phenomenon of anticipatory resoluteness. Let us simply mark, at this stage, that the phenomenon of history is derived, or rather "deduced" from Dasein's ability to face its own death as its ownmost and unsurpassable possibility, as its ability, in other words, to come face to face with itself, independently of the way in which it is with others. In anticipatory resoluteness, Dasein is made present to its own being in such a way that it can take it over wholly and be free for it. This means, in other words, that Dasein understands itself as this being which is both projected against its own end and thrown into a world. Through anticipatory resoluteness, the "there" or the situation of Dasein is made transparent to Dasein. The existential choices and attitudes that would follow from such a resolution are not discussed: they do not belong in the existential analysis. So, once again, Heidegger maintains his analysis at the fundamental ontological level, without introducing anthropological considerations that would illustrate the basic structure laid out. If an ethics or a politics could indeed unfold from this fundamental existential constitution, Heidegger refuses to consider it. Dasein's resoluteness remains empty. Such is the reason why, at least within the context of *Being and Time*, I cannot identify anticipatory resoluteness with the heroism and the decisionism with which it has often been charged, even though, of course, the very possibility of proper existence hinges on the decision with respect to the taking up of one's existence as finitude.

But do those possibilities of existence, which have been disclosed in anticipatory resoluteness, unfold from death itself, or are they already "there", along with Dasein's own facticity? Or does resoluteness reveal them in a new way? In other words: what is the relation between projection and thrownness, between those possibilities that are opened up on the basis of Dasein's authentic projecting against its own death and those possibilities in which Dasein seems to be thrown and which it inherits? Resoluteness, Heidegger says, is the way in which Dasein comes back to itself, back to its original site, from the dispersion in everydayness into which it is for the most part thrown. But such coming back, such gathering is not an inward movement whereby Dasein would cut itself off from the world so as to enjoy the peace and depth of some precious inner life. Rather, it is a movement of disclosure, of clearing, where Dasein authentically ek-sists its own essence, and this means confronts its own facticity. In coming back to itself, Dasein comes back to its own ecstatic yet finite essence. In the movement of such coming back, Dasein discloses authentic factical possibilities, those very possibilities that constitute its own heritage. In other words, it is only on the basis of the anticipation (the running ahead, *Vorlaufen*) of its own death that Dasein can hand down to itself the possibilities that were already his. Such, then, is the paradox of appropriation, of the becoming-proper (of what is inappropriately referred to as "authenticity"): Dasein gives itself to itself, it gives itself what from the start is its *own*, and yet what is its own is also its gift, its heritage, which, as resolute, it takes over. A more traditional way of putting it would be to say that Dasein is free for its own necessity, that its authentic freedom is revealed in its ability to take up and take over the necessity of its own condition. It should be of no surprise, then, that the word Heidegger uses to define such ability is the philosophem that traditionally (at least since German Idealism) serves to designate the unity of freedom and necessity, namely, "fate" (*Schicksal*):

> Once one has grasped the finitude of one's existence, it snatches one back from the endless multiplicity of possibilities which offer themselves as closest to one – those of comfortableness, shirking and taking things lightly – and brings Dasein into the simplicity of its *fate*.
>
> (SZ 384/435)

Snatched back from its fascination for a world that distracts it from its ownmost call, that dulls it and lulls it by way of a never ending production of cheap fantasies, petty satisfactions and good conscience, Dasein comes face to face with its own finitude, with its fatal outcome. It is no longer for Dasein a matter of indulging in the facile (*das Leichte*)[15] and of taking things lightly (*Leichtnehmen*). It is now a question of embracing the hard and the heavy, and of embracing it in the way in which one embraces a destiny. The time of the *fatum* and of its overpowering power (*übermächtige Macht*) has begun to strike. One halts, shrieks and finally wonders: must the opening to the essential finitude of existence take the form of an appeal to the hard and the heavy, *Härte und Schwere*? Cannot existence find its meaning in the affirmation of lightness – lightness of the feet and of spirit, of the mind and of destiny? Must we all embrace our fate like an armour? Is this our fate? Is this fate?

Fatal Dasein, historical Dasein. History is fate, fate is history. It is only insofar as Dasein makes this destiny its own that it can become free for its own history, that it regains its tradition and its inheritance. Thus fate designates Dasein's originary historical happening, which, Heidegger writes in a recapitulative sentence, "lies in proper resoluteness and in which Dasein hands itself down to itself, free for death, in a possibility which it has inherited and yet has chosen."[16] But for this stroke of fate, for this piercing arrow, Dasein would err anonymously amongst the no less anonymous mass of *schwärmende* busy bees.

It is at this point of the analysis, toward the middle of the section, that the text, head on, blind to the consequences, precipitates itself, all too hastily, all too carelessly, in the abyss of steely and *völkisch* rhetoric. It will never quite recover from this journey. Could this have been avoided? Every text – every great text, paradoxically – escapes at a decisive moment, trembles and opens onto an abyss. A text is never a master in its own house. The author is not a shepherd, and yet responsibility always befalls him. Such is the fate of the thinker: absolute responsibility. This is how the much discussed passage runs (I cite it in its entirety, so as then to unravel it):

But if fateful Dasein, as being-in-the-world, exists essentially in being-with-Others, its historical happening is a co-historical happening and is determinative for it as *communal fate* [*Geschick*]. This is how we designate the historical happening of a community [*Gemeinschaft*], of a people [or a nation: *Volk*]. Destiny is not something that puts itself together out of individual fates, any more than being-with-one-another can be conceived as the occurring together of several subjects. Our fates have already been guided in advance, in our being-with-one-another in the same world and in our resoluteness for definite possibilities. Only in communication [*Mitteilung*] and in struggle [*Kampf*] does the power [*Macht*] of destiny become free. Dasein's fateful destiny in and with its "generation" [*Generation*] goes to make up the full, proper historical happening of Dasein.

(SZ 384/436)

This passage calls for at least three remarks:
1. On the *Schicksal* and the *Geschick*. Until now, the historical character of Dasein, what Heidegger designates as the *Geschehen* of Dasein, referred to the destiny of Dasein, and that meant to Dasein's ability to run ahead of itself toward its own death so as to disclose the whole of its being to itself. As Heidegger suggested in the beginning of the analysis, "history" appears to be a concrete working out of Dasein's originary temporality. Now since Dasein is essentially in the world with others, as section 26 established, and since Dasein is essentially fateful or historical, it follows that Dasein's fate is a co-fate (*ein Geschick*) and its history is a co-history (a community).

Yet are things as straightforward as Heidegger seems to suggest? Given the way care has been described so far, how easy is it for it to incorporate Dasein's historicity, particularly as communal fate? What happens in the apparently innocent and legitimate move from Dasein's resoluteness as fate to the common resoluteness whereby a people would constitute itself as destiny? Despite what section 26 established, despite the fact that the world of Dasein is a world shared by others, it is not possible to simply equate Dasein's historicity with a common fate. Why? Because the world that is shared by others is the world of everydayness, the world of the One (*das Man*), that world from which Dasein was precisely to cut itself off if it ever were to grasp itself as a potentiality-for-being-a-whole.[17] For the most part, Heidegger insists, being-with-one-another is a *fallen* mode of being for Dasein. This means that in being with other entities that have Dasein's own way of being, Dasein is not according to its *own* being, but according to the being of this somewhat anonymous and yet all pervasive ("dictatorial," Heidegger says) identity referred to as "the One." In everyday life, one goes by the way things are ordinarily considered, thought, dealt with; one is actually *absorbed* in such things, in such a way that one becomes oblivious of the fact that one exists on the basis of one's own being and this means, ultimately, of one's own nullity. The world in which we are thrown, and in which we are thrown with other Daseins in the way of a concernful absorption, is not in a position to reveal Dasein to itself as this being which has its being to be and which understands its own being as what is most its own. In other words, everyday life, although an ontologically positive phenomenon, does not reveal Dasein in its singularity (in its "mineness"); it does not make Dasein transparent to itself in its totality. The phenomenon that is to attest Dasein's being-a-whole is not everydayness, not Dasein's daily engagement with others, but Dasein's coming face to face with its own finitude and transcendence. This happens not in everydayness, where Dasein is with others, but in anticipatory resoluteness. There, Dasein is revealed in its originary temporality. Dasein's historicality arises precisely out of Dasein's abstraction from its life with others, as an essential modification of that everyday life. "Authentic" temporality is not within-timeness; it is ecstatic temporality.

The question, then, holds: given that authentic temporality and historicality as such emerge from Dasein's breaking loose from the average possibilities of everydayness (with the only way in which Being-with-one-another was described) and facing its ownmost, unsurpassable possibility, how can we move from this solipsistic encounter with one's self to a shared temporality, a co-history? Does resoluteness open onto another way of being with others, a more authentic way, one that would be captured under the names "community" and "people"? Do such words imply a shared resoluteness, in which a given community would exist *qua* community or people? Does this mean that a people comes to be constituted as such only in the anticipation of death as its ownmost possibility? But how can a community face its own death as its ownmost possibility without imposing a peculiar kind of closure upon its singularities? From the moment at which death is inscribed as the horizon that constitutes the community as such, a certain logic is already under way: it is a logic of totalization and immanence, where the existing singularities are projected against a heroic-tragic understanding of their destiny. It is a logic of sacrifice, where the plurality of existences is absorbed into the immanence of the Same.[18]

Two remarks follow from this. First, if Heidegger's conception of destiny indeed presupposes the possibility of death as a horizon for the contitution of authentic commonality, one should point out the tension that such conception introduces with respect to the analysis of death explicitly developed in sections 46–53. For was death not then described as this unsurpassable possibility that is always mine and unappropriable? Did such a description not insist on the peculiar emptiness attached to the phenomenon of death as *possibility*? Second, it would seem that my reading is an attempt to retrieve the ontic signification of what is presented as a purely ontological exposition. To this objection, I would argue that, paradoxically, Heidegger's analysis is ontically overdetermined because it is ontologically too vague and too quick. To put it differently: because Heidegger's concept of history as destiny is not secured ontologically, it is from the start politically oriented. One finds further indication of Heidegger's slippage in this sentence from the passage quoted earlier: "Our fates have already been guided in advance, in our being-with-one-another in the same world and in our resoluteness for definite possibilities." As such, "being-with-one-another in the same world" does not suffice to conclude to the possibility of a living-together in the sense of a community. Once again: to-be-with-one-another in the same world is primarily to exist improperly. What is truly history-creating, then, is "our resoluteness for definite possibilities." More precisely: it is the "our" and the "we" underlying the resoluteness that accounts for the destinal possibility. But how is this "we" constituted? Who is/are "we"? On what basis can Heidegger use the first person plural in the context of the analysis of Dasein? Where does the unity of the "we" lie? Can we say "we" in the same way in which Dasein speaks its own singularity through the "I"? Can "we" be at once singular and plural? "We" are precisely insofar as we resolve ourselves for definite possibilities. Whatever such possibilities may be – and it is not the task of a fundamental ontology to reveal them – they must be rooted in anticipatory resoluteness. And this, once again, brings us to our aporia: what does resoluteness mean for the "we"? Must a community or a nation presuppose death as its own horizon so as to exist *qua* community? Must a community consist in the sharing of such a horizon? Must it perpetuate the model of the communion around a founding sacrifice? And does such a conception not bring Heidegger back to a very common understanding of death: death as that which binds, brings together, works, produces, death as negativity and *poiesis*?[19]

The being-with-Others that is destinal is a community, a people. The community or the people is itself defined in terms of its destinality. Yet destiny is not the sum of individual fates. It is itself something that we inherit, something that befalls us. Since Dasein is from the start with other Daseins, its individual fate is given to it as a common fate, which is tantamount to saying that there is no (purely) individual fate. The destiny of a community is freed through communication and struggle. This means that a people is not simply given, but is constituted through communication and struggle, through efforts and decisions, through a common resoluteness. What this suggests is that there is no such thing as a completely isolated Dasein, that each Dasein is always historically rooted, and that its choices are limited by its historical situation. On the other hand, it also suggests that destiny is not to be equated with some kind of *fatum* that descends upon Dasein from the skies, but that it stems from Dasein's ability to relate to its own historical situation and to other Daseins. There is a certain circularity in history, then, between singularity and commonality, between necessity and freedom, a circularity which Heidegger captures in the notion of *Geschick*.

2. On the *Gemeinschaft* and the *Volk*. One cannot emphasize enough the consequences linked to the identification of history with destiny, of *Geschichte* with *Geschick*. For it is this very identification that gives a political orientation to Heidegger's discussion. To be more specific, the very way in which Heidegger construes history predetermines a specific conception of the political. Indeed, on the basis of Heidegger's destinal interpretation of history, the political comes to be apprehended not as a free association of singularities bound by a contract based on a common interest ("destiny is not something that puts itself together out of individual fates"), but as a "community" (*Gemeinschaft*) or a "nation" (*Volk*). Not as a *Volksgemeinschaft*, though. At least not yet.[20] Why *Gemeinschaft* and *Volk*? Why not *Gesellschaft* and *Staat*? In early twentieth-century Germany, these words (*Gemeinschaft, Volk*) were freely circulating amongst the various academic disciplines and scientific milieus, and were always contrasted with what appeared as their complementary yet often antithetical modes of social organization, society (*Gesellschaft*) and State (*Staat*). Thus, one finds versions of this *Gemeinschaft–Gesellschaft* divide in the works of historians, sociologists and philosophers such as Spengler, Weber or Scheler.[21] Yet all such versions can be traced back to the publication in 1887 of Ferdinand Tönnies" *Gemeinschaft und Gesellschaft*,[22] the reprinting of which in 1912 was to become decisive for an entire generation of *Geisteswissenschaftler*. Although one could easily argue that Tönnies' work is in no way original, insofar as most of its fundamental concepts can be related to much of the tradition's basic motifs, and specifically to Aristotle's *Politics*, there nonetheless remains a distinctly German quality to the book, due to its Germanic rootedness and to what can only be interpreted as a certain romanticized vision of the country life and the Middle Ages, as well as a skepticism with regard to the effects of the industrial revolution on the traditional modes of social organization. These are the traits that will become the focus of concern for many at the turn of the century and that will eventually serve to feed a certain reactionary ideology, often referred to as the conservative revolution or the *völkisch* movement.

According to Tönnies, the history of the West is marked by the combination of two types of social organizations, communities and societies, each type being characterized by basic geographical, economic and sociological patterns. Communities are characterized by ties of blood, place and spirit: they are thus limited to the family and to the village, which is itself the place where agricultural labor, natural and customary law as well as the worship of deities are gathered. The community's economy is domestic and rural, its spiritual life is one of friendship and of religion. As an organic and natural unity, it is a *Volk* and the whole of its spiritual life is identified as *Kultur*. Unlike the *Gemeinschaft*, the *Gesellschaft* is an artificial association based on a free contract motivated by interest. As the platform for the development of commerce and trade, the society's place is the city. Its ties are purely practical and conventional, and its law is one of contracts. The life of the city is spiritless, since it is governed by public opinion, calculative thinking and essentially cosmopolitan newspapers. Where passion, sensuality, courage, genius, concord, piety and imagination prevail in the community, lust for pleasure and power, greed, self-interest, ambition, calculation, thirst for knowledge, vanity and spiritlessness prevail amongst societies. Where the community appears as a harmonious totality governed by need and mutual interest, the society appears as a mechanistic and anonymous organization (the state) governed by money, profit and exploitation. Since with the development of capitalism societies have tended to dislocate and dissolve traditional communities, Tönnies concludes his book in the following way: "In the course of history, the culture of the people (*die Kultur des Volkstums*) has given rise to the civilisation of the state (*die Zivilisation des Staatstums*)."[23] And we have now reached the point where "the entire culture has been transformed into a civilisation of state and *Gesellschaft*, and this transformation means the doom of culture itself if none of its scattered seeds remain alive and again bring forth the essence and idea of *Gemeinschaft*, thus secretly fostering a new culture amidst the decaying one."[24]

A further elaboration of Tönnies' fundamental thesis regarding the decay of culture in civilization can be found in Spengler's *Years of Decision* and in his famous *The Decline of the West*.[25] Even if not through a direct reading of Tönnies, Heidegger was exposed to the motifs of *Gemeinschaft*, *Volk* and *Kultur* at least through Spengler, whom he was reading and lecturing on in the 1920s.[26] The following passages must have caught Heidegger's attention:

[M]an is not only historyless before the birth of the culture, but again becomes so as soon as a civilisation has worked itself out fully to the definitive end which betokens the end of the living development of the culture and the exhaustion of the last potentialities of its significant existence.[27]

If the Early period is characterised by the birth of the city out of the country, and the Late by the battle between city and country, the period of civilisation is that of the victory of city over country, whereby it frees itself from the grip of the ground, but to its own ultimate ruin. Rootless, dead to the cosmic, irrevocably committed to stone and to intellectualism, it develops a form-language that reproduces every trait of its essence. ... Not now destiny, but causality, not now living direction, but extension rules.[28]

In a way that is very similar to what one finds in Tönnies, Spengler associates the word "civilisation" with the emergence of the cosmopolitan, the city, capitalism, profit, intellectualism (what one could call the avant-garde); "culture," on the other hand, serves to define traditional modes of life and social organization, characterized by a fundamental and natural relation to the soil, to one's family and one's rural and religious community.

I am not suggesting that Heidegger is directly borrowing his concepts of *Gemeinschaft* and *Volk* from Tönnies or Spengler. Neither am I suggesting that it is the use of such a vocabulary that made Heidegger's political involvement with Nazism possible (if only because of the fact that some of the most prominent figures of the conservative revolution, like Jünger or Spengler, refused to embrace National Socialism), although I would certainly see it as laying the ground for a positive interpretation of the "movement." Rather, I want to suggest that the very use of such words within the intellectual context of the time is not an incidental one, and that it is made as much in favour of a specific understanding of the nature of our being-in-common as it is made *against* the view – associated with liberalism, capitalism and intellectualism – which articulates the meaning of communal life in terms of *Gesellschaft* and *Staat*.[29] This unthought ideological background of Heidegger's will become easily mobilized in favor of an affirmation of the *Deutschtum*, the links of blood and soil, the essential sacrifice, and the necessity to reconcile science with the German Dasein.

Two testimonies regarding Heidegger's ideological attitude with respect to his time in the late 1920s seem to confirm the scarce indications revealed in *Being and Time*. This is the way Max Müller describes Heidegger in Freiburg in 1928/9:

Heidegger cultivated an entirely different style with his students than the other professors. We went on excursions together, hikes and ski trips. The relationship to national culture [*Volkstum*], to nature, and also to the youth movement were, of course, talked about then. The word national [*völkisch*] was very close to him. He did not connect it to any political party. His deep respect for the people [*Volk*] was also linked to certain academic prejudices, for example the absolute rejection of sociology and psychology as big-city and decadent ways of thinking.[30]

The second testimony is also collected in *Heidegger and National Socialism*, this time by Hans Jonas, a former student of Heidegger's:

> [Y]es, a certain "Blood-and-soil" point of view was always there: He [Heidegger] emphasised his Black Forest-ness a great deal; I mean his skiing and the ski cabin up in Todtnauberg. That was not only because he loved to ski and because he liked to be up in the mountains; it also had something to do with his ideological affirmation: one had to be close to nature, and so on. And certain remarks, also ones he sometimes made about the French, showed a sort of (how could I say it?) primitive nationalism.[31]

3. On the *Kampf*. Still in *Being and Time*, one reads the following: "In communication and in struggle the power of destiny first becomes free". History as the power of a common fate is thus freed through communication and through struggle: *in der Mitteilung und im Kampf*. One might be surprised to see "communication" (*Mitteilung*) and "struggle" (*Kampf*) so closely associated. We have established that the community or the people is defined in terms of a common resoluteness for definite possibilities. Resoluteness is the commonality of the community. Thus resoluteness is the object of both the communication and the struggle. What is communicated is precisely what is shared: it is communicated through its very sharing (*Teilung*).[32] And such sharing, far from being passive and strifeless, is the object of a struggle. How are we to interpret such struggle? What is the ontological validity of *Kampf*? This is a difficult question, since Heidegger does not feel compelled to justify the use of this word, which only appears four times in the whole of *Being and Time*,[33] and does not even provide us with a hermeneutical clue. We must be careful, then, not to jump to conclusions hastily (such as the ones privileging a political overdetermination of the Heideggerian text) nor to overinterpret the two pages where the word appears.

With or against whom or what does the struggling occur? Over what? And what is being communicated?

Does the struggle refer to the attitude of the fateful Dasein expressed a few lines before, that attitude of Dasein which consists in breaking loose from the offhandedness of everydayness when confronted with the finitude of existence and the anxiety attached to it? Is the struggle the struggle of existence itself, the struggle that is required sometimes to bear the weight of existence? Is authentic existence an effort, a struggle? To live one's life as fate, does that not imply a combat with oneself? This hypothesis seems to be confirmed by what Heidegger writes at the beginning of the paragraph immediately following the one I have just quoted from, which reveals Dasein's historical happening as a striking combination of power and abandonment, of might and distress:

> Fate [*Schicksal* – and not *Geschick*: we have now returned to the fate of the singular Dasein] is that powerless overpower [*die ohnmächtige ... Übermacht*] which puts itself in readiness for adversities [*Widrigkeiten*] – the power of projecting oneself upon one's own Being-indebted, and of doing so reticently, with readiness for anxiety.
>
> (SZ 385/436–7)

The struggle, then, seems to refer primarily to Dasein's confrontation with its own fate, the fate of ex-istence (of finitude, anxiety, conscience and guilt). It is an explicit characteristic of fate, but nothing at this point seems to suggest that it constitutes destiny in any substantial way.

A few lines down, the word *Kampf* occurs for a second time. This time, it is not introduced as a substantive, but as an adjective that suggests both an ongoing action and a relation to something else: the "following" (*Nachfolge*) and the "fidelity" (*Treue*). One follows and is faithful to someone or something that can be repeated, to what Heidegger himself calls a "hero" – be the hero Jesus Christ, Gengis Khan, Michael Jordan or Hitler. One pauses and shudders: Could Heidegger have really chosen the latter as *his* hero? Could Nazism have been *his* struggle? At this point, the struggle appears in a context that seems to be marked no longer by the individual fate alone, but by the way in which the resolute existence relates itself to its own time and history:

> The resoluteness which comes back to itself and hands itself down [*sich überliefernde*], then becomes the *repetition* of a possibility of existence that has come down to us. Repeating is handing down explicitly [*die Wiederholung ist die ausdrückliche Überlieferung*: the repetition is the explicit tradition] – that is to say, going back into the possibilities of the Dasein that has-been-there. The authentic repetition of a possibility of existence that has been – the possibility that Dasein may choose its hero [*seinen Helden*] – is grounded existentially in anticipatory resoluteness; for it is in resoluteness that one first chooses the choice which makes one free for the following and the fidelity that struggle [*die kämpfende Nachfolge und Treue*] for that which can be repeated.
>
> (SZ 385/437)

The context within which one finds the second occurrence of the word *Kampf* is marked by a rigorous delimitation of what a tradition is. The word "tradition" serves to translate Heidegger's *Überlieferung*. The latter use of the word tradition is to be sharply distinguished from the *Tradition* Heidegger refers to in section 6 of *Being and Time*.[34] There, the tradition ("metaphysics") is interpreted as a fallen mode of Dasein's understanding of its own being, and hence as an obstacle to the completion of the task ascribed to fundamental ontology. The tradition is thus to be appropriately deconstructed. The *Überlieferung* Heidegger introduces in section 74 is an attempt to retrieve a more original, a more positive and hence *constructive* comportment toward one's history. Tradition is to be understood on the basis of what Heidegger calls a *Wiederholung*, a *repetitio*. To repeat is to claim anew. But one can claim something anew only insofar as that thing has been handed down in such a way that it can be claimed. And such is the reason why the tradition is an *Über-lieferung*, a handing down. Such handing down is made possible only by Dasein's very historicity, that is, by the fact that Dasein *can* come back to something that has been (can have a past, a history, a heritage) only on the basis of its own projection, and that means on the basis of the existential-ontological phenomenon of anticipatory resoluteness. It is only on the basis of Dasein's own temporal self-projection, then, that something like a tradition is first made possible. Thus, a tradition, a past, a "history" in the ordinary sense is not something that is simply delivered over to Dasein, and to which Dasein simply belongs. Rather, the very possibility of a tradition is marked by a peculiar process of repetition, where Dasein, on the basis of its ownmost future, "goes back" to a given situation, but in such a way that this situation is thus disclosed, illuminated in a new way, revealed as a unique historical possibility, and not repeated in the sense of a simple reiteration or a passive obedience. In this process of repetition, it is not a question of remitting one's freedom and ability to decide to the hero one has chosen; it is not a question of abdicating one's own existence for the benefit of another existence in the name of a fidelity to some possibility contained in the past: "The repeating of that which is possible does not bring again something that is 'past'. ..."[35] Rather, Heidegger insists, the repetition is marked by a specific comportment toward the possibility of that existence, a comportment of *Erwiderung*. The translation of that word (*die Wiederholung* erwidert...) is anything but obvious. *Erwiderung* suggests a response, yet a response in which the strifely is inscribed; hence something like a retort or a rejoinder. The counter-ness or the opposition that belongs to the ad-versities which fate must face, and which Heidegger mentioned earlier,[36] is thus confirmed. Is it not in the context of such a strifely or adverse attitude of Dasein in the face of its own historical situation that we must understand the use Heidegger makes of the word *Kampf*?[37] Does the "struggle" not refer to Dasein's ability to engage with its own time in a strifely dialogue – a polemic, in the most literal sense[38] – on the basis of a confrontation with its ownmost future? Is it not on the basis of a thinking of time as ecstasis that Heidegger is in a position to throw a new light onto the nature of the historical present, a nature such that the "today" is neither the stake of a nostalgia for a time past nor the opening toward a bright future, but a constant back and forth, and indeed a struggle, between past and future, between an originary self-projection and a return to one's having-been, in which historical possibilities are disclosed and a heritage is made manifest?[39] Is this not what Heidegger means when he writes that:

> Repetition does not abandon itself to that which is past, nor does it aim at progress. In the instant [the instant is the moment of decision that follows from resoluteness] authentic existence is indifferent to both these alternatives.
>
> (SZ 386/438)

What better illustration of what is meant here by repetition do we have than Heidegger's own relation to the philosophical tradition, and to the need to repeat its long since forgotten question? Yet is the task of repeating the question of being a mere illustration of what a repetition can be, or is it the historical task, that is, the task in which the historical present is most at stake? One cannot but reflect Heidegger's discourse on repetition back onto the very project of fundamental ontology itself as it is exposed in section 1 of *Being and Time*, thereby giving it a more precise historical dimension. One recalls that section 1 states the "necessity for explicitly repeating the question of being," since "this question has *today* fallen into forgottenness."[40] The today, then, the historical today is marked by a peculiar forgottenness, the forgottenness concerning the question of being, which is now in need of its own repetition.[41] In other words, from the very start, the historical is attached to the power of the ontological; the present is defined in terms of a peculiar deficiency with respect to a question to which it has already responded without ever having raised it, a question, then, which it fails to address as a question. If it has become necessary to repeat the question that has fallen into oblivion, it is not with a view to returning to some sheltered origin, to a beginning that would have remained untouched by the process of forgottenness itself. It is not a question of returning to those days when the question was alive and well, as if one could simply leap back into the past and thus suspend the very unfolding of history. Nor is it, for that matter, a question of lamenting the loss of some ontological paradise. Rather, it is a matter of acknowledging the question as that question to which belongs the very covering up of the question, that question which is characterized by a peculiar self-effacement. The history of that self-effacement is the history of metaphysics, ontology proper. Such is the reason why the task in working out the question of being includes not only the interpretation of the meaning of being in general, but also the *Destruktion* or *Abbau* of the history of ontology. Since Heidegger's de(con)struction is often charged with being *anti*-metaphysical and *against* the tradition (while also found guilty of reactionary tendencies), and since such a stance as regards the tradition is often considered (at least by the representatives of that tradition) as the source of his political affiliation, it is of the utmost importance to clarify the stakes underlying the deconstructive project.[42]

Why does the very task of raising anew or repeating the question of being entail that peculiar relation to the history of philosophy which Heidegger describes as deconstructive? And why translate *Destruktion* as deconstruction, and not destruction? The repetition can be carried out only in and as the deconstruction of the history of ontology, since that history is precisely the *how* of the forgottenness of the question. The repetition, and that is the concrete working out of the question, cannot be carried out independently of the historical inquiry of the question, and that means the inquiry concerning its effacement. That history itself may be defined in terms of an effacement, an effacement that leaves traces, is precisely what is at the origin of the need for deconstruction. In that respect, deconstruction is to be understood as an exhibition of the process of self-effacement. It is a retrieval, a clearing of those traces which are inscribed in the movement of the self-effacement of the question. To destroy, then, does not mean to efface the traces, to scorch the philosophical earth so as to fertilize it anew. To destroy means to reveal the history of ontology as that field of traces, the tracing of which belongs to a peculiar effacement. Thus, it is a construction, insofar as it retrieves, reveals and isolates an otherwise confused phenomenon (in that respect, the project of fundamental ontology remains phenomenological throughout):

> In thus demonstrating the origin of our basic ontological concepts by an investigation in which their "birth certificate" is displayed, we have nothing to do with a vicious relativizing of ontological standpoints. But this destruction is just as far from having the *negative* sense of shaking off the ontological tradition. We must, on the contrary, stake out the positive possibilities of that tradition.
>
> (SZ 22/44)

Heidegger's relation to the tradition, to his own time and to the historical possibilities of Western metaphysics are thus far from simple. On the one hand, the tradition is viewed as the history of a *Verfallen*, a fall, yet a fall characterized as the forgottenness and the covering over of a question that is necessarily presupposed and to some extent already answered.[43] Later on, in a series of decisive moves that will need rigorous critical examination, Heidegger will identify the history of such forgottenness with the history of nihilism.[44] On the other hand, history itself, that is, historicity, is rooted in the existential phenomenon of ecstatic temporality, which is itself properly revealed in anticipatory resoluteness. Dasein's very historicity, then, lies in its futurity, in such a way that its past will be revealed to it according to the way in which it comports itself toward its own future. And the reason why, according to Heidegger, the tradition has been oblivious of its own ground is because, proximally and for the most part, it understands existence and what it means to be *improperly*, that is, in a way that does not correspond to Dasein's *proper* way of being; as something that is present-at-hand and in the world like other beings, and not as that being which comports itself toward the world and toward its own being ecstatically. The historical present, in turn, appears as a particular way of being open to one's ecstatic essence, as a particular way of responding to one's historicity: to respond inappropriately or improperly to one's historicity is still a way of being historical, it is still a mode of openness. Fallenness belongs to Dasein as an essential existential and historical possibility of Dasein. Such is the reason why, Heidegger writes, "we cannot do without a study of Dasein's improper historicity if our exposition of the ontological problem of history is to be adequate and complete."[45]

What conclusions can we draw from our reading of those sections of *Being and Time* devoted to the question of history? Can we draw a political profile on the basis of Heidegger's supposedly ontological analyses? Are we now in a position to affirm that such analyses made Heidegger's political engagement possible, or at least to what extent they did not make such an engagement impossible?

In the light of what we have revealed concerning the historical and ideological context surrounding the motifs of the *Gemeinschaft* and the *Volk*, can we conclude that Heidegger's use of such notions in the potentially most political moment of *Being and Time* reveals what sociologists would call a "social fantasy"? Are they indications of *völkisch* and conservative revolutionary tendencies? They at least reveal an affinity, a family resemblance with some of the most easily identifiable conservative revolutionary motifs. Furthermore, to think of history as destiny, community, people, struggle, decision, heroism is to prepare *philosophically* the terrain for an ulterior political decision. Yet in no way can this affinity be put forward as the sole or even major ground for Heidegger's subsequent affiliation with National Socialism. Also, if Heidegger's text seems to inscribe and integrate such reactionary motifs, it also and simultaneously exceeds them in a direction that is proper to Heidegger's very project and that cannot simply be identified as a version or a variation of an ideology. This logic of integration and excess, of the most easily identifiable reactionary tendencies and of their uncompromising transgression governs the entirety of Heidegger's political gesture, and accounts for the fact that, while glorifying the "inner truth and greatness" of Nazism till the very end, while dismissing Bolshevism and American capitalism as two forms of planetary nihilism, Heidegger will develop an immanent critique of Nazism that is nowhere to be found amongst any of the Nazi ideologues.

It is this essentially ambiguous logic, a logic that never allows us to quite corner Heidegger, that has made the Heidegger affair so passionate and virulent. Two examples should suffice to illustrate my point:

1. With respect to the motifs of the "people" and the "nation." Even though these notions are neither subordinated nor even explicitly attached to questions of blood, soil or race, they do seem to presuppose a certain *Deutschtum* based on the possibility of a common resolve for a common history, the origin of which is the phenomenon of death. It is death as the constitutive horizon of the people as such that allows for the heroic-tragic overtones of the passage. Yet, as we have tried to show, such a horizon can only be inscribed in the general economy of Heidegger's project at the cost of a tension with respect to the peculiarity of the analysis of death originally developed at the beginning of the second division. More specifically: what was gained in the first chapter of the second division, namely the status of death as a possibility (and not an actuality) that is in each case mine (and not the other's or the people's), seems to be called into question in the context of history. Death is suddenly folded back onto a very traditional (sacrificial and tragic) conception. The political risk attached to this conception is one of fusion and of communion, one, I should add, that will run through the entirety of Heidegger's writings.[46] The common resolve that is argued for thus itself falls short of the radicality of the analysis of Dasein in its finite and irreducible singularity, and serves to reintroduce a very traditional conception of the people, where the "we" underlying it is united in voluntarism and heroism. This fundamental aspect of historicity will become most manifest in the Rectoral Address.

2. With respect to the notion of repetition. This notion, and particularly the ecstatic conception of temporality that underlies it, seems to undercut two traditional political comportments: reactionism, on the one hand, which is nourished by a thinking of the return (to the origins, to God, to values, to meaning, etc.) and progessivism, on the other hand, whose conception of history as the arche-teleological unfolding of a meaningful process is rooted in a certain appropriation of the philosophy of the Enlightenment. While Heidegger's alleged anti-humanism, so often pointed out by his detractors as the source of his involvement with National Socialism and his inability to speak up against the final solution, can at first glance be derived from his suspicion regarding the universal values of the Enlightenment and the liberal tradition inherited from Rickert, Wildenband and Dilthey, his stand with respect to reactionary thinking seems to be overlooked. Although the reasons and the circumstances for Heidegger's political engagement remain to be addressed within this study, it seems already clear, on the basis of the nature of Dasein's temporality and historicity, that they cannot be derived from what could

be seen as a purely reactionary tendency of Heidegger's thought. In order to understand Heidegger's relation to history, to the past and to the tradition, it does not suffice to consider superficially his remarks concerning the necessity to deconstruct the history of ontology. It is of the utmost importance to understand that such a deconstruction is aimed at retrieving a constructive relation to the past, based on a proper (*eigentlich*) understanding of historicity as originary temporality. And if something is to account for Heidegger's involvement with National Socialism, it is certainly not some "nihilistic" dimension of Heidegger's thought, one that would be the direct consequence of the "deconstructive" project. Rather, it is to be found in the truly *positive* historical possibilities that Heidegger saw in the "movement." But the ontological possibility of such historical possibilities is itself laid out in *Being and Time*. For what the repetition allows for, if not calls for, is nothing other than a *revolution*. In that respect, the task of repeating the question concerning the meaning of being, and that also means the task of destroying the history of ontology, can be seen as political from the very start. The *Kampf* is that which opposes the giants on the question of being, and this struggle is historical and destinal from the start: it carries the political in its wake, it shapes it and molds it. Is it surprising, then, that Heidegger entered the political scene through the gates of the university, that the university was chosen by him as the place where the revolution was to take place? If a revolution is essentially a freeing, if it is a wresting that liberates, then is the repetition of the *Seinsfrage* not essentially revolutionary? Can one not go even further and say that every revolution, as a freeing, is essentially ontological? And is not Heidegger's failure with respect to National Socialism to have thought of it as a revolution, indeed as the revolution that was to allow for a freer relation with being and with the history it commands, when in fact it meant nothing but the sheer destruction of that history?[47] What is implicitly at work in the problematic of the repetition in *Being and Time* is perhaps best expressed and economically recaptured some ten years later, in the 1937/8 winter semester lecture course, at a time when Heidegger had become disenchanted with the actuality of Nazism:

> The future is the origin of history. What is most futural, however, is the great beginning, that which – withdrawing itself constantly – reaches back the farthest and at the same reaches forward the farthest. ... Therefore, in order to rescue the beginning, and consequently the future as well, from time to time the domination of the ordinary and all too ordinary must be broken. An upheaval is needed, in order that the extraordinary and the forward-reaching might be liberated and come to power. Revolution, the upheaval of what is habitual, is the genuine

relation to the beginning. The conservative, on the contrary, the preserving, adheres to and retains only what was begun in the wake of the beginning and what has come forth from it.

(GA 45, 40–41/38)

And Heidegger adds on the following page:

What is conservative remains bogged down in the historio-graphical; only what is revolutionary attains the depth of history. Revolution does not mean here mere subversion and destruction but an upheaval and recreating of the customary so that the beginning might be restructured. And because the original belongs to the beginning, the restructuring of the beginning is never the poor imitation of what was earlier; it is entirely other and nevertheless the same.

(GA 45, 41/39)

Is this not Heidegger's mistake, then: to have mistaken National Socialism for a revolution in the most genuine sense, to have misjudged it to the point of seeing it as an authentic relation to the power of the origin? To say that underlying Heidegger's thought, then, is a revolutionary concern, is not an overstatement. Yet Heidegger's definition of what a revolution is, and by that we mean the temporality and the ontology that underlies it, is irreducible to any traditional model, including the fascistic or other-wise conservative one. To be sure, Heidegger did at some point see in the reality of National Socialism the upheaval necessary to reawaken the German people and possibly the West as a whole to its forgotten and abandoned essence. Yet the peculiar logic of the repetition that calls for the revolution, the way in which this revolution is bound to the begin-ning of philosophy and to the task of thinking, exceeds and, to a lesser extent, even suspends the model into which too often Heidegger's thought is forced. What remains to be seen, then, is how this genuine mis-take actually took place, how, in other words, the truly revolutionary project of repetition was able not only to accommodate itself to National Socialism, but also to be one of its most enthusiastic supporters, if only for a certain period.

2
Archaic Politics

---

left.
Those of *leftist* ideas – along with their *rightist* opponents, who expect violence from the *left* – will probably be surprised to know that the word *left* is originally from AS. *lyft*, weak, worthless. It was applied to the hand that was usually the weaker, as opposed to the *right*: from AS. *riht*, *reht*, straight, just; cognate with L. *rectus*; cp royal.
royal.
The L. words for king, *rex*, *regis*, and kingly, *regalis*, came in OFr. to be *roi* and *roial*. From this through the Normans came Eng. *royal* and *royalty* . . . Directly from L. the same words were adopted in Eng. Thus we have *regal*; *regent*, present participle of the verb *regere*, *regens*, *regent-*, *regi*, *rectum*, to rule, to make straight – since what the king did was right – and a right line was a straight one: as in right angle – we have Eng. *rectitude*, *rector*, *rectify*, *erect*, etc.
Joseph T. Shipley, Dictionary of Word Origins

Where does this concern for the question come from? And the great dignity accorded to the question? To question is to seek, and to seek is to search radically, to go to the bottom, to sound, to work the bottom, and, finally, to uproot. This uprooting that holds onto the root is the work of the question. The work of time. Time seeks and tries itself in the dignity of the question.
Maurice Blanchot, The Infinite Conversation

If the *Destruktion* of the history of ontology that is called for in *Being and Time* is indeed not merely negative or destructive, but is aimed at freeing a more proper relation to one's historicity, and that means to one's present, should the university itself, as the institution that shelters this specific relation to the tradition, not fall under the yoke of Heidegger's deconstructive questioning? Should the university itself not become at once the object and the locus of a questioning aimed at redefining the nature of its relation to its historical situation? Must it not, from within itself, ask as to its relation with the various sciences it shelters, with its own history as well as with the public life of which it is a part? In the demand that science as a whole and philosophy in its relation to the fundamental forces of life and history be rethought, can these forces themselves simply remain untouched? What of the relation between science and power, between the institution and the State, between the university and the juridical, the social and the political? In the light of these questions and of that which, in modernity, links the institution to the material and ideological conditions of existence of the State,[1] should it come as a surprise that Heidegger came to enter the political scene through the gate of the university,[2] and came to see the possibility of the emergence of a new political configuration from out of a transformed conception of science?

Thus, to understand Heidegger's entrance onto the stage of politics, to throw any significant light on his action and his declarations as a prominent figure of the early stages of Nazi Germany would primarily amount to clarifying his conception of science, of the university as an institution and of its relation to the nation as a whole. This, in other words, suggests that the university marked for Heidegger not only the site or the *topos* of a political action and a program of national ambition, not only the locus of a concrete choice and of an involvement of an historically irreversible dimension – not only the site of a politics, then – but the place of a philosophical questioning regarding the nature and the task of the university in the twentieth century, as well as a meditation on the historical and political possibilities freed on the basis of such a questioning. And the rectoral address of 1933, the very address that marks Heidegger's official entry into the arena of politics, despite its steely rhetoric and its nationalistic sentimentality, continues to echo this questioning. Not only to the extent that the address raises crucial questions regarding the nature, the role and the organization of the university of the twentieth century, thus pursuing and decisively reorienting a German tradition that goes back to Kant's *The Conflict of the Faculties*,[3] but also because questioning itself comes to be seen as the most originally disclosive attitude and identified with philosophy as such. Not only is Heidegger's rectoral address not purely occasional; it is philosophical through and through. Yet its specificity lies in its political dimension, a dimension which is twofold. First, the address marks an attempt to gather the essence of the German nation as a whole by way of a repetition of the uniquely historical Greek beginning. Such a repetition, as our study of *Being and Time* has already demonstrated, is not the repetition of a moment that actually took place, but of an historical possibility held in reserve at the very dawn of history. The political that is at stake in the address, then, is entirely subordinated to the philosophical, to the possibility of its reawakening on the basis of a reflection concerning its essence. Second – and this is perhaps the most distinctive trait of the address – the meditation concerning the essence of the German nation takes the form of a politics, of a political programme and a political action in the most traditional sense. Thus, the address is not only a philosophical reflection on the essence of the political. It is also a call and an exhortation to the actualization of this essence. The address is this unique text in which Heidegger explicitly develops the necessity of a politics. The politics that is called for is one that we shall call "archaic." It is a politics of the beginning in its most rigorously philo-sophical sense, a politics that has little if anything to do with what was then happening under the name of National Socialism. Where does the confusion come from, then? Was Heidegger misled? No, for to say that Heidegger fell for the wrong politics would not suffice. Rather, in Heidegger's own positive commitment, it is a matter of acknowledging the ever so thin boundary separating the philosophical meditation on the historical *Wesen* of a people from a simple nationalism; it is a matter of marking the moment at which the concern for the affirmation of the distinctly German essence touches upon the filth of nationalism. More than ever, then, the boundary between the national, or between what Hölderlin calls *das Nationelle*[4] and nationalism, the boundary between that which relates to the essence of the nation, namely the *"heim"* (the *Heimat* and the *Heimweh*, the *Heimlichkeit* and the *Unheimlichkeit*, the *Heimkunft* and the *Heimischwerden*) and the forces of blood and earth, is one that is in need of rigorous delineation. This task is one that became central to Heidegger's own thinking after the period of the rectorate, and one that precisely consisted in a meditation on Hölderlin's *Dichtung* as that of the essence of the German nation. His political misadventure will indeed be followed by a double gesture. On the one hand, the national, particularly in its biologistic version, will be submitted to the strongest critique. Along with the deconstruction of biologism, politics itself, that is, the very possibility of an actualization of a historical possibility on the basis of a metaphysics of the subjectivistic will, will itself be called into question. Heidegger's withdrawal from politics will have been itself philo-sophical throughout: politics as we know it today must be given up on, because in it pervades a concept of the will that is most detrimental to the possibility of an authentic repetition of the Greek moment and of the freeing of a new beginning. On the other hand, Heidegger will not give up on the possibility of thinking the national altogether, and that is the essence of the German nation understood as a historical-destinal config-uration. It is in this context that Hölderlin, as the poet of the Germans, will become the central destinal figure for Heidegger. This thinking of the nationell will remain politically ambiguous, for if it will indeed be directed against Nazism understood as a metaphysics of race, it will also be directed equally against the liberal democracies and against the Soviet nation, for both will come to be seen as completed forms of the nihilistic will to domination. What is aimed by Heidegger's critique is the very form of the nation-state as the locus where this domination is carried to its extreme. What is at stake is the possibility of thinking the nationell independently of this nation-state. It is in this context that Heidegger's meditation on the Greek *polis* in the 1930s and 1940s should be understood.[5]

By focusing on the rectoral address, this chapter wishes to establish three things. First, the address is not simply an occasional text. This will be shown by way of a sketch of a double genesis that underlies the text, that is, in terms of both a German tradition of the question of the university and a personal itinerary that goes back to Heidegger's concern with life-philosophy in the early 1920s. Second, the address is through and through *philosophical*. The philosophical is here measured in terms of an ability to *question*. Third, the address is of course "political," but the political that is at stake here is entirely subordinated to the philosophical: the political is identified in terms of the *repetition* of an historical possibility, that of questioning.

An Old Question

The Address and the Tradition

Heidegger's rectoral address, as a philosophical text on the university, is in no way unique, although it is exemplary. It is indeed preceded by a long tradition that goes back to Kant's *The Conflict of the Faculties* and that runs through virtually the whole of German idealism, all the way to Nietzsche's "On the Future of our Teaching Institutions" (1872). The book of this extraordinary unity of concern remains to be written. It should be a long and detailed book, one that I cannot write here. I simply wish to focus on the political aspect of this legacy, and of the way in which it relates to Heidegger's address. Specifically, I want to suggest that the address marks the completion of this tradition. It is the last philosophical gesture aimed at retrieving the university from its fragmentation into a manifold of disconnected disciplines, the last gesture in which philosophy is seen and affirmed as the very essence and unity of the university as a whole. After Heidegger, and according to his own predictions, philosophy becomes, or rather is confirmed in its status as a science, or even a discipline. It no longer designates this science underlying all the other sciences and providing them with their unity, this concept of *Wissen* and *Wissenschaft*, irreducible to any given science. Philosophy falls prey to the technical organization of the field of knowledge, that field which is governed by the imperatives of the state, of production and of calculative thinking, in short, of what Heidegger calls "technology." The address will have marked an attempt to model the university after the project of fundamental ontology itself, where the various sciences, as positive sciences, would be brought back into the domain of their essence, back into fundamental ontology. The failure of the rectorate will have also marked the failure of a non-technical mode of organization of the university, of a university that would not entirely be submitted to the imperatives of the *Gestell* or the capital state. It will have marked yet a further turn of the screw in the subordination of the sphere of knowledge to that of planetary domination.

What becomes decisive with Kant, and will constantly be reaffirmed, is the way in which philosophy comes to be seen as the very unity and universality of the institution as a whole, as the very way in which the various sciences come to organize themselves into a totality. At a time when the sciences were beginning to develop themselves for themselves, and assert their domain over against that of philosophy traditionally defined as the all encompassing science, philosophy reacted by thinking of itself as the inner link and articulation of the various fields. The common observation, whether in Kant, in Schelling[6] or in Heidegger, is that the university as it currently exists is the locus of a random gathering of disciplines lacking inner articulation and unity. Schelling even speaks of "chaos." Philosophy is seen as the concept or the idea underlying the possibility of an institution that would not simply be an arbitrary collection of sciences, but a living totality. The university is associated with a living organism. Thus, for Kant, for example, the faculty of philosophy expresses the universality of the university by exposing the infinite act of a finite subject which totalizes and unifies the regional sciences, the decision that grants knowledge with its destination. What must preside over the university as a whole is the Idea of Reason, the teleological Idea of an infinite Progress. The Idea is the principle that serves to unify the university as a whole. It is the very principle underlying the possibility of a Uni-versity. This conception of the university as an institution of learning held together by the power of the Idea will remain central for German Idealism. Because of this power of unification, Philosophy comes to designate not one science amongst others, but science itself. Philosophy is *Wissenschaft* itself, the essence or the concept of science (see Schelling, First Lecture). All of the major texts written on the question of the German university between 1802 and 1816[7] are permeated by the spirit of that which Schelling calls the "uni-totality" (*die Ein- und Allheit*), or the spirit of the System (First Lecture). The very concept of Uni-versity suggests that the multiplicity turns itself toward a unity. In accordance with its concept, the university was to realise or actualize the systematic demand of philosophy, actualize the philosophical as such. As will later be made manifest, Heidegger does not suggest anything other than such a completion of the philosophical. The difference, however, is that "the rooting of the sciences in their essential ground" is the deed not of a systematic rationality, but of the essence understood as questioning. Yet the university is there to actualize and affirm this essence, this essence which is none other than philosophy itself.

Yet what makes the discussion of German Idealism particularly relevant is the historical context in which its texts were written, a context that has some bearing on the way in which the university comes to be thought in national terms. Until Kant, the university is thought from a cosmopolitan viewpoint. It is the university of universal reason, and not the German university in particular. Yet with the French invasion at the beginning of the nineteenth century the question of the university in Germany gains a distinctive national flavor. The peace of Tilsitt forces Prussia to abandon the duchy of Magdeburg, where its most important university was sheltered: the Royal University of Halle. The military disaster is therefore aggravated by a cultural threat. Consequently, the administrators of the University of Halle ask the Prussian kingdom for their transfer to the other side of the Elbe, in those territories that are not occupied by the French. Thus, the University of Berlin, conceived as early as 1802 by the minister Beyme for reasons of national prestige, becomes an intellectual necessity and a potent way of producing a response to the invader. The problematic of the German university becomes a speculative and systematic response to French imperialism. Once the decision to transfer the university is taken (4 September 1807), Beyme turns to various representatives of the cultural world to ask them how they would envisage reorganizing the university. Fichte writes a long and detailed initial report, that is followed by a critical response and a counter-project on the part of Schleiermacher. Von Humboldt, asked by Beyme to deliver his final report, decides in favor of Schleiermacher. The modern foundations of the German university were thus laid by the theses of Schleiermacher. It is that very university which was to be annihilated by the Nazis in 1933, that very university which Heidegger offers to revolutionize in the name of "the essence of the German university." The conception that presides over the University of Schleiermacher and von Humboldt is liberal and devoid of nationalistic considerations. Fichte's report, on the other hand, is authoritarian and many of Schelling's remarks suggest that only the Germans might be in a position to create the truly systematic and conceptual university. This division between two conceptions of the university is far from being absolute and stable (it is difficult to reduce Schelling's or Hegel's views to this alternative). Furthermore, the designations "liberal" and "authoritarian" should not be misleading. They do not primarily suggest a political divide, that is, a divide along political sensibilities, but primarily conflicting readings of Kant and different ways of appropriating the Kantian heritage. In other words, the debate is philosophical throughout, even if the stakes might be political.

As far as our problematic goes, and with respect to Fichte's "Deductive Plan" to begin with, it suffices to say that the university, organized along the lines of the family (section 37) and the living organism (section 56), seems to indicate obligations (section 20), various types of subordination between the various elements of the system (for example, in section 21, that of the "assistants" to the "professors"), hierarchies (between the various disciplines, between the various classes of students), even the possibility of a repression on the part of bodies of surveillance and justice (sections 36 and 37). In short, the "totality" that is spoken of here can easily appear as totalitarian. And one can only be struck by the similarities between the university proposed by Fichte and the inner organization of the Prussian State itself. Fichte himself actually thinks the university in the context of its inscription with a larger totality, that of the nation (section 9) and of the State (see the long note at the end of the first section). Schleiermacher's conception is quite different: he insists on the limited role of the State – limited to financial support – in order to guarantee the independence of the institution; on the necessity to provide the professors with the largest possible freedom, not to impose on them any set programs or methods, not to limit the competition between professors amongst a given area, and not to submit students to internal tribunals and obligations (obligations that Heidegger and the Nazis will seem so eager to reactivate). Most of all, perhaps, Schleiermacher insists on the independence of research (the academy) with respect to teaching (the university) and of teaching with respect to the practical goals of the other schools. These are the very principles one finds in Humboldt. "Autonomy" (*Selbständigkeit*) becomes the philosophem under which this liberal position comes to be gathered. As will become obvious in our reading of the address, Heidegger's *Selbstbehauptung* can be read as a reaction to and a counter-model for the "autonomy" as a guiding principle for the organization of the university. Whereas Schleiermacher's and Humboldt's system insists on the autonomy of the various sciences, Fichte wishes to see those sciences unified under a common, *philosophical* concept of science. Can we conclude that Heidegger's conception of science and of the university is Fichtean? As we shall see, many of its traits could be compared with those of Fichte's conception: the *Führerprinzip* itself, the bias against autonomy, the vision of a totality that would not be limited to the walls of the university, the vision of philosophy as a unifying ground. Yet the major difference will lie in the fact that, for Heidegger, the university of the German people does not lie in a principle of rationality and systematicity, but in a reawakening of and to its historical beginning. The question of the university is not played out in the production of its concept, but in our ability to bring it back into the site of its essence. "Science," then, is not thought of in terms of a unifying principle of an organic totality. Heidegger's conception of the university is not organic but archaic. Which does not mean that it has nothing to do with "life." On the contrary. But life is not *bios*, it is *factical* life.

Life and the University

From the standpoint of Heidegger's personal philosophical itinerary, one can wonder as to how the university could have *not* become a question for him. After all, Heidegger's life, life itself for Heidegger, particularly for the "young" Heidegger, was the university. In those years, in Freiburg and Marburg, when Heidegger was not yet a writer, the name "Heidegger" was associated only with a teacher. To be more specific, with a certain way of teaching, with a certain authority and yet a great passion in the voice, with a certain flame and a certain fire, that of life-philosophy, the flame of life itself. In his teaching, Heidegger upset the habits, lifted the image of the competent master addressing an interested audience, erased the image of the philosopher who, having ascended the ladder of professorship, irons philosophy out and reduces it to a simple discipline, a dusty and rusty corpus of texts and arguments. No, with Heidegger, philosophy was life itself! That is where it took its point of departure, that is what it wanted to illuminate. Life, Heidegger demonstrated, is not incompatible with philosophy, and the university is the place where this exhilarating encounter happens:

> I work in a concretely factical manner, from out of my "I am"
> – from out of my spiritual, indeed factical nexus of life, from
> out of that which thereby becomes accessible to me as the living
> experience in which I live. As existentiell, this facticity is no mere
> "factical Dasein"; Dasein is proper to existence, which means
> that I live it – such is the "I ought" that is never spoken of.
> With this *facticity of being-thus*, i.e., with the historiological,
> existence rages; but this means that I live the inner obligations
> of my facticity, and that I live them as radically as I understand
> them. Proper to this facticity of mine is – this I mention only in
> passing – my being a "Christian theo*logian*." In this there lies a
> definite concern for self, a definite radical scientific character –
> *in* this *facticity* there lies a rigorous objectivity; in it there lies
> the historical consciousness of "spiritual history" – and all this
> I am in the nexus of life of the *university*.
>   'Philosophising" is connected with the university only in a
> factically existentiell manner, which does not mean that I claim
> that there can be philosophy only *there*, but that philosophising,
> precisely on the basis of its fundamental existentiell meaning,
> finds a proper facticity of actualisation within the university, and
> thus also its boundaries and its limitations.

This does not exclude the possibility of a "great philosopher," a creative one, emerging from the universities; and it does not exclude the possibility that philosophising within the university will be nothing but *pseudo-science*, i.e., neither philosophy nor science. What university philosophy is in such a case can only be revealed by way of one's life.[8]

No doubt, then, there are some great philosophers that left the university or even never made it to the university. Similarly, the corridors, the lecture halls and the offices of the university are filled with individuals that can claim to be "philosophers" solely on the basis of the fact that they are philosophy professors. Yet unlike Nietzsche, or Kierkegaard, Heidegger never attempted to turn away from the institution, never turned it down. Even while objecting to its dominating mood, even while raging against its rigidity and scorning its dinosaurs, Heidegger always felt committed to the institution, as if at stake there were a responsibility, perhaps responsibility itself, in the form of an ability to respond to life by way of thought. To flee the university, Heidegger writes in 1921–2, is easy, all too easy.[9] It is a vain flight. One only wonders whether a few years later, in 1933, such a flight would have been as easy and as vain, or whether "science" would have been better served in exile. Yet it is precisely then that Heidegger decided not only to stay, but to become concretely involved in the "revolution." That move was by no means opportunistic. It was through and through philosophical, and thence comes its profoundly disturbing character. But in the 1920s, for the young Heidegger, as well as for an entire generation of students who attended his courses, the university was where it was all happening. It was not – not yet – the politicized university, but, as Krell puts it, the university of life.[10] As early as 1919, in the "War-Emergency Semester" that lasted from January 25 till April 16, Heidegger opened his lecture with a "Preliminary Observation" on "Science and University Reform." There, postponing any discussion regarding university reform – a postponement that will end with the rectoral address and with the call for a total *Gleichschaltung* of the German universities, on the basis of the fact that "we are not mature enough today to achieve *genuine* reforms in the university sphere",[11] Heidegger insists that the renewal of the university can take place only if scientific research is wrested from worldviews and redirected toward the essential and primordial phenomenon of life understood not in the biological sense but in the factical or existential sense, and that is with the meaning of the being of human existence as the ultimate goal of the investigation. In his 1921/2 lecture course Heidegger insists even further on this essential connection between the university and factical life.[12] The university is even to serve as an access-situation (*Zugangssituation*) to the principal definition of philosophy:

If there is to be philosophising, here and now, then it can determine itself only in the direction of the factical nexus of life,
which we designate by the term university.

(GA 61, 64)

Yet in the same lecture course Heidegger is already aware of a fundamental difficulty, a difficulty which is reformulated in the 1929 address
to the faculty of the university of Freiburg and confronted most explicitly in the 1933 rectoral address. This difficulty has to do with what might
be identified as an essentially historical nature of the university, a nature
such that the philosophising that might take place within it will always
be determined by the tradition underlying and supporting the institution.
Does philosophy derive its possibility from the university as the institu-
titon that shelters the tradition (is philosophy university-philosophy?), or
does the university itself presuppose philosophy as a concrete mode of
relation to factical life? These questions presuppose that we first question
the university with respect to its being-structure, with respect to what
tradition and history mean for it. And since the university is a nexus of
life, the question of its historical character can itself be addressed only
on the basis of a concrete analysis of the historicity of factical life.[13]

From 1919 to 1933, Heidegger, in several occasions and sometimes at
length, always in lecture courses and public addresses, came to formulate
some illuminating remarks on the nature, the task and the future of the
university as the locus in which a certain conception of science comes to
be determined. In his inaugural lecture to the Freiburg University faculties on July 24, 1929,[14] Heidegger identified the university as a community
of researchers, teachers and students, whose very existence (*Dasein*) is
determined by science (*Wissenschaft*). And already in 1929, Heidegger
diagnosed in the university a certain distance from and indifference to
its essence:

The scientific fields are quite diverse. The way they treat their
objects of inquiry differ fundamentally. Today only the technical
organization of universities and faculties consolidates this
burgeoning multiplicity of disciplines; the practical establishment
of goals by each discipline provides the only meaningful source
of unity. Nonetheless, the rootedness of the sciences in their
essential ground has atrophied.

(Wm 104/96)

Uprooted, cut off from their own ground, the sciences are now moribund
disciplines artificially kept alive and held together by way of a purely
technical organization. But what is this ground that is today forgotten?
Science. Although the 1929 lecture gives some indication of what Heidegger

understands by science, it is really in the 1933 address that this concept comes to be developed explicitly. Both in terms of the question of the university in its relation to the historical Dasein and of the concept of science, the rectoral address constitutes an extension of "What is Metaphysics?" It is really in that address that we find Heidegger's previous remarks most explicitly and most economically captured. They, perhaps more than anything else, can help us decipher the political magnitude of Heidegger's position. As for the "facts" surrounding the period of the rectorate, they are now well established. The circumstances of Professor Heidegger's appointment as the Rector of the University of Freiburg in April 1933, the detail of his action, his declarations and his relation with his colleagues as well as with the Nazi officials during the period of the rectorate are carefully recounted in Hugo Ott's biography of Heidegger, to which we can only refer.[15] Ott's book reveals the magnitude of Heidegger's involvement, the depth of his faith in Hitler, the enthusiasm for the heroic and sacrificial pathos of Nazism, the grand and somewhat comical *mise-en-scène* of his adherence to the NSDAP on 1 May 1933, his personal telegram to Hitler calling for the *Gleichschaltung* of the Association of German Universities and his attachment to the *Führerprinzip*, his disgraceful political speeches in full support of the most radical aspects of Nazi politics, to say nothing of the indifference manifested over the sad fate of Husserl, of the sinister report written on Eduard Baumgarten and sent to the association of the Nazi professors of Göttingen, or, last but not least, of the no less ignominious report concerning Hermann Staudinger, the chemistry engineer of international reputation who had made public his anti-nationalist convictions during World War I. But most perplexing perhaps is the evidence contradicting Heidegger's post-war version of his own political activities as a rector and his attitude toward the regime after 1934: starting in 1945, Heidegger carefully and consistently minimized his political responsibility during the period of the rectorate, truncated the circumstances of his resignation, and falsified the nature of his relation to the "movement" after 1934. Once again: the "facts" can hardly be disputed. The texts remain to be confronted.

Finis Universitatum?[16]

The rectoral address, entirely dominated by the question concerning the task, the essence and the organization of the German university, envisages this question from the perspective of its "self-assertion" (*Selbstbehauptung*). By self-assertion, Heidegger understands the *will* to the *essence* of the university. Why is the affirmation of the essence of the university tied into the philosophem of the will? Is affirmation necessarily voluntaristic? What does this essence of the university consist in? And what is the essence of the specifically German university? Can the task of the "German" university be formulated on the basis of the essence of the university, in which case the Germanness of that university would certainly not be its most decisive aspect, or must the university be thought on the basis of a certain preconception of Germanness, whatever such a conception might be? This is a crucial question, for it determines the nature of the relation between science and power, between the institution and politics. Is Rektor Heidegger bringing the university of Freiburg into line by placing it under the yoke of Nazi ideology, or is he developing a non-aligned conception of the role and the nature of the university, one that will prove unliveable in the longer run and will be the cause of his resignation some ten months after the address is delivered? There is perhaps no straightforward answer to this question. On the one hand, it is quite obvious that Heidegger would not have been chosen to succeed to Sauer had his sympathies for the new regime not been known at the time. Furthermore, we now know that a great number of his actions and declarations during the period of his rectorate were aimed at implementing and speeding up the process of the *Gleichschaltung* of the universities planned in Berlin.[17] On the other hand, though, the address does present itself as a philosophical reflection on the university, and on the metaphysical essence of knowing itself. Although taken into account and to a certain extent thematized, the national and the social are themselves envisaged in the light of such an essence. In no unequivocal way can the address be identified with a Nazi oath of faith. While openly supporting the ongoing "revolution," while serving its cause and integrating much of its rhetoric, the purpose and the scope of the address exceed the Nazi official line in directions that I shall try to indicate. This, however, is not to suggest some subterranean resistance to the Nazi regime on Heidegger's part; nor is it to suggest some politically disruptive dimension of Heidegger's speech. But it is to locate the point at which Heidegger saw the historical possibility of a radical transformation of the German university aimed at reawakening an urgency for its *essence* and, through such a reawakening, at a new foundation of the German Dasein as a whole.

Self-assertion

The question, then, is that of "the self-assertion of the German university". Every term of this title – "assertion," "self," "university," "German" – needs to be clarified. Do we know what such terms mean? Do they speak for themselves? If the university needs to assert itself, it is because it has not yet done so. It has not yet imposed itself, it has not yet found a way of affirming itself. Yet the university already exists, it is already there, as we hear Heidegger begin his address. Yet, what is given in the existence of this university, insofar as something is given at all, is not the German university, not the university itself, *kat'auto*, but something else, something other than the university or the essence of the university. What is given is the university in the age of technology, the university of the *Gestell*. To assert the university, then, would be to reveal it and posit it according to the power of its essence – an essence which, of course, would not simply be foreign or external to the university of the today, but with respect to which the today would be most oblivious. The self-assertion of the German university, or the assertion of itself, is not the positing of the university over against something that would by nature be external to it, and in the opposition to which it would come to be determined. The self-assertion does not primarily point in the direction of its "independence" with respect to power, to politics, to religion, etc. The self-assertion is not an assertion *against* or *over against*, but an affirmation *according to*. To what? To a principle that would be its very own: its *essence*. The university would come to be and assert itself only in appropriating for itself what most belongs to itself, only in opening itself to what is properly given to it. In its self-assertion, the university would obey and respond exclusively to the law of its essence, which is not the juridical or the political law, but, as we shall see, the law on the basis of which something like the juridical and the political can come to be. This law, the law of the essence of the university, is the essence of the law. It is the law of a fundamental relation, of a relation so fundamental and so old that without it there would be no relation to the whole of being, and this means no history, no politics, no right, and least of all, no "autonomy" or "independence" with respect to such regions. Throughout the address, Heidegger will dismiss the appeal to autonomy and independence on the basis of its secondary or derived nature. The *nomos* that is in question here is of a different nature. It is true autonomy, the autonomy that arises out of the affirmation of the essence of the university. What is most striking about this self-assertion is that its mode of positing is that of the will, as if assertion itself were necessarily of the will. Specifically, the very term "self-assertion" is one that belongs to the metaphysics of the will, that metaphysics that Heidegger will precisely confront and submit to the most rigorous questioning starting in 1935. The extent to which the deconstruction of the metaphysics of the will is central to Heidegger's reorienting of the question of the political is something that will be made evident in the following chapter. This confrontation will take the form of a sustained reading of Nietzsche, yet only to the extent that, for Heidegger, the will to power as thematized by Nietzsche is the last philosophical expression of a historical unfolding that finds its roots in the very opening of modernity. The term "self-affirmation" (*Selbstbejahung*) is one that can be traced back to Schelling and to his metaphysics of the will. In his remarks contained in the Appendix to the Schelling lecture course (1936), Heidegger notes that Schelling's "self-affirmation" goes back to the modern interpretation of being in the sense of the Leibnizian *exigentia essentiae*, that is, to a conception of being as that which presents itself on the basis of its ability to re-present itself in its essence.[18] "Self-affirmation" means: "To will oneself."[19] It is this conception of self-affirmation, then, profoundly rooted in the metaphysics of the will, that presides over Heidegger's political discourse. The voluntarism that seems so overwhelmingly present in the address, and that seems to echo and amplify the willful rhetoric of National Socialism is a metaphysical overdetermination that can be traced back to the very origins of modernity, a tendency which remains unquestioned and unproblematized in the address. As our following chapter will attempt to demonstrate, it is this very metaphysics that will become the crux of Heidegger's *Auseinandersetzung* with Nazism starting in 1935.

"We"

Furthermore, this voluntarism is accompanied by, and to a certain extent subordinated to a "we," that is, a first person plural that is perhaps far less universal than the singularity and mineness of Dasein, a pronoun that has come to replace Dasein as the name that designates the proper, the proper name. Was the appeal to this "we" inevitable? Does Heidegger, once elected rector of the University of Freiburg, become compelled to say "we," and to speak in the name of a "we" that is no longer the "I" of Dasein? And does politics begin in this move? In other words, does politics begin when and where an "I" says "we"? If it is true, perhaps, that there is no "I" that is not fundamentally a "we," the "we" to which this "I" belongs can only be a matter of extreme perplexity and radical questioning. In the name of what/whom can one say "we"? What is it that allows me to say "we"? Who are "we"? This is precisely the question that leads *Being and Time* into the designation of "man" as Dasein, as this singular being to whom mineness belongs essentially. Yet now, in 1933, the "we" seems to point in a different direction, in the direction of the national: "we," the community of German professors and students. Yet how can this determination not resonate as the most abstract and ontologically emptiest of all determinations? True, section 74 of *Being and Time* had already laid the ground for an ontological understanding of the *Volk* and the *Gemeinschaft*. Yet in the very use of the "we," Heidegger has moved from an ontological description of historicity to a historical and political decision: Heidegger now designates who "we" is, and speaks in the name of a specific *Volk* and a definite *Gemeinschaft*: the *Volksgemeinschaft*. One could object: the rectoral address is a "ceremony," it officially marks the opening of an academic responsibility and is the outcome of an election; Heidegger thus represents a certain general will, a will that designated him as the leader of a community. Hence the "we": it was Heidegger's responsibility and duty to speak in this way. In effect: Heidegger's "we" in the address is not the discreet and polite "we" that is required by the academic discourse, the "we" that corresponds to the logic according to which science does not belong to anyone in particular, but rather to everyone. Heidegger's "we" is *political*. In this "we," that is, in its very utterance, independently of any declaration of intention and of any programme, politics has already begun. If there is an irreducibly political gesture, one in which the "right" comes to be distinguished from the "left," it is perhaps in the "we" in the name of whom one decides to speak that it is first brought about: either I say "we" in the name of the nation, of the people, of the majority of citizens, whether this people or this majority comes to be expressed "democratically" or otherwise, in which case I am driven by a logic of the "right," that is, by this logic according to which the "we" would be the expression of a quantifiable reality, or the signifier of an identifiable and verifiable signified; or – and this is how one could begin to (re)formulate the leftist imperative – I say "we" in the name of those who are without a name and thus without a "we," the "wes" that never have a voice in the logic of political representation (which is a political logic of representation), the "wes", then, that can never be made into *a* we, the "wes" that are not *we*. We must distinguish between the "we" first person plural, and the "we" whose plurality is or has no person. This latter logic, "illogical" in that it is paradoxical, is also apparently usurping: for what allows "me" to say "we" is precisely the recognition that in the logic of the "we" there are those for whom to say "we" is their very im-possibility. Politics is perhaps played out in the recognition of this impossibility, or rather in the confrontation between these two irreconcilable logics of the "we."

What, then, about Heidegger's "we"? Who is this "we" in the name of whom it has become urgent to take up the highest academic responsibility? In a way, and in all appearance, Heidegger's "we" seems to conform itself to this logic for whom to say "we" goes unproblematically and is a matter of willful affirmation: "We," the German *Volksgemeinschaft*. Yet things begin to gain complexity when it becomes a question of defining this nation/people: it is not that which is gathered in a pregiven "we," but that for whom the "we" comes to be constituted in its relation to being. The "we" *is* – *we* are – insofar as we are, thus insofar as, for us, in our "we are" (our being), our very being is at issue. For us, being is at issue, and it is in that respect that "we" are. It is in the extent to which there is, for us, being – or presence – and in the way in which, for us, presence is (unfolds according to its essence or destines itself), that something like a "we," as a response to this summoning, comes to constitute itself. "We," for Heidegger, can be – there can be a "we" – only on the basis of the way in which presence gives, sends or destines itself. It is on the basis of such a historical-destinal unfolding that we are disposed and dwell on this earth in a definite way. This dwelling marks the site of the national (of the political) as such, the site of that which, in *Being and Time*, Heidegger designated as *Geschick* or communal destiny. Heidegger's error and errancy will have consisted in remitting the possibility of the national understood destinally into the hands of Hitler's national populism, in having identified the place of the political with the "we" of the *Volksgemeinschaft*. That amounted to replacing the "we" of the nation-state with that of the totalitarian state, without the "we" being taken up in all its problematicity, without realizing that the latter "we" remained caught in the very logic of representation it was overturning and rejecting in the most violent of all gestures. By contrast, the move to Hölderlin's poetry, enacted as early as 1934, can be seen as an attempt to problematize the "we" on the basis of which a discourse concerning the national – the nationell – or the essence of the *Vaterland* becomes possible.[20]

Technè

The question remains, however, as to what the essence of the university consists in. The question also remains as to how this essence determines the Germanness of the university. Does Germanness, and thus "Germany" itself not come to be determined in the light of this relation to the essence? Is it not in a certain responsibility with respect to the law of the essence that something like Germany comes to be constituted? Is it not in a certain ability to *will* its own essence that the German nation comes to constitute itself as such? Would this not also suggest, then, that the university, as the locus of the will to essence, is at once the place of the political?

What, then, is the essence of the university? Science (*Wissenschaft*). Not the sciences themselves, not this plurality of disciplines that refer to themselves as sciences, but science in the singular, science as essence. Thus the will to the German university is the "will to science as the will to the historical spiritual mission of the German *Volk*."[21] The question, then, is that of the relation between science and the mission of the German people. As we shall see, this spiritual mission is nothing outside science itself. Exactly how problematic this identification of the will to science with a truly German mission is, is something that will need careful examination. Why, in other words, should science be geared toward voluntarism, spiritualism and nationalism? If Heidegger's statement can indeed be viewed as promoting a nationalistic interpretation of science and of the university as a whole, it also suggests that the *Volk* itself, the German nation or people comes to be as such only in and through its will to science. From the very beginning, then, Heidegger locates the possibility of the national and the political, of the *Volk* and the *Volksgemeinschaft*, at the level of a common will to science. And this, as we shall see, is none other than philosophy understood authentically and primordially. In that respect, Heidegger's appeal to the self-affirmation of the German university is a distant echo of the systematic and national university of Schelling and Fichte. The spirit and the destiny of the German nation lie in that nation's ability to conform to science authentically understood, that is, to science understood on the basis of its concept or essence. The national is played out in this historical possibility: it is, for Germany, a question of actualizing or realizing philosophy as such, a question of bringing philosophy back into the open and of submitting the whole of the German Dasein to its power. This, as we shall now begin to see, is the authentically philosophical gesture of repetition of the historical possibility held in reserve in the Greek beginning.

What, indeed, is science? In essence, it is nothing German. Nor is it anything national. Unless one thinks of Ancient Greece as a nation, which it was, but precisely in the historical-destinal sense, that is, in the sense of its ground-breaking relation to the truth of beings – a relation which it defined as *technè*. Science is *technè*. The essence of science was first spoken and experienced in what Heidegger calls "the Greek beginning." That beginning is a beginning insofar as it bespoke *technè*. It is not any beginning, but the very beginning of Western history. This, however, is not to say that Ancient Greece marks something like the "origin" of "world-civilization" or even "European civilization." The question is not historiographical. Least of all would it be a matter of evaluating the level of intellectual, social, political and religious "maturity" of a definite "culture" and of privileging the Greek moment in what would no doubt appear as some nostalgic longing for a paradise lost. Rather, it is a matter of acknowledging how, in Ancient Greece, science emerges in the very specific form of man's ability to question beyond beings into the truth of beings and to grasp himself as this being to whom a certain understanding of being belongs – this ability, then, of transcending the realm of *phusis* in order to ask about and experience the truth of *phusis*. Science is transcendence proper, or metaphysics: with the birth of what was to be called philosophy, the Greek man thinks of himself as the meta-physical animal. This, Heidegger says, is what the old word *technè* captures. It is archaic, not simply because it is old, but because it has become *decisive* – decisive to the extent that a history, history in the sense of an essential and insistent *sending* continues to unfold from it. *Technè* is essentially archaic; the *archè* is itself technical. By *technè*, we need to understand the emergence of a thinking and questioning confontation with the whole of being. For the first time, in Ancient Greece, man rises up (*sich aufsteht*) against the totality of what is and stands erect in the midst of that totality by way of his questioning attitude.[22] It is there, in the full assumption of his verticality, that man finds his proper dwelling. It is in the wake of such a meta-physical stance that the *polis*, as the place in which the sharing of this archaic attitude occurs, is first made possible. Later on, through his reading of Hölderlin, Heidegger will identify this archaic dwelling with that of poetry. The Greek moment, then, marks man's awakening to the power of being, his standing firm amidst the whole of what is.

It is this original verticalization, this long since forgotten erection that is in need of its own repetition. German man must learn to hold fast in the midst of being, to stand upright in his world, to steel himself before the weight of his history and his destiny. For Heidegger, life will have meant nothing but this: an upright state (if not a state of right), a rectitude or a standing erect, in brief, a stiffness or a stiffening of which the rectorate, precisely, formed the perversion and properly tyrannical caricature, an encampment right in the midst of presence and of the tempest which unleashes itself there (and doubtless the work camps, so dear to Rektor Heidegger with their dressy scouting appeal and their "bonding," *bündisch* virility, would, in his eyes, have had a metaphysical foundation). To endure beings as a whole and the force of being that agitates it, to suffer the slings and arrows of destiny, far stronger than any will, without averting one's eyes or submitting: here is what existing or knowing, in other words questioning, will have meant for Heidegger. He wanted to build the university of transcendence and of finitude, the university of the meta-physical ground in which all disciplines are rooted. Yet this ground is precisely that which opens onto the groundlessness of its own transcendence, or of its freedom. It is precisely here, at the very heart of transcendence, that Heidegger's heroic pathos comes to take shape: his counter-bourgeois philosophy puts on the costume of hardness and heaviness, of virility and of confrontation. One cannot blame Heidegger for having wanted to bring the university back to the place of its essence, that place without place (as Heidegger will later characterize the Greek *polis*), *unheimlich* and unfamiliar: being in its (temporal) ekstasis, existence in its finitude. Yet one can blame him for having translated this place into a pathos and a rhetoric that would be simply grotesque had they not had vital (that is, human) consequences.

By turning itself toward the (Greek) beginning, the German Dasein would not simply turn to something of the past and reawaken it. One can turn to a beginning only if this beginning has already leapt ahead of us, only if its archaic power is such that it is always preceding us, always opening the way to the future. In other words, one can repeat the beginning only when one is already led and guided by the beginning. Such is the logic of the *archè*: its commencing is an ordering, its unfolding is ekstatic:

> The beginning is still. It does not lie *behind* us as something long past, but it stands *before* us. The beginning has, as the greatest moment, which exists in advance, already passed indifferently over and beyond all that is to come and hence over and beyond us as well; it stands there as the distant decree that orders us to recapture its greatness.

(SDU 12–13/32)

Is this distant decree easily perceived? Is the voice of the beginning accessible to all ears? Or do we need to learn how to listen and hear? Who can teach us? What is required of us in order for our ears to become attuned? Is this attunement not the very stake of the revolution that is taking place in the university? If the ongoing revolution is to have some genuine orientation, it must be that of the transformation of the entire German historical existence, that is, a transformation in one's relation to the totality of being such that we shall be brought face to face with the frailty and uncertainty of beings. This originary attitude, in a way the simplest one, is also what is hardest to attain, precisely because we have lost the simple power of questioning.

But what has happened since that beginning? How have we grown so estranged from what is most essential? What has happened to man's original wonder at the power and mystery of nature, to his primitive confrontation with the overwhelming force of *phusis*? First, Christianity, and then technology, have removed science from its origin. Heidegger's attacks on Christianity and technology, still somewhat veiled in the rectoral address, will become most explicit in the *Contributions to Philosophy*, where Christianity and Machination (*Machenschaft*) are reinterpreted in the light of the history of nihilism and of the abandonment of being (*Seinsverlassenheit*).[23] As far as technology goes, and in the context of the possibility of a relation to the beginning, how technology can be inverted with a view to liberating a new relation to its essence is more immediately graspable, since in it the Greek *technè* still rules. What becomes central, as early as 1933, is the way in which technology, as the metaphysical *Prägung* of the today, relates to *technè* as the originally disclosive attitude of the historical Dasein. The key to this relation lies, of course, in Heidegger's reworking of the question of truth in the early 1930s, and in the way in which this question will be allowed to shape the discussion concerning *technè* and technology as a discussion concerning different modes of disclosing (*aletheuein*). If *technè* and technology both designate modes of truth, in that through them beings come to be disclosed in a specific way, Heidegger, starting in the address, will always play *technè* against technology, will always be engaged in showing how, despite itself, technology still holds the power of *technè* in reserve, and that the freeing of this essence held in reserve would mark the possibility of a step beyond and away from technology.[24] *Technè* will always designate the power of the *archè* for Heidegger, and the address is just one instance, indeed a very political one, in which Heidegger tries to think the possibility of a counter-movement to that of the *Gestell* on the basis of a reactivation of that fundamental ontological-existential attitude. At stake in the "revolution" for Heidegger was precisely this: a counter-movement to the global seizure of technology, yet one which was itself entirely dependent upon the metaphysics of the will to power that it was to overcome. National Socialism signified this promise: that of a new historical configuration in which those fundamental forces of life and earth still held in reserve would be liberated. National Socialism signified this hope: that of a nation and a people that would become attuned with the wondrous power of truth. What is most specific to the address is the way in which this counter-movement is sustained by a metaphysics of the will, and the way in which *technè*, as the essence of science, is identified with questioning. The address is perhaps the locus of this twofold privileging with respect to the notion of *technè*: the privilege of the will and that of the question. Soon after the failure of the rectorate, and that means after the failure of Heidegger's techno-politics, *technè* will be thought against voluntarism, and bent in the direction of its other essence, art. With *Introduction to Metaphysics* (1935), art becomes the determination in which the historical comes to be thought. Art, whether in its original form, namely the Greek tragic poem or, most decisively perhaps, in the thinking poetry of Hölderlin, marks this attempt to free thought from the will to power as well as from that peculiar form of contemporary questioning which calls itself philosophy and which Heidegger identifies with questionlessness or sheer calculation. *Technè*, whether as tragedy or as myth – as *Dichtung* – comes to be thought in (the) place of the political, in (the) place of technologized politics:

> What is the basic attitude in which the preservation of the wondrous, the beingness of beings, unfolds and, at the same time, defines itself? We have to see it in what the Greeks called *technè*. Yet we must divorce this Greek word from our familiar term derived from it, "technology," and from all nexuses of meaning that are thought in the name of technology. To be sure, that modern and contemporary technology could emerge, and had to emerge, has its ground in the beginning and has its foundation in an unavoidable incapacity to hold fast to the beginning. That means that contemporary technology – as a form of "total mobilisation" (Ernst Jünger) – can only be understood on the basis of the beginning of the basic Western position toward beings as such and as a whole, assuming that we are striving for a "metaphysical" understanding and are not satisfied with integrating technology into the goals of politics.
>
> (GA 45, 178–9)

If, starting in 1934–5, *technè* still means knowledge, it is no longer, or at least no longer primarily associated with questioning. Rather, it is identified with a certain stance with respect to *phusis*, yet one which does not seek to overpower it or exploit it, but which merely wishes to retain the holding sway of *phusis* in unconcealedness. Ultimately, then, it is subordinated to the self-manifestation of beings, that is, to the truth of beings. This trajectory also marks a shift of emphasis from the necessity of a repetition of the *archè*, inherited from fundamental ontology, a repetition through which a new historical configuration might begin to emerge, to the problematic of the other beginning (*der andere Anfang*), one which problematizes even further the question of the relation to the "first" or Greek beginning.

Yet, as we know, the beginning still stands before us, for its power has reached far beyond us. This means that its power and its greatness can still be recovered. To win back the greatness of the beginning, to bring science back into life and to open life onto its essence is to will the essence of science, and that is the great questioning confrontation with the whole of being: science must (again) become "the fundamental event of our spiritual-national existence [*unseres geistig-volklichen Daseins*]."[25] Essentially, nothing has changed since 1921/2 and since Heidegger defined the task of philosophy in the opening pages of *Being and Time*: it is still a question of reawakening a fundamental attitude toward the world and toward life, of bringing fundamental moods back to life, those typically Greek moods of "wonder" and "admiration."[26] But, as we know from the structure of repetition, this reawakening is not an invitation to return to the beginning (how could one return to the beginning when the beginning has invaded our future?). Rather, it is an invitation to wrest contemporary science (that is, science as a fragmented field of multiple sciences or disciplines) from its questionlessness and to reassert the primacy or the worthiness of questioning as the highest form of knowledge, and not simply as the preparatory step to the answer.

What does questioning do? It shatters (*zerbricht*), but also gathers and grounds; it breaks the various sciences open, but with a view to a more fundamental attunement to the basic forces of human existence as a whole. In a remarkably apocalyptico-messianic passage, Heidegger sketches the revolution of the university to come in the following way:

> Such questioning will shatter the encapsulation of the various fields of knowledge into separate disciplines; it will return them from the isolated fields and corners into which they have been scattered, witout bounds and goals; and it will ground science once again directly in the fruitfulness and blessing of all the world-shaping forces of man's historical existence, such as: nature, history, language; the *Volk*, custom, the State; poetry, thought, belief; sickness, madness, death; law, economy, technology.
>
> (SDU 13–14/33)

Questioning, then, blows the scientific landscape to pieces. It frees the forces of life from the fetters they have progressively been forced into.

But this upheaval, this trembling is only with a view to reconciling science with such forces. It is to open science to the totality of life, but it is also to gather such forces under a common experience of wonder and awe. Elsewhere, in what constitutes perhaps Heidegger's most enthusiastic and unconditional support for National Socialism and its *Führer*, in the midst of his most gruesome declarations, one finds, as if hidden away, the following passage:

> For us, questioning means: exposing oneself to the sublimity of things and their laws; it means: not closing oneself off to the terror of the untamed and to the confusion of darkness. To be sure, it is for the sake of this questioning that we question, and *not* to serve those who have grown tired and their complacent yearning for comfortable answers. We know: the courage to question, to experience the abysses of existence and to endure the abysses of existence, is in itself already a *higher* answer than any of the all-too-cheap answers afforded by artificial systems of thought.[27]

Questioning means: exposedness, awakenness to the world, both in its sublimity and its darkness. Questioning is for the sake of questioning only. It is not to serve the technical imperatives of the time; it is not to be brought into the logic of use and usefulness. Nor even is it to open the way to answers, to those all too comfortable academic answers. As we have already suggested, originary questioning is a way of being (*Seinsweise*) and is itself a response to the way in which being is at issue for a historical Dasein. Let it not be forgotten that questioning is shattering. Yet even here, even when speaking of world-shaping forces and freedom, of marvelling and wonder, Heidegger cannot help leaving a certain dreary heaviness behind him: science understood as questioning is "the most extreme danger," an awakening of the fundamental forces of sickness, madness and death. This is what Heidegger calls the "world of spirit."[28] Yet can't spirit be light, healthy and joyous – alive? What happened to factical *life*? Can't spirit be *spirituel*, witty, heedless and innocent? *L'esprit de sérieux* versus the joyous science. For Heidegger,

> "spirit" is neither empty acumen nor the noncommittal play of wit nor the busy practice of never-ending rational analysis nor even world reason; rather, spirit is the determined resolve to the essence of Being, a resolve that is attuned to origins and knowing.
> (SDU 14/33)

This hearkened and resolute nature of spirit is only aggravated when related to the national:

> And the *spiritual world* of a *Volk* is not its cultural super-
> structure, just as little as it is its arsenal of useful knowledge
> [*Kenntnisse*] and values; rather, it is the power that comes
> from preserving at the most profound level the forces that are
> rooted in the soil and blood of a *Volk*, the power to
> arouse most inwardly and to shake most extensively the
> *Volk*'s existence.
>
> (SDU 14/33–4)

Spirit, that very German spirit, not only speaks the language of darkness, of sickness and of death; it also bespeaks blood and earth. It is nothing spiritual, nothing ethereal, nothing light: it is weighty, not witty, it is of the body and of the soil, it is attached, riveted as it were, to the frailty and the finitude of human existence. The strength of the German *Volk* lies in its ability to assume fully the extent of its condition, to suffer the blows of destiny by way of an essentially disclosive attitude which Heidegger calls "questioning." The challenge awaiting the German people lies in the nation's ability to confront the essentially tragic nature of history. Life is tragic in that it is both finite and transcending: man must become free for his own transcendence, and yet his heroic stance in the midst of beings is always threatened by necessity, that is, by his own mortality as well as by the force of destiny. It is in the light of such comments that we should understand Heidegger's reference in the address to Aeschylus' *Prometheus*, according to which, in Heidegger's translation, "knowledge is far weaker than necessity" (*technè d'anankès asthenestera makrò*). Heidegger's reference to Prometheus is not incidental. It is also promised to a long future. The address marks perhaps the point at which the tragic has already begun to "work" the question of *technè*, in a way that will become fully manifest in the 1935 lecture course *Introduction to Metaphysics*.

The university, as the place where questioning is waiting to be reawakened, has a leading role to play in the revolution of the German historical existence. The "true" revolution is primarily and above all a revolution of essence and of spirit. This revolution requires strength, resolve and unity. For what could conceivably be more difficult than to place oneself under the law of essence, to let one's existence be governed by the shattering power of the essence? Yet this difficult path is the only path to freedom genuinely understood: not to the so-called and much praised "academic freedom," which is essentially "negative," insofar at it means predominantly "lack of concern," "arbitrariness" and "lack of restraint,"[29] not to this lower kind of freedom, then, which Descartes characterized as "*liberté d'indifférence*," and Kant as "*Willkür*," but to this positive and resolute freedom for the law of one's essence. To tragic freedom, then.

Onto-technocracy

Yet Science redefined as questioning is not only to shatter the old conception of the university as a place for theoretical speculation fragmented into various disciplines, disconnected from one another as well as from the fundamental forces of the nation. What is affirmed in the self-affirmation of the university is more than just the university itself. What is affirmed is the political as such. In other words, along with the affirmation of the essence of the German university as questioning, because the true revolution in the university consists in becoming attuned to such forces, the "new freedom" is one that binds the students to what Heidegger, certainly in agreement with the official line of the party, but also, and most of all perhaps, in a way that gathers the three types of citizen central to the constitution of Plato's *Politeia*, designates as the two remaining fundamental domains of the *Volksgemeinschaft*: labor and defense. Yet if one can indeed recognize the three types of the *technites* (the artisans), the *phulakes* (the guardians) and the *philosophos* (the philosophers) in Heidegger's organic description of the new state, a major difference with Plato's *Republic* lies in the fact that for Heidegger every philosopher needed to be a worker and a soldier as well. The conception that is put forward here is thus more in accordance with a Nazi principle than with a Platonic one, if one recalls Socrates' insistence in the *Republic* (423 d) that to every one citizen must correspond one job.

This is how Heidegger describes the first two obligations:

> The first bond [*Bindung*, which also means obligation] is the one that binds to the *Volksgemeinschaft*. It entails the obligation to share fully, both passively and actively, in the toil, the striving, and the abilities of all estates and members of the people. This bond will henceforth be secured and rooted in student existence through labor service.
>
> The second bond is the one that binds to the honor and the destiny of the nation [Nation] in the midst of the other peoples of the world. It demands the readiness, secured in knowledge and ability and firmed up through discipline, to go to the end. This bond will in the future embrace and pervade all of student existence in the form of *military service*.
>
> (SDU 15/35)

Heidegger's lack of an original and reflected political vision – and visibility – is startling: the philosophically inane and reactionary rhetoric of discipline, self-sacrifice, courage, service and honor only reveals Heidegger's blind faith in Nazi ideology and his unconditional embracing of its most radical aspects.[30] Furthermore, the considerations regarding labor and defense are so rudimentary and simplistic, so much in line with the most basic Nazi understanding of these "forces," that one can only marvel at Heidegger's lack of education and independent thought with respect to such matters. The "vision" that is offered here is indeed that of the *Volksgemeinschaft* – of a community of blood and earth whose inextricable unity is revealed in its forces of labor and defense, in its rigorously disciplined and resolute legions of workers and soldiers, marching to the sound of a single martial tune praising the virtues of a revitalized and resolute Germany, ready to confront its uncompromising destiny. The importance Heidegger attached to the military organization of the community as a whole, and of the university in particular,[31] is now a well established fact. Also known is the so-called "scientific camp" the Rektor-Führer organized in Todtnauberg in October 1993 with its peculiar mix of virile comradery, paramilitary discipline and spiritual-scientific guidance, a camp which, in effect, was the effort to realize concretely and provide an example of what Heidegger meant by the unity of the three obligations and services of the German youth.[32] Very much impressed by the heroism and the self-sacrifice of the German soldier romantically, if not mystically recounted in Jünger's *Storms of Steel*, certainly distressed by the sight of a bankrupt, weakened and crippled Germany, Heidegger, like most other Germans, found a sign of rejuvenation and hope in the self-confidence, the steely pathos and the appeal to the national pride of Nazism. For many, without necessarily implying overt hostility and imperialism, military power primordially meant the recovery of honor and dignity, of faith in oneself and in one's destiny, of pride in one's abilities and resources as a nation. As for labor, Heidegger had a no less idealized and partial view of what he failed to recognize as a complex and multifaceted phenomenon, a view that was informed by Jünger's *Der Arbeiter* more than by Marx's *Das Kapital*. Idealized, first of all, to the extent that Heidegger saw in labor an "obligation" and a "service," not a reality with a logic and a law of its own (the law of Capital), a reality that is itself productive of ideologies; second, partial insofar as labor is seen as a power of political unification disconnected from its concrete material and economic conditions of existence, and transcending the boundaries of class and the imperatives of production. This raises the question regarding the possibility of taking any political responsibility, or making any political choice, without linking, from the very start, politics with a concrete situation, one which is as economically and materially mediated as it is historically decisive. It is to emphasize the absolute necessity of a material analysis of the various ontic forces constituting the historical-political field. It is only at the cost of such a vigilance, combined with a deconstructive awareness of the dominant ideological discourses, that the worst and politically most dangerous naïvetes might be avoided. Having failed to take into account the specificity and the irreducibility of the ontic, having envisaged the emergence of National Socialism solely in terms of a renewed dialogue with the most hidden powers of being, Heidegger became blind to some of the most central aspects of the regime he so enthusiastically supported. Similarly, as much as his desire to reopen the university to the rest of society may seem legitimate, we have to wonder whether his disconnectedness from the world of economic realities and international politics does not exemplify his point concerning the isolation of German academia in the 1930s in a most concrete way – an isolation which, paradoxically, made the rise of National Socialism all the easier.

In any case, and to come back to the address, which we never quite left, through work, military service and transformed science, Germany was to become the heir to the European spiritual throne left vacant since the extinction of the Greek *polis*. The third bond and service, only alluded to so far, is that of knowledge, and the one to which Heidegger devotes the longest treatment. What contrast one finds between the rudimentary nature of the reflections concerning the first two and the rich and nuanced account of the third! If through the evocation of the first two services Heidegger demonstrates his unconditional fidelity to the regime, the last service, which most consistently echoes the whole of the address, reveals, albeit cryptically, the specificity of Heidegger's conception of the fundamental goals and orientations of the revolution. At stake, in this third service, is nothing other than leadership or guidance itself, leadership in its essence. What is the essence of leadership? Essence itself. Essence leads. What is the true access to essence? Questioning. It is from within the university, insofar as it opens onto the most extreme questioning, that the people can take the full measure of their destiny and learn to endure the difficulty of their existence. Thus, insofar as the university constitutes the matrix of an originary and therefore exemplary relation to the overpowering power of being, a matrix within which the forces of the historical existence find their truth, the university can claim to guide the guides and the guardians of the nation. This, as already suggested, amounts to a resumption of the Platonic *politeai*: the workers and the defenders of the *polis* united under and guided by the power of knowing itself; the leaders themselves lead by the light of being, of the Good, of the True. This "vision" is nothing but the ancient – Platonic – model of an architechnocratic republic:[33] power to those who are attuned to the highest principles. Yet whereas in Plato this power is described as *epistemè* and *sophia*, and is distinguished from the *technè* of the artisan, *technè*, in the context of Heidegger's address, designates the highest and most truthful comportment. This retranslation, or rather reappropriation of the ancient *technè* does not go as far as to call into question the Platonic model of the organization of the *polis*. On the contrary. This is what Heidegger said in his 1931–2 lecture course:

As far as the "state" (this is how we translate *polis*, in a way
that is not quite adequate) and the question of its inner possibility are concerned, that which, according to Plato, prevails
as the highest principle, is that the genuine guardians of the
being-with-one-another of men, in the unity of the *polis*, must
necessarily be philosophising men. This does not mean that
philosophy professors should become chancellors of the Reich,
but that philosophers must become *phulakes*, guardians. The
domination of the state and the ordering of this domination must
be ruled by philosophising men who, on the basis of the deepest
and widest knowledge, a knowledge that interrogates freely, bring
the measure and the rule, and open the paths of decision. Insofar
as they philosophise, they must necessarily know, in all rigour
and clarity, what man is and what his being and his potentiality-
for-being are.

(GA 34, 100)

No other power, no other authority than the university itself – granted
that it is the university of true *technè* – can grant the university its ground,
its destination and its law. The university, if it is to be at all, is
self-grounding, self-determining and autonomous. This, then, is what
Heidegger means by autonomy: the ability on the university's part to relate
to the law of its essence, and to affirm it as its sole law. To bring this
law into the open and to open the university as a whole to its law means
to revolutionize the institution. For the traditional university is a university that is oblivious of its essence and its beginning. The revolution for
Heidegger, if it was to have any meaning, was to be a revolution of (the)
essence. It is the essence that was to be reawakened and brought back to
life; it is life itself that was to be reconciled with its long since forgotten
essence (and this, I believe, explains why Heidegger long after the war
continued to insist on "the inner truth and greatness of this movement,"[34]
which had to do with the "essence" of the movement, and that is to say
precisely with the movement's relation to the essence).

It is on the basis of this renewed conception of science, and with the
law of essence firmly held in view, that Heidegger attempted to lead his
revolution within the university. If Science itself is a *Führer*, it demands
obedience and discipline. How compatible is the understanding of science
as essential questioning and uncertainty, as fragility and risk in the face
of being, with the ultra-disciplined and univocal organization which it
requires at the level of the institution? Why, in other words, should "questioning" go hand in hand with *Gleichschaltung*? These questions point to
the vision with which Heidegger tried and ultimately failed to shape the
German university as a whole. If not only the rector, albeit as *Rektor-
Führer*, but also the university as a whole, is to open itself to the call of

being once heard in Ancient Greece, then the whole of the forces constituting the university must undergo a radical transformation, and not only
a reformation. Such forces include the student body, the faculty, and the
disciplines themselves. Each faculty, by way of a relation to its essence,
must provide "spiritual legislation" to the specific disciplines that fall
under its scope. This order of grounding and guidance is strikingly remi-
niscent of the ontological order of grounding Heidegger sketches in section
3 of *Being and Time*, where the positive sciences are said to depend upon
their respective regional ontologies, which alone can open up the domain
of investigation which the sciences always and necessarily presuppose.
Thus, Aristotle is seen as having provided the concepts of *phusis* and
ousia in which the physical and meta-physical sciences found their proper
ground. Similarly, Kant provided the concept of nature, and the ontology
corresponding to it, in which Newtonian physics revealed its presuppositions. Closer to us, Husserl himself revealed the transcendental ground of
all investigations concerning the *psuchè*, and thus the ground proper to
psychology as a unified though polymorphous science. Here, in the context
of the structure of the university, the faculties are to serve as the place
for the articulation of such regional ontologies. As such, they are not artificial categories under which disconnected disciplines can be subsumed.
In submitting themselves to the regional-ontological legislation of the
faculty, the disciplines find their proper point of anchorage and are able
to relate to one another. Therefore, they are able to free themselves from
the enclosure, the encapsulation and the abstraction in which they were
thus far trapped. Yet the faculties themselves, as regional ontologies, still
lack their proper grounding. This, as we recall from *Being and Time*, can
be obtained only by way of a *fundamental* ontology, in other words by
the type of investigation that reveals the meaning of being necessarily
presupposed and operative in the sciences as well as in the regional ontologies themselves. Fundamental ontology, or philosophy proper, is in a
relation of grounding with respect to all regional ontologies, which are
themselves in a similar relation with respect to the manifold of positive
sciences. That which *Being and Time* expressed in descriptive ontological
terms is now offered as the basis for a transformation of the fundamental
structure and constitution of the university: the rector must be a thinker
of being (a philosopher) *and* a *Führer* because being has always *guided*
in advance our historical existence, has always called upon us in such
a way that we relate to beings and to one another according to that
original illumination. We understand being, always already, albeit pre-
ontologically and pre-conceptually. We live, think and act in the light of
being. We are thus being's followers and disciples. The "discipline"
Heidegger invokes is the self-discipline of the disciple; the spiritual legislation he calls for is the ap-propriation of that law which is ours from
the start. The various disciplines are disciplines to the extent that they

remain open to the law of their essence. As for the students, they are the concrete singularities whose relation to the truth of beings is determined by their submission to that of being. Ultimately, then, the university is not a place for the accumulation and transmission of knowledge; rather, it is the place where the *Führung* of being that has always already taken place and illuminated beings as a whole is explicitly brought back to its truth. This, perhaps, is the reason why Heidegger refuses to envisage the teacher–student relationship as one of learning in the sense of communicating a pre-defined and pre-articulated knowledge. Knowledge in the highest sense is philosophy understood as attunement to the truth of being. And this has nothing to do with science as a collecting and processing of information, nothing to do with the university of the *Gestell*. Because science is *essentially* attunement and self-exposition to the truth of being, teachers and students emerge out of a common ground and a common necessity. Teachers are indeed to a certain extent guides and leaders: they lead the way into given areas of being and help students find their own way through the area thus opened up. Yet because the originary light and ground of both the teachers' and the students' activities are identical, the relation between teachers and students is not only one of following. It is also one of "resistance" (*Widerstand*):

> All leadership [*Führung*] must allow following to have its own strength. Every following, however, carries resistance [*Widerstand*] within it. This essential opposition between leading and following must neither be covered over nor, indeed, obliterated altogether.
>
> (SDU 18/38)

Thus, the true and most fruitful relation between teacher and student is one that Heidegger characterizes as "struggle" (*Kampf**), a relation which aims to keep the opposition between leading and following alive. Why must this opposition not be overcome? Because only in and through it does true questioning arise and is science made possible. Thus, it is in the very sustaining of the opposition, in the very affirmation of its strifely nature that the university can come to affirm itself on the basis of itself. Bearing in mind section 74 of *Being and Time*, and the reading of it we provided in Chapter 1 of this study, it is not surprising, in the context of the address, to see Heidegger reformulate what was then expressed in terms of a "kämpfende *Nachfolge und Treue*"[35] and an *Erwiderung*.[36] It was then a question of understanding Dasein's relation to its own history as "repetition" and to the "heroes" it chooses for itself. Here, in the address, the same vocabulary is put to work to define the relation between teachers and students, and between leaders and followers in general: *Folgen, Führen, Widerstand, Kampf*: the structure of resistance and opposition is built into that of leadership. *Kampf* alone has the gathering power sufficient to bring about a true unity and a genuine community:

> Struggle alone will keep this opposition open and implant within the entire body of teachers and students that fundamental mood out of which self-limiting self-assertion will empower resolute self-examination to true self-governance.
>
> (SDU 19/38)

No doubt, the Heraclitean *polemos* finds here a novel field of application. But is this not because *polemos* designates the nature of not only ontic relations, but of being itself as a strife between concealment and unconcealment, and of man's relation to being as one of mutual and strifely ap-propriation, as "the tightest gathering" (*die straffste Sammlung*)[37] of the extremes? Is *polemos* not another word for being itself? Can the university be perceived as a *Kampfgemeinschaft*, as a "community of struggle between teachers and students",[38] otherwise than on the basis of the university's essence as a questioning power exposed to the empowering overpowering power of being?[39]

In the end, there will have been, on Heidegger's part, the desire to wrest science from its lack of questioning and its extreme technologization, from this tendency which has engulfed every thought in obviousness; there will have been this will to reaffirm questioning as the most essential attitude, this will to render philosophy permeable to the body of forces surrounding it, to the "world" as a whole and in the largest possible sense, in this sense so rich and so rigorously articulated by Heidegger himself throughout the 1920s. Yet this effort of repetition was ultimately subordinated to the voluntarism and the nationalism of the time, this mimetic task was actualized by way of a most repressive politics that signified the annihilation of a certain conception and a certain practice of the university that went back to von Humboldt, to a confusion and above all a fusion of knowledge, of power and of work, in other words of the university, of politics and of labour. That Heidegger saw in this fusion the possibility of a historical upheaval which, finally, would haul the German nation to the heights of the Greeks, that this identification had for him a value and a meaning that was above all metaphysical, this is beyond doubt. The political naïvete lay in the belief that something like a politics of repetition were possible, as if politics itself, with its metaphysics of the will and of actuality, were in a position to actualize the essence of philosophy, to bring it into the open and inscribe it concretely in the State structure. At the time of Heidegger's rectoral address the total "politicization" of the German university was already well underway. This politicization of science ultimately meant the application of the racial principle as the fundamental criterion and sole point of valuation of the institution as a whole. At that point, at the point when Rosenberg's and Krieck's views will have become predominant, Heidegger will no longer wish to have anything to do with leadership. Meanwhile, though, Heidegger's address resonates like a pathos-filled call to the will to essence of the university, like a burning desire to convince and to find the political legitimacy to construct the university of essence. In vain. The battle for the university of essence was already lost. The true revolution will not have taken place. But can one ever revolutionize the essence? Can a movement of essence ever be the result of a political or historical will? Can the essence be summoned and called upon by man himself, or is man himself not always summoned by the essence? Can there ever be a politics of essence, that is, a politics that would have the essence as its object, if politics itself is nothing but a certain manifestation of essence, if it is always claimed by its power? Furthermore, can the essence be willed as an object of the will, when the will is always already made subject to the power of the essential unfolding of the essence? These questions began to develop as a result of Heidegger's failure to revolutionize the university and the nation's inability to remain faithful to its historical challenge. Can one go as far as to see the whole problematic of "the other beginning" (*der andere Anfang*), which can emerge only out of an *Auseinandersetzung* with "the first beginning" (*der erste Anfang*), a problematic so carefully laid out in the *Contributions to Philosophy*, as the direct result of what Heidegger interpreted as the "movement's" failure to properly respond to the historical challenge of the time? Possibly. The words and the images will nonetheless remain, painfully and irreversibly inscribed in the flesh of thought: *Volksgemeinschaft, Blut, Boden, Opfer, Heil Hitler!*

3
After Politics

Even the fact that in the *Republic* philosophers
are destined to be *basileis*, the highest rulers, is
already an essential demotion of philosophy.
            Martin Heidegger, *Basic Questions of Philosophy.*

It is not until the mid-1930s that Nietzsche began to come under the
scope and scrutiny of Heidegger's deconstructive project of the philosophical tradition. This, however, does not suggest that Heidegger had
not read Nietzsche. We know that as early as the beginning of the 1910s,
Heidegger had encountered the newly expanded edition of unpublished
notes by Nietzsche issued under the title *The Will to Power*. Yet between
those years and 1936, there is no trace of any lecture course nor any
essay on Nietzsche, even though Heidegger sometimes refers to Nietzsche
and occasionally even praises him, as in his *Habilitationsschrift* on Duns
Scotus[1] or in *Being and Time*.[2] Did Heidegger at the time perceive
Nietzsche as an exception to the deconstructive task? When one knows
the range of thinkers with whom Heidegger felt compelled to engage philosophically (from the Presocratics to Husserl, from Plato to Jaspers), one
can only wonder as to why Nietzsche did not fall under the scope of such
a philosophical confrontation. Along with Spinoza and a few other notable
figures of the tradition, Nietzsche seems for a while to have escaped
the battle of giants Heidegger thought philosophy to be. Yet for a
while only, since for approximately twelve years, from 1936 to 1948,
Heidegger's thought will have developed by way of a long and difficult
Auseinandersetzung with Nietzsche, a confrontation which extended
well into the 1950s. In the end, Nietzsche remains the figure to
whom Heidegger will have devoted the largest number of pages, the figure
over whom he will have poured the largest amount of sweat, with results
that often raise suspicion and controversy amongst interpreters. In this

extended battle, something essential was obviously at stake. It is not my intention to unravel here the variety of stakes underlying Heidegger's repeated and uncertain readings of the Nietzschean corpus. Rather, I wish to focus on the political aspect of this confrontation, one which Heidegger himself expressed in 1945, and which has become the focus of attention since commentators have started to pay attention to Heidegger's political itinerary. Heidegger's statement, written in the form of a letter to the Rector of Freiburg University dated 4 November 1945, reads as follows:

> Beginning in 1936 I embarked on a series of courses and lectures on Nietzsche, which lasted until 1945 and which represented in even clearer fashion a declaration of spiritual resistance [to the Nazi regime]. In truth, it is unjust to assimilate Nietzsche to National Socialism, an assimilation which – apart from what is essential [and it is of course this 'essential' aspect that requires rigorous examination, as opposed to the alleged political or biological aspects of Nietzsche's thought] – ignores his hostility to anti-Semitism and his positive attitude with respect to Russia [and, one might want to add, his virulent attacks on German Nationalism]. But on a higher plane, the debate with Nietzsche's metaphysics is a debate with *nihilism* as it manifests itself with increased clarity under the political form of fascism.[3]

Although one needs to remain cautious with respect to Heidegger's retrospective evaluation of the nihilistic nature of National Socialism *per se*, since the liberal democracies of the West as well as the Workers' State of the Soviet Union are for Heidegger *as,* if not *more,* nihilistic than National Socialism itself,[4] which, after all, contained an "inner truth and greatness," a privilege Heidegger never granted to any other form of political organization, one can only take seriously the political ramifications of Heidegger's interpretation of nihilism.

Bearing the question of nihilism and of its political significance in mind, let us follow more closely what seems to be Nietzsche's progressive entry into the horizon of Heidegger's thinking. In the rectoral address of 1933, traces of Nietzsche's vocabulary begin to surface in Heidegger's own discourse. Thus, alongside the notions of "resoluteness," "fate," "beginning," "essence" and "being," one finds the Nietzschean motifs of "will" and "power" (even though the "will to power" as such is not mentioned). Whether this somewhat surprising semantic development corresponds to a controlled entry of Nietzsche in Heidegger's thought, or simply to a concession made to the willful and steely rhetoric of National Socialism remains unclear at this stage. In any case, at stake here is a political as well as a philosophical responsibility toward Nietzsche: it is precisely in the context of a base political appropriation and a grotesque deformation of Nietzsche's thought that references to the thinker of the will to power needed to be avoided altogether or, more appropriately perhaps, played against its ideological (nationalistic and biological) parody – which is precisely what Heidegger will end up doing, notably through a critique of Bauemler's then fashionable *Nietzsche, Philosopher and Politician*.[5] Still in the rectoral address, and more importantly perhaps, since this occurrence no longer seems to simply partake in the *Zeitgeist*, Heidegger refers to the "death of God" in an attempt to describe the abandonment of man today in the midst of what is.[6] In 1936–7, looking back at his use of the proposition in 1933, and emphasizing its political dimension, Heidegger wrote the following:

> Europe always wants to cling to "democracy" and does not want to see that this would be a fateful death for it. For, as Nietzsche clearly saw, democracy is only a variety of nihilism, i.e., the devaluing of the highest values, in such a way that they are only values and no longer form-giving forces ... "God is dead" is thus not an atheistic doctrine, but instead the formula for the basic experience of an event of Western history. With full consciousness did I use this proposition in my Rektor's address in 1933.
>
> (GA 43, 193)

From 1933, and particularly in *Introduction to Metaphysics*, the references to Nietzsche begin to accumulate. In the 1935 lecture course, one finds no less than ten direct references to Nietzsche and the last section of the last chapter, entitled "Being and the Ought" (*Sein und Sollen*), constitutes at bottom a critique of the notion of value and of its overwhelming presence in philosophy since Kant and particularly Fichte.[7] Nietzsche himself, by making the notion of value the focus of his enterprise, albeit in the form of a "revaluation of all values," remains unequivocally caught within the horizon of his time, and therefore is never able to access the truth of it. It is also in the conclusion of that book that, to my knowledge, Heidegger for the first time personally assumes the term "nihilism," yet in a gesture which from the start poses the entire complexity of his relation to Nietzsche:

> From a metaphysical point of view, we are staggering. We move about in all directions amid beings, and no longer know how it stands with being. Least of all do we know that we no longer know. We stagger even when we assure one another that we are no longer staggering, even when, as in recent years, people do their best to show that this inquiry about being brings only confusion, that its effect is destructive, that it is nihilism. ...

But where is nihilism really at work? Where men cling to familiar beings and suppose that it suffices to go on taking beings as beings, since after all that is what they are. But with this they reject the question of being and treat being like a nothing (*nihil*) which in a certain sense it "is", insofar as it unfolds essentially [*sofern es west*]. To cultivate only beings in the forgetfulness of being – that is nihilism. Nihilism thus understood is the *ground* of the nihilism which Nietzsche exposed in the first book of *The Will to Power*.

By contrast, to press inquiry into being explicitly to the limits of the nothing and to draw the nothing into the question of being – this is the first and only fruitful step toward a true overcoming [*Überwindung*] of nihilism.

(EM 154–5/202–3)

In a way, as far as the question of nihilism goes, Heidegger will not say anything more that what is expressed in this passage from *Introduction to Metaphysics*. Yet it will take him some twenty years to unpack and fully thematize his brief opening statements. From the start, "nihilism" appears as a notion with multiple entries and almost contradictory meanings, which Heidegger will nonetheless try to hold together. Three such meanings are here emphasized. First, in the mouth of those who are absorbed in the thickness of beings to the point of philosophical blindness (and, no doubt, this blindness includes most of what is presented as "philosophy"), "nihilism" serves to designate that which impedes their gesticulating busyness and upsets the secured world of their values, that which, in other words, leads "nowhere" (that is, leads to no secured ground or absolute certainties). From the perspective of such men, the question concerning being is the empty, pointless and nihilistic problem *par excellence*. The word "nihilism" is here worth a condemnation, and presupposes values on the basis of which something can be dismissed as nihilistic. Yet true nihilism consists precisely in acting and thinking in the way of such men, that is, as if being were nothing – or rather, since being is indeed no-thing (no particular being), to act as if it *were* not (as if it did not rule or unfold),[8] and thus as if its questioning made no difference (when difference as such always dwells within its reign). In that respect, true nihilism is nothing but the forgetfulness of being. Third, there is also of course Nietzsche's concept of nihilism, which Heidegger only alludes to here, insisting that it can only be understood on the basis of the truer sense of nihilism. In addition to all three senses sketched out in this passage, Heidegger raises the difficult question concerning the overcoming of nihilism by suggesting that a "first and fruitful step" toward such overcoming lies precisely in thinking being *with* the nothing. This concern regarding the possibility of an overcoming of nihilism will remain at the very heart of Heidegger's thought well into the 1950s, without ever reaching the point of an unequivocal opinion.

The relation to Nietzsche is now engaged. Starting in 1936, Heidegger devotes himself to it entirely, to the point of absolute consumption by the thinker who in the process had become Heidegger's "most intimate adversary." Never will a thinker have commented on the works of one of his predecessors in such an unrelenting and lengthy manner. The heart of Heidegger's analyses on nihilism date from the 1940s,[9] even though one finds preliminary analyses in the 1936/7 lecture course on *The Will to Power as Art* (section 20). I wish to organize my remarks around two major lines: the first has to do with the various types and meanings of nihilism Heidegger identifies; the second with the delicate question of the overcoming of nihilism.

Nihilisms

Technological Nihilism: The Final Phase

Nowhere is this ultimate stage of nihilism described better than in Ernst Jünger's "Total Mobilization"[10] and *The Worker*[11], which impressed Heidegger to the point that he read and discussed *The Worker* with a small circle of university teachers in the winter of 1939 to 1940. In his letter to Jünger of 1955,[12] Heidegger pays homage to his friend's 60th birthday and to his work in the following terms:

> Much of what your descriptions brought into view and to language for the first time, everyone sees and says today. Besides, *The Question Concerning Technology* owes enduring advancement to the descriptions in *The Worker*. In regard to your "descriptions" it might be appropriate to remark that you do not merely depict something real that is already known [*ein schon bekanntes Wirklichkeit*] but make available a "new reality" [*"eine neue Wirklichkeit"*].
>
> (Wm 219/45)

What exactly was this "new reality" in Heidegger's view? The description of European nihilism in the phase that followed the First World War, and that is the revelation of nihilism, at first exclusively European, in its planetary tendency. In that respect, *The Worker* can be seen as the continuation of "Total Mobilization." Originally experienced and revealed in the magnitude of the First World War, where every force and energy was concentrated on the war effort so that no domain of the economic and political life was to be spared, total mobilization quickly became for Jünger a planetary condition that encompassed the phenomenon of war but

reached far beyond it. What the world was witnessing at the time of the
First World War was the phenomenon of planetary domination revealed
through the figure (*Gestalt*) of the Worker (*Arbeiter*). Every epoch is
marked or stamped by a particular "figure" which shapes the world in a
specific way. The epoch in which Jünger then believed the world was
entering, the stamp with which time, space and men were being coined,
all led to the sole figure of the Worker. The Worker is not the represen-
tative of a class, a new society or a new economy; it is a universal and
original figure, one that shapes and informs the world according to a logic
and a rhythm of its own. Thus, if our epoch witnessed the birth of the
party of workers, the organization of workers and even the State of
workers, it is only as the symptom of a more profound tendency attested
in all the areas of our contemporary life: "Work" is here seen as the mark
of the unconditional ruling of will to power, and not as a socio-economic
condition. The Worker is the fundamental figure through which the will
shapes, increases and releases its power over the whole of beings. The
world as a whole – and that means the earth (nature), politics, economics,
culture, men themselves – is mobilized in such a way that it is increasingly subjected to the total planning and global organization of the will
to power. The world is now envisaged solely as matter and as a reserve
of energy that can be exploited, manipulated and transformed according
to the Worker's will to global planning and domination. It is no coincidence, then, if the Worker also takes the more immediately destructive
figure of the soldier, and if war appears simply as one form of mobilization and domination amongst others. In the summer of 1941, as the
conflict was progressively and inevitably entering the stage of its global-
ization, Heidegger addressed his students in the following way:

> 'Workers" and "soldiers" open the gates to the actual. At the
> same time, they execute a transformation of human production
> in its basic structure; of what formerly was called "culture".
> Culture only exists insofar as it is plugged into [*eingeschaltet*]
> the operations that secure a basis for a form of domination. That
> we use the term "plug in" [*einschalten*] to name this connection,
> an expression from machine technology and machine utilization,
> is like an automatic proof of the actuality that finds words here.
> "Workers" and "soldiers" remain obviously conventional names
> that nevertheless can signify, roughly and in outline, the humanity
> now arising upon the earth.
>
> (GA 51 37–8/33)

From the perspective of the essential configuration of the modern age, the
Second World War must be seen as the continuation and the confirmation of the total mobilization already operative in the First World War.

Yet the planetary conflict from the heart of which Heidegger addressed his students eventually marked the last stage in the development of man's power over the earth. For if that conflict was eventually brought to an end, it was only by way of an escalade in the means of mass destruction as well as by the threat of the complete annihilation of an entire nation, if not of the planet as a whole. Is it not a symptom of our epoch that only the actual possibility of a catastrophe of world magnitude could bring the most deadly of wars to its end? Yet the "peace" that followed from the death of hundreds of thousands in Hiroshima and Nagasaki did not bring the fury of might to an end. That peace was and still is the confirmation of the total mobilization that characterizes our epoch. Brought to its knees by power, Japan has become the very emblem of power, of this kind of power consisting of a meticulous organization and a military discipline, of an optimization of its resources and of an exemplary treatment of planetary information. The distinction between war and peace has become increasingly difficult to draw. War seems to be carried out as much if not more on the economic terrain as it is on battlefields. The fiercest battles are now being fought on the "markets": the labor market, the securities market, the real-estate market, the culture market. The whole of reality has become a market, saturated to the point of having to invent and simulate for itself an alternate space, the space of virtuality. The voices of technology – in this case of Capital – are impenetrable. Europe itself has become a Common Market, the market of the smallest common denominator of exchange. The "shares" of such markets are being fought for, much in the same way in which nations used to fight (and still do) for territories. One has become entitled to wonder whether the *Führer* are indeed those whom we continue to label as such, or whether they are now only left with the menial task of managing and orchestrating the ordering, the bringing to heel and the empowering of all the sectors of being. And let us not be fooled into thinking that such wars do not bring their share of victims – victims who do not necessarily die, but who find themselves condemned to survive on the periphery of these planetary phenomena, cast out into the sombre zones of para-techno-capitalism.

In identifying technology with the way in which the figure of the Worker mobilizes the world according to its inner necessity, Jünger's analyses converge with those of Spengler, who had published his *Man and Technology*[13] one year before *Der Arbeiter*. Toward the end of his book, in a chapter entitled "The Last Act," Spengler provides the following description of our Faustian civilization:

> The whole of the organic agonises in the all encompassing organisation. An artificial world penetrates and poisons the natural one. Civilisation has itself become a machine that does or wants

to do everything mechanistically. One now only thinks in terms of "horsepower." One no longer sees a waterfall without transforming it into the thought of electric power. One does not see land full of pasturing herds without thinking of the evaluation of their meat-stock, no beautiful handiwork of their native inhabitant without the wish to replace it by a modern technical procedure. Whether it makes sense or not, technical thinking wants realisations.[14]

Heidegger may have had this passage in mind when, many years after its publication, he gave the following description of the way in which nature is revealed to man in the age of technology:[15]

The revealing that rules in modern technology is a challenging forth [*Herausfordern*], which puts to nature the unreasonable demand that it supply energy which can be extracted and stored as such. The earth now reveals itself as a coal mining district, the soil as a mineral deposit ... even the cultivation of the field has come under the grip of another kind of setting-in-order, which sets upon nature. It sets upon it in the sense of challenging it. Agriculture is now the mechanized food industry. Air is now set up to yield nitrogen, the earth to yield ore, ore to yield uranium, for example; uranium is set upon to yield atomic energy, which can be released either for destruction or for peaceful use. ...

The hydroelectric plant is set into the current of the Rhine. It sets the Rhine to supplying its hydraulic pressure, which then sets the turbines turning. This turning sets those machines in motion whose thrust sets going the electric current for which the long distance power station and its network of cables are set up to dispatch electricity.... What the river is now, namely, a water-power supplier, derives from the essence of the power station. In order that we may even consider the monstrousness that reigns here ...

(TK 14–15/296–7)

What monstrousness does Heidegger have in mind here? In what sense can technology be declared "monstrous"? And why associate technology with nihilism? At this stage, nihilism can only be envisaged in the most simple sense, and that is as a phenomenon linked to the *effects* produced by global technology. Following Jünger's descriptions of the age of the Worker, Heidegger provides his most economic description of the actuality of nihilism in section XXVI of "Overcoming Metaphysics."[16] Technology defines the way in which the "world," perceived solely as extended space, is mobilized, ordered, homogenized and used up so as to enhance man's will to hegemony. The ordering takes the form of a total planning or an equipping (*Rüstung*), which consists in the division of the whole of being into sectors and areas, and then in the systematic organization and exploitation of such areas. Thus, each domain has its institute of research as well as its ministry, each area is controlled and evaluated with a view to assessing its potential and eventually calibrated for mass consumption. Resources are endlessly extracted, stocked, distributed and transformed, according to a logic which is not that of need, but that of inflated desires and consumption fantasies artificially created by the techniques of our post-industrial era. Beings as a whole have become this "stuff" awaiting consumption. Nothing falls outside of this technological organization: neither politics, which has become the way to organize and optimize the technological seizure of beings at the level of the nation; nor science which, infinitely divided into ultra-specialized sub-sciences, rules over the technical aspect of this seizure, nor the arts (which are now referred to as the "culture industry"); nor even man as such, who has become a commodity and an object of highly sophisticated technological manipulation (whether genetic, cosmetic or cybernetic). The hegemony of technology, which can take various forms according to the domains of being it rules over, seems to be limited only by the power of its own completion. It is, for technology, a question of organizing the conditions of its optimal performance and ultimate plan – whether these be the totalitarian or imperialistic politics of yesterday, the global economics and the new world order of today, or the uniformalized culture and ideology of tomorrow. Yet behind this seemingly ultra-rational organization rules the most nihilistic of all goals: the absence of goals. For why is such an ordering set up? What are all those plans for? For the sole sake of planning. For no other purpose than the artificial creation of needs and desires, which can be fulfilled only by way of an increase in production and further devastation of the earth. Under the sway of technology, man – the man of metaphysics, the rational animal – has become the working animal. For such a man, there is no other truth than the one that produces results, no other reality than that of use and profit. His will, this very will that constitutes his pride and that he erects as an instrument of his domination over the whole of the earth, is nothing but the expression of the will to will. Yet what this man does not realize is that his labor and his will spin in a vacuum, moving him ever more forcefully away from his provenance and his destination, from his position amidst beings and from the relation to being that governs it. Busy as he is at using up and producing, at manipulating and consuming, today's man no longer has the eyes to see what is essential (namely presence in its epochal configuration) and can no longer greet the discrete echo of presencing which resounds in thinking and poeticizing alone. At best is he in a position to accumulate "experiences" (*Erlebnisse*), which he flaunts as his "truths."

Complete Nihilism: Nietzsche

Both Jünger and Spengler saw technology as the culmination of the will to power in the subordination of the earth. Even though their texts do not explicitly engage with Nietzsche, his vocabulary is put to work and assimilated with the last phase of a historical process. Heidegger, who was first exposed to the discussions concerning technology through the reading of Jünger and Spengler, was *de facto* confronted with its Nietzschean background. Yet in the end he took this background more seriously than Jünger and Spengler ever did, so seriously, we might add, that his approach to technological nihilism in fact became a long confrontation with Nietzsche, as well as with the entire history of metaphysics that preceded him. Although Heidegger's first readings of Nietzsche favored the perspective of the possibility of an overcoming of nihilism through art understood on the basis of Nietzsche's aesthetics, he soon began to associate Nietzsche's name with the completion of the metaphysical nihilism that rules in the age of technology. In other words, Heidegger was not so much interested in describing nihilism in its actuality as he was in revealing its metaphysical (that is, Nietzschean) background. This task took the form of a long and renewed interpretation of the will to power as will to will: if technology constitutes the last phase of nihilism, Nietzsche's metaphysics, as the metaphysics of the will to power, constitutes its penultimate phase, insofar as it prefigures the will to will that underlies the calculation and the organization of beings as whole.

For Nietzsche, Heidegger insists, nihilism names an event in occidental history. What does this event consist in? In the devaluation of the uppermost values, in the annihilation of all goals.[17] Because the "uppermost" or the transcendent has become null and void, those beings whose value and truth were measured in the light of this transcendence are now worthless and meaningless . The "death of God" is another name for this event. By the death of God we need to understand the death of transcendence as such: not only of the Judeo-Christian God, but also "ideals" and "norms," "principles" and "rules," "ends" and "values" which are set "above" beings so as to give beings a purpose, an order and meaning. Nihilism is the history of the death of God, a death which is slowly yet inexorably unfolding. It may be that this God will continue to be believed in and, as Nietzsche says, that his shadow will continue to cover the surface of the earth. Yet this death resembles that of stars, which continue to gleam long after they have died. As an event that determines the essence of our time, nihilism cannot be equated with a point of view or an attitude. Rather, it is to be understood as the fundamental trait that defines the whole of being in its manifestation or truth. And if the way in which the whole of being is revealed and made manifest to man in history is precisely what defines metaphysics, then we must conclude that nihilism marks the end or the death of metaphysics. The end of metaphysics does not mean its cessation or its interruption. On the contrary, metaphysics continues to rule, much in the same way in which the dead star continues to gleam. Yet the way in which it continues to rule is through the collapse of the realm of the transcendent and the ideal that sprang from it. As a result, all previous aims and values have become superfluous.

It is precisely at this point, at the point of the absolute collapse of all ruling values, that the historical possibility of a new valuation arises. It is precisely at the moment of the completion of nihilism that the counter-stroke to all preceding metaphysics can be carried out. This possibility, whereby nihilism will be overturned and overcome, and at the same time fulfilled, Nietzsche defines as "classical nihilism." This nihilism loses the purely nihilistic sense in which it means a destruction and annihilation of previous values. "Nihilism" in this renewed sense calls for a "revaluation of all values hitherto." This revaluation is not equivalent to a replacement of the old values by new values. Since the old values have become "old" or superfluous only as a result of the collapse of the realm within which they were contained and from which they originated – namely the space of the "beyond" or the "above": transcendence – the new values cannot simply take the place of the old ones. Rather, a new principle for a new valuation must be established. A basis for defining beings as a whole must be secured. It is only on the basis of such a principle that a new light can be thrown on everything that is, and that thinking can be wrested from the nihilism that has invaded metaphysics. But if the interpretation of beings as a whole cannot originate from a transcendent that is posited over and above them, whence can the new values be drawn? From beings themselves. Beings themselves must be thought out in such a way that they can allow for the inscription of a new table of values and a new standard of measure for ranking such values. This new principle, which unites beings and defines them as what they are, without reference to a transcendent realm, Nietzsche calls the "will to power". By will to power, we must not understand the mere yearning and quest for power by those who have no power. We must not understand this formulation teleologically, as if power were the goal that we would set out to achieve. Rather, we must understand power as the affirmation of power through which power struggles to increase its power. Power is essentially self-overpowering: a never-ending process of increase, overtaking and overcoming of power. As the basic trait of everything that is, the will to power is also the force that posits values, valuates and validates. Something can have or can be a value only on the basis and from the perspective of the will to power, of the type and the quantum of force or power it releases. Because "transcendence" in general has been abolished, only the "earth" remains. Thus – and here Heidegger introduces a major twist to the Nietzschean text, a *coup de force* that many wish to identify as a fundamental misreading – the new order that defines beings as a whole must be "the absolute dominance of pure power over the earth through man – not through any arbitrary kind of man, and certainly not through the humanity that has heretofore lived under the old values,"[18] but through the "Overman." And Heidegger immediately adds the following, thus taking the analysis in the direction of an essential complicity between Nietzschean nihilism and technological nihilism:

> With nihilism . . . it becomes necessary to posit a new essence for man. But because "God is dead," only man himself can grant man his measure and center, the *"type"*, the "model" of a certain kind of man who has assigned the task of a revaluation of all values to the individual power of his will to power and *who is prepared to embark on the absolute domination of the globe.*
> (N II 39/N IV 9)

The overcoming of nihilism through the shaping of the overman is at bottom a humanism, indeed the last phase and the fulfillment of humanism, where "man", albeit in the form of the overman, becomes the center of all things and the absolute value. Nihilism in its "classical form" prefigures technological nihilism, and the figure of the overman is simply the prefiguration of the figure of the Worker. Nietzsche's conceptualization of nihilism is the general metaphysical background of the age of technology and the text underlying Jünger's entire work. It is not my intention here to challenge Heidegger's (mis)reading of Nietzsche on the question of nihilism and its connection with the Overman, on the various meanings of "earth" for Nietzsche and on the specific signification of the "will to power." Rather, I wish simply to point to the moment at which Heidegger intervenes with the strongest hermeneutical violence so as to mark the relation of metaphysical subordination between Nietzsche's conception of nihilism and the technological nihilism Jünger describes in *The Worker*. It is, paradoxically, one might think, only at the cost of an anthropological reading of the will to power as it manifests itself in the Overman, and that is, for Heidegger, as the unleashing of man's power and the domination of his will over the earth, that Heidegger is able to take Nietzsche in the direction of a prefiguration of the fulfillment of nihilism in technology.

Yet, "the most pressing issue that still remains unclarified is why Nietzsche's valuative thought has far and away dominated all 'world view' thinking since the end of the last century."[19] In other words, it remains to be understood why valuative thought has become so central and evident to contemporary thought, and what the consequences of such a type of thinking are. This very question also raises suspicion over Nietzsche's own genealogical thought aimed at revealing the origin of values. For if the very notion of value is one that essentially belongs to the nineteenth century, does it not become a retrospective construction to talk about the "values" of Ancient Greece or Christianity? Does the task not then become that of a more originary genealogy, not that of the origin of values, nor even that of the value of values, but that of the origin of the value of values? Such a task points to the uncovering of the *essence* of valuative thought as such. In other words, the question is not to know how the question of values can throw some light on the history of thinking (as the history of the ascetic ideal or nihilism), but to see how the history of thinking (metaphysics) can itself account for the possibility of the emergence of valuative thought in the nineteenth century and how this specific type of thought marks the completion of nihilism. Thus Heidegger upsets the Nietzschean problematic by reversing its presuppositions, by showing how the origin of valuative thought is itself nothing valuative and how the essence of nihilism is itself metaphysical. Valuative thought, the first major articulation of which Heidegger saw as early as 1919 in the thought of Fichte, but which runs through the whole of the nineteenth century and well into the twentieth century (in the so-called *Wertphilosophien* Heidegger objected to so strongly in his early Freiburg years,[20] as well as in the "phenomenology of value" of Scheler), find its most complete and rigorous articulation in the thought of Friedrich Nietzsche. The paradox is that the essence of nihilism comes to be completed in the thought of he who most rigorously revealed and deconstructed the inner logic of nihilism and yet who was able to do such a thing only by reaffirming the absolute valuative standpoint redefined as will to power.

The question is thus now: Where does valuative thinking have its metaphysical source? How does the whole of being come to be determined as will to power? What occurs and reigns in Western metaphysics, that it should finally come to be a metaphysics of will to power? Why is the latter something that inherently posits values? Why does the thought of will to power emerge along with valuative thought? With these questions, Heidegger's *Auseinandersetzung* with Nietzsche begins:

> If it should be shown to what extent the interpretation of the being as will to power first becomes *possible* on the basis of the fundamental positions of modern metaphysics, then as far as the question of the origin of valuative thought is concerned we would have achieved the important insight that Nietzsche has not and cannot have given an answer to the question of origins.
>
> (N II 114 /N IV 73)

To be more specific, the will to power and the valuative thought attached to it carry out the final development of Cartesian subjectivity, and that means the positing of the human subject as the unshakable ground of all certainty. By transforming everything that is into the "property and product of man," Nietzsche simply aggravates the central position of man within beings as a whole. As a metaphysics of the will to power and the Overman, Nietzsche's thought marks the completion of philosophy as anthropology: it is only in the wake of an understanding of beings as a whole at the very centre of which man rules as the ultimate stand-point of evaluation and certainty, as the "master and possessor of nature" (Descartes) and over which he extends the power of his will, that Nietzsche's metaphysics is made possible.

Consequently, must we not admit that technological nihilism, as the unleashing of the will to will over the whole of being and the domina-tion of man over the earth, is at bottom a humanism? Must we not conclude that the essence of nihilism as we know it today is grounded in the history of metaphysics, if metaphysics indeed consists in the process whereby man comes to be determined as the ultimate and sole standard for the valuation and the truth of beings? And does it not then become urgent to change the perspective, dis-locate or dis-place the central position of man within the whole of being, so as to initiate an overcoming (*Überwindung*) of nihilism? And would this dislocation not amount to the possibility of another beginning and another relation to beings, to a silent and discrete, almost imperceptible event, yet one that would mark an inversion or a bending of history, or rather a "turning" (*Wende*) within history?

The Essence of Nihilism

These questions find their most rigorous treatment in the *Contributions to Philosophy*. There, Heidegger envisages the essence of nihilism on the basis of the history of beyng (*Seyn*) as the history of "the abandonment of being".[21] This history is none other than that of "the first beginning," the end of which unfolds as nihilism in the form of planetary technology. Yet the first beginning finds its origin in the very withdrawal or aban-donment of beings by being, and its truth is the one expressed by the history of metaphysics. Metaphysics is the way in which the abandon-ment of being happens as the forgottenness of being. *Seinsverlassenheit* is *Seinsvergessenheit*. Yet this forgetting is not simply a form of absence or an effacement: it rules and reigns over the whole of being in such a way that the truth of being becomes unattainable. In its completed form, nihilism in the form of technology, it rules as will to power, as the most disastrous unleashing of power amidst beings as a whole. How does it come to rule in this way? What must be the essence of European nihilism if it is such that it comes to completion in the form of the will to will?

This essence, which Heidegger will eventually identify as "en-framing" (*Ge-stell*),[22] is first thematized as "machination" (*Machenschaft*) in the

Contributions to Philosophy.[23] By "machination," Heidegger understands the way in which the truth of beingness comes to be interpreted on the basis of the ever more radical abandonment of being, and which culminates in a metaphysics of "lived experiences" (*Erlebnisse*) and "worldviews" (*Weltanschauungen*), with man standing as the ultimate standpoint and center of all interpretation concerning beings in their being-ness. Through the gradual forgottenness of his essence (his relation to the truth of being, or to presence in its presencing), which for the first time he is in danger of losing, man has become the grand manipulator of beings as a whole. Machination is the historical-metaphysical process whereby the whole of being becomes a domain for scientific investigation, technological manipulation and the proliferation of "ideas" "values," and "views" about the "world." But for the earth to become a region sub-mitted to the scientific gaze and the willful power of man, the whole of being must first be revealed and envisaged in a certain way. In other words, if beings as a whole are envisaged today as that which can be interrogated with a view to an ever more precise and pressing process of manipulation, transformation and reproduction, such beings must first be *posited* as such. Beings as a whole have indeed become a *positum*, and "science" "positive" science.[24] In that respect, it matters little whether science be understood in the sense of a "cultural value" (*Kulturwert*), as in most liberal democracies, of a "service to the people" (*Dienst am Volke*), as in a communist regime, or of a "national science" (*völkische Wissenschaft*), as in the biological ideology of Nazism. In other words, it makes no difference whether science be seen from the perspective of Capital and of its logic of accumulation, whether it be considered from the standpoint of the systematic and technical organization of the earth through five-year planning, or indeed from the viewpoint of the preser-vation and the perpetuation of the master race. In every case, the whole of being must be posited as standing reserve (*Bestand*), as that which can be endlessly manipulated, transformed, processed or disposed of according to the various needs and idiosyncracies of the many forms in which machi-nation manifests itself. Not only the earth, but man himself – whether as the entrepreneur of Capital, the Worker of the Socialist State (Stakhanov) or the disposable non-Aryan – has become subjected to this process of machination: a commodity like any other commodity, an instrument of global planning, disposable waste (industrial, biological, political). In every case the earth and man himself have become this stuff under the yoke of the will to power. "Science" is nothing other than the "setting-up of the correctness for a domain of explanation."[25] The only relevant question, with respect to the relation between the various sciences and the kind of worldviews, ideologies and politics they serve is to know which one, amongst the latter, will be able to mobilize the greatest means and forces so as to provide science with its most extreme and final condition, a task which might indeed very well take several hundreds of years to be completed. After the collapse of the so-called totalitarian states, the advantage, in this struggle for power, seems to be on the side of Capital. But who can be sure that a more systematic, technical and global form of organization of the whole of being will not appear some day, thus rendering democracy as a form of technological organization redundant?

How science became "positive" science is something that can be grasped only by looking at the way in which, starting with Plato, beingness or truth came to be understood as *idea*, and how, as a result, the whole of being came to be interpreted as representedness (*Vorgestelltheit*) – how, in other words, the origin of technological nihilism coincides with the emergence of philosophy as metaphysics. It is a question, then, of thinking the interpretation of the truth of beings as *idea with* the essence of technology as *technè*. In other words, it is a question of thinking the essence of technology (*Machenschaft, Gestell*) in its co-emergence with the birth of metaphysics as idealism, which Heidegger often refers to as "Platonism." By situating the origin of nihilism in Platonism, Heidegger is in fundamental agreement with Nietzsche, even though, unlike Nietzsche, he will insist on the fact that what is lost in the positing of the *idea* as the beingness of being is precisely the *einai* of *ousia*, the being of beings as a whole, or presence in its presencing. Rather, the *einai* of *ousia* becomes what is posited beyond being and yet allows being to be *what* it is, its essence. Above and beyond beings, essence can (must) consequently be interpreted as "the good." Essence has become an ideal and a value, the very object of thought and its ultimate point of reference. Being as presencing is no longer in view: only presence remains, whether as the presence of what comes into presence and leaves presence, or, increasingly, as what *is* and never becomes: absolute presence in the form of essence. As that which stands beyond being, as that which makes being visible and meaningful, the idea soon starts to be interpreted as origin and cause, as well as "the good" and "the beautiful." Ontology becomes onto-theology, the science of the most common and highest kind of being: Aristotle transforms Plato's *idea* into a prime mover, into a substance that is essentially at rest in the form of thinking thinking itself. Such is the first end of the first beginning. The rise of Christianity only confirms the fundamentally Platonic structure of Western metaphysics: God comes to be equated with the *idea*, and serves as cause as well as the source of meaning in general. But something essential is added, since the cause is now *causa efficiens*: *ex nihilo aliquid fit*. Every being is now an *ens creatum*, a created being. God himself is a "caused" being, even though it is *causa sui*. Causality is introduced as the paradigm for the explanation of what is and for revealing the meaning of beingness. It is precisely at this point, at the point where the whole of being comes to be interpreted mechanically, as a world functioning like a machine, with a great clockmaker winding up its mechanisms, that machination starts to deploy its essence: not only God, but man himself becomes the one being who can machinate, and that means deploy his power of creation and trans-formation. For that purpose, to demonstrate the magnitude of his might,[26] man needs will. Descartes is the one who will grant him with this will.[27] With Descartes, the *idea* becomes *perceptio* and the whole of being becomes that which can be represented, an *object* of representation. No longer pre-sentation (as presencing, or even as presence in the sense of *eidos* or "out-ward appearance"), but re-presentation, no longer pro-duction, as coming into presence (as *poiesis*), but re-production now constitute the essential relation to the truth of beings. Beings now stand as this sheer surface that can be re-presented and thus re-produced, as this object or this *Gegen-stand* that simply stands there before us. The subject as *thinking* subject (as *cog-ito*) is now the cause of the whole of being, not as efficient cause, but as the condition of possibility for its representation. Being is now equivalent to being true in the sense of being "clear and distinct," a position that can be attained only because the subject has been posited as a thinking thing certain of itself. In short: *esse=verum; esse=certum; esse=ego perci-pio=cogito me cogitare*. The intellect or the understanding lays the foun-dations for the deployment of the will. The whole of being becomes the *Gemacht* of man, his product or his thing, insofar as now man defines the meaning and the purpose, the origin and the destination of that which comes into presence. It is not only transcendental philosophy that is announced in the rise of modernity, but also Hegel's idealism, which raises the idea to the level of the absolute, and consciousness to the level of world-history. In the present age, all ideologies, worldviews and "philosophies" are at bottom effects of Platonism. To be more specific: philosophy itself has become nothing but *Weltanschauung* and ideology, nothing but *Wertphilosophie*. Even the so-called existential philosophies are at bottom disguised forms of *Erlebnisse* or "lived experiences." Nihilism reigns in the form of the forgottenness of its essence, in the form of "ideas" and "ideals," of "values" and "worldviews." Whether Christian or non-Christian, whether anti-Christian or post-Christian, the fundamental philo-sophical positions at the end of this millennium remain a Platonism. With the emergence of all such views, machination is entering the completion of its essence, whether the mode of representation is mechanistic, pragmatic or biological.[28]

Yet Platonism as the metaphysical expression of Western nihilism is itself grounded in a phenomenon which Heidegger defines as "the most profound mystery of the current history of Western man."[29] This "phenomenon" is the most profound mystery insofar as it precisely does *not* manifest itself, insofar as its phenomenality is such that it can only manifest itself as what it is not. In other words, to this phenomenon, which Heidegger identifies with the very essence of the history of the

West, belongs a peculiar self-effacement, a covering-up or a withdrawing of itself, through which something (beings as a whole) happens – through which "there is" (*es gibt*). In this peculiar phenomenon, then, it is a matter of acknowledging the presence of a certain nullity at work, a nullity or a withdrawal that never occurs or manifests itself as such, but only in the presencing of beings. This unique phenomenon, which governs the history of the West, and the essence of which remains covered up by the very unfolding of that history, Heidegger calls the abandonment of Being (*die Seinsverlassenheit*). The question arises, then, as to whether nihilism, far from finding its roots in some attraction toward the nothing, toward the nihil and its nihilation, does not actually stem from a certain blindness with respect to the essentially negative essence of being, from a certain forgottenness of the nothing inscribed within the very structure of being, in short, from a certain inability to take the question of the nothing and, as a consequence, the question of being itself, seriously. Or, as Heidegger himself puts it,

> The question arises whether the innnermost essence of nihilism and the power of its dominion do not consist precisely in considering the nothing merely as a nullity, considering nihilism as an apotheosis of the merely vacuous, as a negation that can be set to rights at once by an energetic affirmation.
>
> Perhaps the essence of nihilism consists in *not* taking the question of the nothing seriously.
>
> (N II, 53/N IV, 21)

What, then, if nihilism were precisely the history of man's inability to hold fast to being as the movement of the abandonment of beings? What if man's doings and thinking were nothing but a way of holding on to beings by way of representations and reproductions, a history which would furthermore be on the verge of entering the stage of its completion in the form of the total absence of questioning with respect to presencing and the total domination and control over beings as whole? Heidegger writes:

> Beings *are*, but the being of beings and the truth of being and consequently the being of truth are denied to beings. Beings *are*, yet they remain abandoned by being and left to themselves, so as to be mere objects of our contrivance. All goals beyond men and peoples are gone, and, above all, what is lacking is the creative power to create something beyond oneself. The epoch of the highest abandonment of beings by being is the age of the total questionlessness of being.
>
> (GA 45, 185)

And in another passage:

> Nihilism, conceived and experienced in a more original and more essential way, would be that history of metaphysics which is heading toward a fundamental metaphysical position in which the essence of the nothing not only *cannot* be understood but also *will* no longer be understood. Nihilism would then be the essential nonthinking of the essence of the nothing.
>
> (N II, 54/N IV, 22)

Overcoming Nihilism?

In a seemingly desperate and hopeless statement, Heidegger writes the following:

> Being has so profoundly abandoned beings and has left beings so much to the discretion of the machination [*Machenschaft*] and the "lived experience" [*Erleben*] that every manifest attempt to save Western culture, every "cultural policy" [*Kulturpolitik*] must necessarily become the most insidious and also the highest form of nihilism.
>
> (GA 65, 140)

If nihilism has advanced to the stage where politics and the realm of the *vita activa* in general can only reinforce it instead of overcoming or overturning it, the question concerning the possibility of an overcoming of nihilism becomes all the more pressing. Since politics or action in general only serves to deepen the power of the will to will and the machination to which presence as a whole is subordinated, whence can a turning in history happen? If it can no longer be a question of calling upon the will as a power of transformation, where can the transformation come from and what shape can it take?

The question concerning the possibility of an overcoming of nihilism is one that is at the center of Nietzsche's thought as well as Jünger's. Yet if both Nietzsche and Jünger identified and thematized nihilism in one of its essential stages and aspects, both failed to think nihilism according to its essence.[30] Because they failed to do so, their thinking always fell short of a genuine overcoming. The overcoming of nihilism is subordinated to the thinking of its essence. To be more specific, thinking is not viewed as a preliminary step toward the overcoming, but as the overcoming itself. As far as Nietzsche goes, overcoming means opposing a countermovement to the devaluation of all values in the form of the revaluation of all previous values. Yet the standpoint to which Nietzsche remains riveted is that of valuation, without ever being in a position to think the origin and essence of valuation, which is essentially complicitous with and is a result of the abandonment of being. The putative overcoming of nihilism through the establishment of the will to power as absolute value only serves to confirm the most extreme omission of being in its default. If nihilism is essentially a default of being itself, that is, of its truth (as disclosedness and unconcealment), does it make any sense to *want* to overcome it? What kind of will would be powerful enough to bend the very course of being and bring it under its sway? Can the history of being be overcome through will-power? At this point, in the face of these very questions, the Nietzschean enterprise begins to shatter, since it offers to overcome nihilism only by willing against it, and so by reinscribing its very horizon (the will to will). In our destitute time, marked by the hegemony of the will to will over presence, any recourse to voluntarism merely confirms the epochal configuration of presence.

If nihilism does not allow itself to be overcome by way of will and decision, it is not because it is insuperable, but because "all wanting-to-overcome is inappropriate to its essence."[31] Since it cannot be a question of simply stepping beyond nihilism, of crossing the line so as to find oneself on the other side of the horizon, the question concerning the possibility of an overcoming of nihilism remains. Yet it remains not in the way of a moving beyond, but in the way of a stepping back – not as an *Überwindung* of nihilism, but as a *Verwindung* or an appropriation of the essence of nihilism. This step back into the essence of nihilism is the only genuine response to the historical unfolding of nihilism. Not will, but thinking itself is the way in which nihilism comes to be experienced on the basis of its essence. This is how, in a statement that anticipates the *Stimmung* of texts such as *Gelassenheit* and *Was heisst Denken?*, Heidegger describes the rhythm of thinking in the age of technological nihilism:

> Instead of rushing precipitously into a hastily planned overcoming of nihilism, thinking, troubled by the essence of nihilism, lingers a while in the advent of the default, awaiting its advent in order to learn how to ponder the default of being in what it would be in itself.
>
> (N II, 368/N IV, 225-6)

Thinking runs counter-stream. Its time is not that of the machine, not that of the *Zeitgeist*. Its time is not that of actual nihilism and of its threat of the total "an-nihil-ation [*Ver-nicht-ung*] of all beings, whose violence, encroaching from all sides, makes almost every act of resistance futile."[32] In this time of destruction, of misery and folly, thinking remains without effects. Its "power" cannot be measured in terms of effects. For thinking only experiences the essence. Yet in the experience of the essence (truth), thinking experiences the actual (presence) in a more originary way. Thus thinking is not entirely without effects: in experiencing the actual on the basis of its essence, thinking opens the whole of being to its truth and grounds it in the truth of being. This silent, almost imperceptible shift is nonetheless decisive. When brought back to its essence, the today opens itself onto another time, or rather onto another dimension of time: the time of deep history, the time of the essence of being, epochal time. In this deepening of time, man, hitherto riveted to the present of absolute presence, is now open to the possibility of an epochal constellation to come. From being a *Heutige*, man becomes a *Zukünftige*, a man of the future.

In the step back from metaphysical representing and from its completion in technology, thinking echoes the silent unfolding of presence. As a result, everything becomes more fragile and uncertain, more questionable and question-worthy. For to relate to presence as such is to relate to the default of being or to being in its withdrawal. Yet this relation is the relation to man's own essence, since man comes to be and experiences presence only on the basis of the withdrawal of being. To be more specific: man is needed by being as the abode of being. To a large extent the turning within being can happen only if man has turned himself toward being: "The salvation must come from where there is a *turn* with mortals in their essence [*wo es sich mit dem Sterblichen in ihrem Wesen wendet*]."[33] Being needs man in order to turn man to itself. Thinking is the way in which man comes to turn toward the truth of being. This happens by way of a letting-be and a letting-go, by way of a certain detachment which is essentially an attunement to the silent voice of being, a gathering around the gift of its presence. To think means: to open oneself to presence as to the gift of being.

Yet even thinking, understood in the most originary sense, or, for that matter, poetizing, to say nothing of all other human "activities," cannot of themselves bring this mutation about. The overcoming of nihilism, which indeed calls for a conversion of man in his essence, can happen only in a "turning (*Kehre*) in the essence of being itself."[34] The possibility of another beginning and another epoch of being is just that: a possibility. The decision concerning such a mutation in the historical unfolding of being is not ours. What form might this transformation take? In "Overcoming Metaphysics," Heidegger goes as far as to suggest that a new beginning might occur only on the ruins of the first one, only as another epoch following the collapse of the technological age:

> Before being can occur in its primal truth, being as the will must be broken, the world must be forced to collapse and the earth must be driven to desolation, and man to mere labor. Only after this decline does the abrupt dwelling of the origin take place for a long span of time.
>
> (VA 73/68)

Yet most often, and particularly in the *Contributions to Philosophy*, Heidegger suggests that the new beginning can run parallel to the first one, not as another epoch, not as the after of technological nihilism, but as the very confrontation with the essence of nihilism. For ours is perhaps the last epoch of being, if it indeed designates the epoch in which the historical possibilities of metaphysics have come to exhaust themselves. More than another epoch, then, a new beginning would perhaps mark the emergence of another domain of time altogether, and an experience of presence that would be simply otherwise than metaphysical.

Yet, at this point, everything happens as if our postmodern condition were nothing but the experience of the unlimited acceleration of time, an acceleration that results in the "spatialisation" of the planet (and of the universe as a whole), that is, in the absolute domination of space in the form of total and readily available presence. The need of being is no longer needed. The essential unfolding of presence has withdrawn, and we are left with beings in the form of standing-reserve. As a result, man is for the first time confronted with the greatest of all dangers, a danger far greater than that of the total and destructive unleashing of power over the earth, and that is the danger of the threat of the annihilation of his essence.[35] The essence of man consists in being needed by being. So long as we do not envisage the destination of man according to his essence, so long as we do not think of man together with being, but solely with the unrelentless releasing of beings, nihilism will continue to prevail, both in essence and in actuality. In essence, as the most extreme manifestation of the *Seinsvergessenheit*; in actuality, as the politics of world domination, which our "democracies" seem to carry out with particular effectiveness. Thus, a politics that concerns itself only with "man," and not with the *essence* of man is bound to nihilism as to its most intimate fate. Does this mean that Heidegger promotes something like a politics of being? No, insofar as politics is always and irreducibly ontic: it concerns man's relation to man. Yet this relation is itself made subject to the way in which being claims man. There can be no politics of being, whether in the sense of a politics inspired by being or with being as its object, because being cannot be the stake of a political program or will. A politics of being is as meaningless as an ethics of being. Yet neither ethics nor politics can be without the prior disclosure of the epochal configuration within which they emerge. In this sense, ethics and politics are always of being. Both ethics as dwelling and politics as place point to man's necessity to find an abode on this earth and to dwell amongst beings. And if Heidegger is so weary of ethics and politics, it is precisely insofar as these modes of dwelling no longer satisfy man's essence, no longer provide man with an abode that is adequate to his essence, in other words, no longer constitute the space of his freedom understood as freedom for his essence (for his relation to the default of being), but are entirely summoned by the power of machination. Unless we come to think of ethics and of politics as the site of a conversion toward the essence of being, a site in which man would find his proper place.

The period of the rectorate will have marked the entry of Nietzsche onto the scene of Heidegger's thinking in the form of a historical and political voluntarism. It took Heidegger no less than fifteen years to dismiss entirely this temptation and to denounce the will to power as the ultimate burst of European nihilism. Whereas in 1933–5, and even up to the end of his life, but only according to its essence, Heidegger viewed Nazism as an alternative to the planetary domination carried out by the politics of the two emblematic superpowers, the techno-social pragmatism of the United States and the Worker's State of the Soviet Union, he eventually saw Nazism, particularly in its imperialistic and destructive phase, as the symptom of an identical historical destination. The confrontation with Nietzsche was a confrontation with National Socialism, not because Nietzsche would have been a precursor of Nazism (Heidegger is careful throughout to condemn any nationalist or biologistic reading of Nietzsche), but because Heidegger's own political engagement was itself made possible by the weight of the will to power as will to will that reigns over the world in the twentieth century. The confrontation with Nietzsche is a confrontation with our epoch as the ultimate figuration of planetary domination and with the will underlying such domination. Nietzsche is unsurpassable, because the metaphysical essence of our age deposited itself in him. By way of a long meditation on the meaning and the essence of will, not as a psychological faculty, but as a metaphysical given, the origin of which goes back to the dawn of modernity, Heidegger was able to wrest his thought from the illusion of the possibility regarding the transformation of the world, of man's relation to being and of men amongst themselves through the sheer assertion of an historical or otherwise political will. From that point on, and to the extent that politics can oppose politics only as counter-will, and thus as *more* will, the transformation, if it is at all possible, will not be political. Nor will it belong to the order of the will. Rather, it will be of the order of the wait and of preparation, it will indeed be passive in the eyes of the will to will, but of this passivity whose forces plunge deep into that which, in our history, is being held in reserve. The emphasis undergoes a certain shift, and the tonality is modified: from an exhortation to resoluteness and great decisions we move to a meditation on salvation, on the new beginning, on the return of the holy. Nihilism cannot simply be left behind, for this still suggests a resort to the will to power. Yet from the very heart of European nihilism, from the very depths of its planetary completion a certain reversal or inversion, a turning is awaiting its time. It is no longer this revolution that consists in overturning and overthrowing, in bringing change by way of a destructive frenzy. It is now simply this turning within history, whereby thinking comes to echo the origin. It is now this silent and singular mutation whose decisiveness is matched by no other event. It is the advent of *Gelassenheit*.

Now if we might be inclined to endorse Heidegger's deconstruction of politics in modernity as being complicitous with a certain metaphysics of the will, a metaphysics which is ultimately hegemonic and destructive, we might also be willing to wonder whether the task of thinking that emerges from this diagnosis is not ultimately heading toward a philosophical dead end, one which, to be more specific, seems to rule out the very possibility of praxis. First of all, and as Heidegger himself seems to suggest, once the suspicion regarding the very possibility of change brought about by politics has been established, is there an alternative to historical trans- formation beside those of "salvation" (*Rettung*), of the coming into presence of a new historical-destinal constellation and of *Gelassenheit* as the proper response to the presencing of presence? To renounce the polit- ical and its metaphysics of the will to will so as to remit one's historical destiny in the hands of "thinking" and of the "god to come," is it not to ask at once too much and too little? Too much, in that thinking cannot come to be thought in the place of acting altogether, and too little, in that thinking cannot be spared from the task of critically analyzing and evaluating the content of the concrete. Could we not think of a concept of praxis, and of a power of historical transformation, that would not presuppose a metaphysics of the will to power? Second, the suspicion that is cast over modern politics as a whole amounts to a totalizing gesture that unables Heidegger to make significant differences between various regimes and ideologies, those very differences that alone can command and motivate specific choices and interventions. For is it not on the basis of a diagnosis encompassing the whole of Western history that Heidegger came to regard politics and ideologies as different as that of Soviet commu- nism, liberal democracies and Christianity as symptoms of one identical calamity, and thus that he was never in a position to consider the specific differences between such ideologies as worthy of philosophical thinking and ethical-political preference?

4
The Free Use of the National

Not even do we renew the world by taking over the Bastille
I know that renew it only those who are founded in poetry.
　　　Guillaume Apollinaire, "Poème lu au mariage d'André Salmon."

They, with a Hydra's vile spasm at hearing the angel Giving too pure
a sense to the words of the tribe.
　　　　　　　Stéphane Mallarmé, "Le tombeau d'Edgar Poe."

The year 1934 does not only mark Heidegger's resignation as *Rektor* of
the University of Freiburg. It is also the year in which, for the first time
in his philosophical itinerary, and in a gesture that initiates a decisive turn
in his thought, Heidegger decides to devote an entire lecture course to
poetry. This does not mean that Heidegger's turn toward poetry was not
announced in previous texts and lecture courses: the brief allusion to the
motif of "Homesickness" (*Heimweh*) in Novalis and the characterization
of poetry as the "sister" of philosophy in the 1929–30 *Fundamental
Concepts of Metaphysics*,[1] the crucial reference to Aeschylus' *Prometheus*
in the rectoral address are only examples of such incursions in the domain
of poetry. Yet such references remained occasional and marginal. How
are we, then, to understand Heidegger's first systematic engagement with
Hölderlin's *Dichtung* in 1934?[2] All commentators seem to agree on the
fact that this choice carries a political significance, even though the 1934/5
lecture course on Hölderlin's hymns *Germanien* and *Der Rhein* (GA 39)
is not devoted to questions of an explicitly political nature. Yet what this
significance amounts to in particular is something that remains open for
discussion. An immediate response would be to interpret Heidegger's
poetic turn as a move away from political activism, as a retreat into the
secluded and sheltered sphere of "pure" poetry. Yet this hypothesis proves
unsustainable when one looks at the specific poems to which Heidegger

turns, namely two national hymns from Hölderlin's later period. This indication can help forge yet another hypothesis, one that would focus on the national dimension of the poems themselves, and that would help raise the following question: How are we to understand the fact that, having endorsed the cause of National Socialism a year before, and having himself deployed a discourse that appealed to the forces of blood and soil of the particularly German *Volksgemeinschaft*, Heidegger now finds it necessary to turn to Hölderlin so as to raise this question of the national anew? Does the very move toward the question of poetic language and, more specifically, toward Hölderlin's singing of the *Heimat* and the *Vaterland*, mark the recognition of a historical (and political) possibility in excess of both the specifically Nazi nationalism of the *Blut und Boden* and a more philosophical nationalism, such as the one developed by Fichte?[3] Is the move to Hölderlin, then, a move away from the questions addressed in 1933, or is it an attempt to raise these same questions in a more originary manner? And what does this tell us about the relation between philosophy, poetry and politics? Such, then, is the hypothesis governing this chapter: by way of a sustained reading of Hölderlin, a reading that is in no way homogeneous nor limited to the 1934–5 lecture course, Heidegger launches the question of the national anew, away from the politics of nationalism.[4] Heidegger's reading of Hölderlin's great hymns, of his correspondence and his theoretical fragments, corresponds to the elaboration of the national question according to its proper ground (not the soil, or the blood, but the earth, and the divine) – a question which is entirely historical-destinal (*geschichtlich*) and this means, ultimately, not onto-theological, but aletheophanic. At stake, then, in this reading, is the possibility of thinking the national "before" any decision regarding the nation-state and independently of the question regarding the juridical status of nationality. The poetry of Hölderlin is unique because it is counter-metaphysical: not because it opposes metaphysics in any way, but because it has leapt ahead of and beyond the time of metaphysics into a new historical configuration, thus opening the way to what Heidegger, in the *Beiträge*, designates as "the other beginning." Starting in 1934–5, the true *Führung* is to be found in poetry understood as *Dichtung*. The poetry of Hölderlin reveals Germany's historical situation to itself: abandoned by the gods, the country sinks ever deeper into the prosaism of its busy everydayness, and no longer has an eye for what is essential. The poetry of Hölderlin names the central and decisive event of the time, this very event which Nietzsche will later designate as "the death of God." This is an unprecedented event, the full measure of which still needs to be grasped. It presupposes and demands a disposition or a "fundamental tone" which Hölderlin designates as "sacred mourning" and "fervor." This tone, which sustains Hölderlin's poem, is in itself a response to the event, a way of sheltering and preserving it, not like an irreversible loss that would arouse in us nostalgia and lament, nor like a momentary crisis awaiting to be overcome, but rather like a lack or a default in the light of which everything comes to be measured, like an absence more present than any actual presence, like a destitution (*Not*) that is at the same time an urgency (*Not*) and a necessity (*Notwendigkeit*), a lack that signifies the very actuality of a place and of an epoch and which, consequently, far from calling for its own erasure, is awaiting the affirmation of its own urgency and necessity. To affirm this event is to endure it, to dwell on and in it: it is to find there one's proper dwelling. It is to this new inhabiting, through which the earth comes to be revealed in a new light, that Hölderlin's poetry invites us. The fundamental stake is indeed that of a proper dwelling for man on earth. And if Hölderlin designates this dwelling as poetic, then this is primarily because of the recognition of the fact that the nature of this dwelling is first decided in language (*Sprache*), and that our relation to the earth, and this means to the world where the whole of being comes to manifest itself, is primarily a relation of language. Language, in this case, is not to be understood as a means of exchange and expression, as a principle of semiotic economy, but as this given in which we are invited to dwell, as this originary place from which presence arises for man. The question of man's dwelling, in the world or on earth, a question that never ceased to haunt Heidegger's text, from the early days of fundamental ontology to the rectoral address, is now brought back to the site of its originary disclosure: poetry. And insofar as the question of the homeland and the national is itself sub-ordinated to this originary dwelling, it too comes to be determined in the sole wake of the question of poetry. The state – if one can thus designate the space not of the management of an accidental encounter between individuals, but of the sharing of a common event in a community whose sole common being would be this very sharing – is itself secondary with respect to the unfolding of such an event, which it necessarily presupposes.

The Poet of the Poets

We recall that one of the central motifs of the rectoral address, indeed the motif that sustained the whole of Heidegger's discourse on the nature of the German university was the concept of *Wissen*, which Heidegger understood as the translation of the Greek *technè*, in which the great Greek beginning was most economically captured. *Technè*, as we recall, was the concept in which the logic of *mimesis* governing Heidegger's discourse was made most visible. What appeared to be most decisive about that concept is that it was in no way reducible to a naming of the essence of the German university: it designated the very origin of history, an origin to the height and challenge of which the German people as a whole was to elevate itself. This historical concept of *technè* is one that Heidegger will retain as a central axis of his thought until the very end, particularly in the question concerning technology and the possibility of its own over-coming:

> From earliest times until Plato the word *technè* is linked with the word *epistèmè*. Both terms are words for knowing in the widest sense. They mean to be entirely at home in something, to understand and be expert in it.
>
> (TK 12–13/294)

Despite this continuity, technè, as the word that serves to designate man's essential and originary comportment with respect to the truth of beings, begins to undergo a slight yet decisive shift in the 1934/5 lecture course, a shift that comes to be explicitly thematized only in the 1935 *Introduction to Metaphysics*. We have already alluded to the decisiveness of this shift in the previous chapter. What does the shift consist in? It consists in the introduction of language (*Sprache*), and specifically of poetry, as the determination in which the historical-destinal nature of *technè* comes to be grasped.[5] On one level, after 1933, whether in *Introduction to Metaphysics* or in "The Origin of the Work of Art,"[6] Heidegger seems simply to repeat what was already sketched out in 1933 on the nature of knowing: "*Technè* means neither art nor skill, to say nothing of technique in the modern sense. We translate *technè* by 'knowledge'."[7] As in "What is Metaphysics?" or in "The Self-Assertion of the German University," knowledge, far from signifying a gathering and an accumulation of information, points to that in which "the norms and hierarchies are set," that "in which and from which a people compre-hends and fulfills its Dasein in the historical-spiritual world [*in der geschichtlichen-geistigen Welt*]." [8] This latter sentence is strikingly remi-niscent of the rectoral address. Yet, while reaffirming the meaning of *technè* as knowledge, and that is as a certain way of standing and dwelling amidst the truth of beings, Heidegger also introduces a major modifica-tion. This is how the passage from *Introduction* quoted earlier continues:

> We translate *technè* by knowledge. . . . Knowledge in the genuine sense of *technè* is the initial [*anfängliche*] and persistent [*ständige*] looking out [*Hinaussehen*] beyond what is present-at-hand at any time. In different ways, by different channels and in different realms, this being-outside [*Hinaussein*] puts into work [*setzt ins Werk*] what first gives the present-at-hand its relative justifica-tion, its potential determinateness, and hence its limit. Knowledge is the ability to put into work [*das Ins-Werk-setzen-können*] the being of this or that being. The Greeks called art in the true sense and the work of art *technè*, because art is what most

immediately brings being (i.e. the appearing that stands there in itself) to stand in something that comes into presence (in the work). The work of art is work not primarily because it is wrought [*gewirkt*], made, but because it brings about [*er-wirkt*] being in a being. To bring about here means to bring into the work [*ins Werk bringen*], that work in which, as that which shines forth [*als dem Erscheinenden*], the ruling surging forth, the *phusis*, comes to shine [*zum Scheinen kommt*]. It is through the work of art as the being that is [*das seiende-Sein*] that everything else that appears and is to be found is first confirmed and made accessible, explicable, and understandable *as a being* or a non-being [als Seiendes *oder aber Unseiendes*].

(EM 122/159)

What is decisive here, decisive to the point of irreversibility, is the introduction of art as a putting into work of being. This new and henceforth essential connection between art and truth as disclosedness constitutes the focus of the 1935–6 "The Origin of the Work of Art." There, art appears as *das Sich-ins-Werk-Setzen der Wahrheit*, as truth's putting itself to work, into the work – truth's putting itself to work in putting itself into the work of art. What was, until 1934–5, the privilege of questioning (which, as we recall, is not a privilege of the question as a form of inquiry, but a privilege of the being for whom its own being is a question for it), namely the ability to stand amidst the whole of being so as to reveal it in its truth, is now equated with the power of art and, more specifically, with poetry as *Dichtung*. Prior to – and that is to say, older than – the *thaumazein* and the questioning of the philosopher is the work of the poet, whose saying constituted the originary speech (*Ursprache*) of the Greek historical Dasein. Such was, at the very dawn of Western history, the role played by Homer's poetry or Sophocles' *Antigone*, the thinking poetry in which the Greek Dasein was given its historical configuration. This does not mean that poetry now replaces philosophy and that, in the place of the specific task of thinking, we could install the task of poeticizing. Nor does it mean that poetry itself is not questioning, or thinking. Rather, it means that both philosophy (or rather thinking) and poetry (or rather poeticizing) are co-originary and of equal necessity, in that both find their ground in the essence of language as *Sprache*. Both consist in an inhabiting of language in and through which language itself is brought to its essence. It is the investigation of this ground, a ground that is absolutely non-foundational, in that it can never be secured, that forces Heidegger into a revaluation of the originarity of philosophy as *technè*. For to say that both poetry and philosophy, as distinct human activities, presuppose language is to acknowledge an origin that is more originary than those activities themselves.[9]

The urgent question, then, becomes: what is language? How does it unfold? What is its essence? It is in pursuing these questions that Heidegger comes to thematize the essence of language as poetry, as poietic or disclosive of the truth of beings in general. It is while thematizing the essential unfolding of language that Heidegger comes to realize that language is precisely the *there* of the truth of beings for man, the place in which beings are first made manifest for man. If man is still interpreted as Dasein, if man is still the being for whom being is an issue, the mode of his stance in the midst of beings, his dwelling, in other words, is now poetic: language is the condition of his ek-stasis and the *Da* in which being comes to shine in its truth. Language is now the there of being and the site of man's encounter with the world. Knowledge itself presupposes the originary event of language, the site of this unfolding where presence comes to be an issue for man. It is only where there is language that *there is* – that a world is given, that presence is at issue for man. If man understands being, it is because he stands under it: he always falls under its yoke, withstands its power and stands by it. If man stands in the midst of beings, it is because he understands being. Man: the (under)standing being. Yet this understanding, originally understood, is poetic: being gives itself in language. Language has this poietic power, which Heidegger identifies with man's very historicity. Poetry and philosophy themselves presuppose this initial opening, in which they are thrown, and in which they find the site of their own essence. Language, in that respect, at least when understood as originary speech (*Ursprache*), is an event: whenever there is language, whenever language takes form and figure, there is a world and beings come to be disclosed in their truth; whenever language unfolds, not as the language of everyday chatter, but as the language in which beings find their ontological site, a new beginning emerges, history happens, and men are disclosed in their essential togetherness and reciprocal appropriation with the truth of being. This co-belonging of being and man is what Heidegger, in the middle of the 1930s, begins to designate as *Ereignis*, the event of ap-propriation. In poetry, words become historically productive, poietic in the most literal sense: through them, a world actually comes to be for man. Man himself, in this happening of language, comes to be constituted as a historical existence or as a people. It is in this sense that poetry can be declared "the originary language of a people" (*die Ursprache eines Volkes*):

> The poetic is the fundamental joint [*das Grundgefüge*] of the historical Dasein, and that means: language as such constitutes the original essence [*das ursprüngliche Wesen*] of the historical being of man. The essence of the being of man cannot first be defined and then, afterwards and in addition, be granted with language. Rather, the original essence of his being is language itself.
>
> (GA 39, 67–8)

Poetry, then, far from being *primarily* a mode of expression or a literary genre, a mode of language amongst other modes, is the very essence of language, the very way in which language unfolds according to its essence. The other modes of language, whether prose or everyday language (*Gerede*) – that mode of language that is *used* to pass on information, to express feelings, desires or orders – are only "fallen" modes of language, already situated at a certain distance from the essence of language. If language is, to use Hölderlin's own words, "the greatest danger," it is precisely because of this double bind: language opens up a world, ex-poses man to the forces of nature and, simultaneously, allows for the possibility of the concealment of this original disclosure and ex-posedness. Language, the language that in coming into being brings a standard on earth, is always and inevitably turned into its opposite, a something that exists amongst many other things, a commodity and a tool, a "thing" readily available. Yet this non-essence of language belongs to language as its counter-essence: from the very outset, the essence of language as poetry is threatened by its counter-essence, by the fact that, from the start, what is opened up by language in a moment of irruption and disruption is closed off by the familiarity of ordinary discourse, which subsequently becomes the rule and the measure of language:

> But the poetic saying falls [*verfällt*], it becomes "prose," first in the true sense, and then in the bad sense, and finally becomes chatter [*Gerede*]. The scientific conception of language and the philosophy of language start off from this daily use of language and hence from its fallen form, and thus consider "poetry" as an exception to the rule. Everything stands on its head.
>
> (GA 39, 64)

If the power of the beginning is now identified with the emergence of poetry, if, in other words, the possibility of a new historical configuration is made dependent upon the disclosedness of a world in language (as was the case in Greek tragedy), the question is one of knowing how this initial moment can become the stake of a genuine repetition. Yet if that which needs to be repeated is no longer, as was the case in 1927, or in 1933, the moment of *Wissen* or questioning that took place in Ancient Greece under the name "philosophy," but the still more originary moment of tragedy, in which the Greek Dasein came to constitute itself, one wonders whether it can remain a matter of repeating such a moment. For what does it mean to repeat poetry? To repeat a question, the question of being, that very question that fell into forgottenness in the very moment at which it was raised, is understandable: to take up the question, to posit it and articulate it in a more originary manner, from the standpoint of the meaning of being, to thus initiate a new beginning in the history of that question, to reorient its course and, with it, that of the West, is a project that seems entirely legitimate. Yet when the beginning is no longer simply associated with a question, but with the emergence of a particular language, the (historical) task of repetition becomes infinitely more complex. Or is it that the historical task no longer consists in repeating the Greek beginning? Or that repetition itself needs to be understood differently: not as the repetition of a pre-existing beginning (what would it mean to repeat that which has already begun?), but as the repetition of beginning itself, as the instituting of a new beginning? And if history happens in the happening of language as poetry, could it be possible that history has already begun anew? But then: where and when? Can history have begun anew, can time have undergone a transformation without our noticing, behind our back as it were? Can history be thus played out: in retreat and silently, far from the sound and fury of world-history? In 1933, Heidegger saw the possibility of such a beginning in the noisy and shattering emergence of National Socialism. Yet the world that was brought about, what was then practiced under the name "politics," lacked the one fundamental dimension that would have transformed it into a movement of an historically decisive nature: a *Dichtung*, a *Sprache*. Instead of opening itself to the historical powers of its own language, the Germany of the third Reich trapped itself in a frenzied celebration of its forces of blood, of soil, of work and of war, without ever realizing that the way of Germany's authentic destiny had already been opened up, in the quiet yet insistent voice of Hölderlin's poetry, a voice that Heidegger came to recognize as the one that most urgently demanded to be heard.

The Poet of the Germans

Thus Hölderlin is not only the poet of the poets and of poetry for Heidegger. He is also the one destinally decisive voice in the history of the West after Sophocles. A German voice! Not that we would know what "German" means before or outside of Hölderlin's poetry: it is precisely in this poetry that the German being comes to be constituted as such. Hölderlin is the poet *of* the Germans, in the double sense of the genitive: he is the national poet because he is the poet of the national, the poet who poeticizes and produces the essence of the German people. As a result of this twofold characterization – poet of the poets and of the Germans – Hölderlin must become a power in German history; to contribute to this latter task, Heidegger writes, "is 'politics' in the highest and ownmost sense." [10] Politics, then, as a concrete human activity, is not altogether abandoned. Yet it is made entirely subordinate to the historical and destinal power of the poetic. How exactly is one to proceed in order to institute Hölderlin as a power in the German people is something that Heidegger does not seem concerned to develop. Unless this is to happen by way of an attunement to the fundamental tone of the poem, to the particular voice that speaks in the poem. The two distinct traits of Hölderlin are not disconnected: if Hölderlin is the poet of the national, it is because he is the poet of the essence of poetry; by revealing the essence of poetry, Hölderlin reveals the possibility of a new historical dwelling on earth.

With respect to the period of the rectorate, Heidegger's poetic turn is decisive in that it enables him to address anew at least three questions that were central to the address as a whole: the first question has to do with the possibility of defining the historical present and of finding a proper response to its decisiveness, a response that is now moving away from political activism and in the direction of poetic attunement; the second question is that of the possibility of the saying of a "we," of which we suggested that it remained unproblematized in 1933, thus allowing Heidegger's discourse to lapse all too carelessly into nationalism; this possibility is now envisaged in the context of poetic language, which shifts the "we" of the German nation away from a metaphysics of blood and soil and, most importantly perhaps, which raises the question of the time of the "we" anew, in an attempt unprecedented since the analyses of co-historicity in *Being and Time*; the last and perhaps most important question is that of the stance and the mode of dwelling of man in the world: in identifying man's dwelling on earth as poetic, Heidegger decisively turns the essence of politics away from politics itself and tries to gain a site of historical disclosure that would be more originary than that of the nation-state and of its politics. It is in the light of this originary dwelling that the questions of the *Heimat* and of the *Vaterland* – of what I wish to call the national – come to be rethought. It is to these two questions that I now wish to turn.

Historical Context: The Absence of the Gods and the Fundamental Tone

In a central passage of his rectoral address, Heidegger referred to Nietzsche's "death of god" in a way that remained enigmatic and unthematized. This is how the passage runs:

> And if our ownmost existence itself stands on the threshold of a great transformation; if it is true what the last German philosopher to passionately seek God, Friedrich Nietzsche, said: "God is dead"; if we must take seriously the abandonment [*Verlassenheit*] of man today in the midst of beings, what then does this imply for science?
>
> (SDU 13/33)

In a way, the 1934/5 Hölderlin lecture course takes absolutely seriously this abandonment of man today in the midst of beings, which Heidegger refers to as the death of God. Yet the formulation that is retained in the lecture course is not that of Nietzsche, but of Hölderlin:

> Gods who are fled! And you also, present still,
> But once more real, you had your times, your ages!
> No, nothing here I'll deny and ask no favours.
> For when it's over, and Day's light gone out,
> The priest is the first to be struck, but lovingly
> The temple and the image of the cult
> Follow him into darkness, and none of them now may shine.
> Only as from a funeral pyre henceforth
> A golden smoke, the legend of it, drifts
> And glimmers on around our doubting heads
> And no one knows what's happening to him.[11]

Between the death of God, and the flight of the gods, the difference seems minimal. Yet it is perhaps here that the break with the tone of the rectoral address is played out. It is the same event that is named in both cases. To be more specific, both Nietzsche's and Hölderlin's formulations respond to the same event. As such, they are both historical: the poetic thinking of Nietzsche and the thinking poetry of Hölderlin fall under the yoke of the same historical transformation. The event is the one that Heidegger begins to describe in his address, and continues to thematize throughout the 1930s, and particularly in the *Beiträge*, under the name *Seinsverlassenheit*, "abandonement of/by being." Yet this specific formulation is to be found neither in the address nor in the first lecture course on Hölderlin. There, Heidegger only speaks of a *Verlassenheit*. This *Verlassenheit* names the historical situation of the West (a situation which, as we shall see, is almost impossible to date). The move from Nietzsche's specific formulation of the event of abandonment to that of Hölderlin is not only a matter of words: it is itself a move, a turn – a transformation. More specifically, it is the beginning of a transformation, one that will require some ten years and numerous volumes dedicated to the interpretation of both Nietzsche and Hölderlin to be fully completed. My intention is simply to point in the direction of this beginning. In what sense is this move more than a matter of words? What does the transformation that is slowly taking place consist in? To put it briefly and crudely: What is at stake is the move, still hesitant and incomplete, from the (Jüngerian) interpretation of Nietzsche that underlies the rectoral address, an interpretation that privileges the philosophems of will and power as ways of overcoming the historical bereavement of Europe, to a meditation on Hölderlin's poetry in which the present, perceived as destitution (*Not*), calls for a response of a radically different kind: neither will nor power, neither guides nor revolutions, but "sacred mourning" and "fervor," *heilige Trauer* and *Innigkeit*. This move away from political activism is at the same time a move into the essence of the national, which is to be thought in terms of the proximity or the distance of the sacred and the divine. Ultimately, then, the political is subordinated to the theophanic.

The event of the flight of the gods cannot be separated from what Heidegger calls the fundamental tone (*Grundstimmung*) of the poem in which this flight is experienced. The fundamental tone is the tone or the mood that carries the whole of the poem, the tone that pervades the poem as a whole and that gives the voice (*Stimme*) of the poem its particular timbre. Thus, the tone is something more than just the expression of something that exists outside of it, something more than just the repetition of a historical fact: it is a response to the event, it is a greeting and a welcoming of the event. In that sense, it is itself historical and belongs to the historical event. Heidegger characterizes the fundamental tone of the hymn *Germanien* as one of "mourning" (*Trauer*). He is cautious to distinguish this mood from any psychological determination, much in the same way in which *Being and Time* insisted that the moods of Dasein be understood existentially-ontologically. Thus, to mourn is not to despair; it is not mere nostalgia in the face of the absence of the gods. Nor is it an attempt to overcome the loss of the beloved. Finally, it is not this diffuse yet insistent and almost unbearable sadness that we designate under the word "melancholia." Mourning, as sacred mourning, as *Grundstimmung* of a poem determined in the historical-ontological sense remains irreducible to the vocabulary and the grip of psychopathology. Rather, the tone that is at stake here serves to describe the way in which a historically decisive event – the flight of the ancient gods – is gathered and preserved. The tone that carries the poem has always exceeded the limited sphere of the personal emotions in order to become the site in which the historical present finds its shelter. At the same time, the tone of the poem opens the historical Dasein to the decisiveness of the event:

> The flight of the gods must first become an experience, the experience must first hit the Dasein in the fundamental tone in which a historical people as a whole endures the distress (*Not*) of its godlessness and its sundering. It is this fundamental tone which the poet institutes in the historical existence of our people. Whether this happened in 1801, whether this is not yet perceived and grasped in 1934 is irrelevant, for the number of years is indifferent to the time of such a decision.

> (GA 39, 80)

Thus the tone of the poem invites us to experience this event of an unmatched decisiveness, this truly historical transformation: the absence of the gods. The gods have fled, the presence of the gods is now something of the past. The time has come for us to mourn: time itself – the historical present – must become the site of this mourning. Yet precisely insofar as the relation to the gods that have fled is one of mourning, the historical present that is characterized here remains under the power of that which it mourns. As such, the renunciation of the ancient gods remains an openness to the gods to come:

> To be permitted no longer to invoke the ancient gods, to want to resolve oneself to renounce them, what is it besides – it is nothing besides – the only possible and resolute preparedness for the awaiting of the divine; for the gods can be renounced as such only if they are maintained in their divinity, and the more so the greater the fervour.
>
> (GA 39, 95)

The poet, the one who abides by the demand of the fundamental tone, lives in a time of the between, that time that is marked by the flight of the ancient gods and, in the very renunciation of those gods that have fled, by the awaiting of the new gods. Time itself, then, unfolds as the history of this double absence: the historical present itself is the site of this twofold absencing. As such, the time that is described in the poem is one of fragility and uncertainty, of abandonment (*Verlassenheit*), dereliction (*Verödung*) and absence of force (*Unkraft*),[12] a time that is marked by the stamp of a twofold default, that of the evanescence of a once epoch-founding event, and that of an event to come, of a future that is in no way ascertained, but only historically possible. This, however, does not mean that the historical attunement to the event of the flight of the gods ought to be one of passivity. The tone that is described here is not the buddhism or asceticism that Nietzsche characterizes as the ultimate stage of (passive) nihilism. Rather, the renunciation of the ancient gods is itself the preparation of the ground for the coming of the new gods; it is itself a certain readiness and anticipation in the face of a historical possibility, a comportment that is not unlike the *vorläufende Entschlossenheit* described in *Being and Time*. Yet this readiness is now progressively stripped from the activistic and voluntaristic overtones in which it was draped in 1933. The mourning that is at stake here is and remains a relation to the gods, both in the form of those gods which have fled and can no longer be called upon, and of those gods to come, and upon which one cannot yet call. Paradoxically, it is in the very renunciation of the gods that the divine is most preserved, and indeed treasured. It is in the name of this paradox that Heidegger can designate both

Hölderlin and Nietzsche as those who, having endured the historical weight of renunciation, still dwell in closest proximity with the sacred. Such has become the task: to will and implore no longer the ancient gods so as to "enter and simply stand in the space of a possible new encounter with the gods."[13] Never, in a way, has the divine been more present than in this time of the absence of the gods: never has the earth been so exposed to its fundamental exposition to the sacred and the divine than in the moment of its uttermost bereavement.

What conclusions can we draw from this initial exploration of the fundamental tone of Hölderlin's *Germanien*? What are the implications of the historical situation revealed in the poem? The *Grundstimmung* can be said to reveal something about the poem as a whole, not as an object of literary investigation, but as the site in which a historical *and* destinal configuration comes to gather itself. Specifically, this gathering is twofold: spatial, first of all, in that the flight of the gods has forced upon man a different relation to the earth, to his dwelling upon it, and hence to what is called the *Heimat* and the *Vaterland* (the homeland and the nation), in which man's historical dwelling finds its particular existence; temporal, also, in that the *Grundstimmung* that emanates from the poem is the expression of more than just the duration of a mood, or even of a life-time disposition: it comes from before the actual "I" of the poet and of its hymn and points far beyond the time of its own existence. The two dimensions gathered in the poem are naturally one: the "I" that speaks in the poem is not the individual "I" of the poet, but the "we" in which the German historical Dasein as a whole comes to recognize itself as a nation. To be more specific, the lament that resonates in the *Grundstimmung* is one with that which emanates from the depths of the homeland abandoned by the gods. It echoes and amplifies the grief of the deserted homeland. There, in the intimacy and the self-gatheredness of the poem, this grief finds its proper site. Such is the reason why the "I" of the poet so naturally comes together with the "we" of the homeland:

> The "I" that speaks here is lamenting with the homeland, because this "I-self" [*Ich-selbst*], insofar as it stands in itself, experiences itself precisely as belonging to the homeland. The homeland – not as the mere place of birth, or as the simply familiar landscape, but rather as the power of the earth, on which man, each time according to his own historical Dasein, "poetically dwells'"[*In Loveable Blue. . .*, VI, 25, v. 32].
>
> (GA 39, 88)

At stake, in the togetherness of the destinal dimensions of space and time is what I wish to designate, after Hölderlin's own formulation, as the *Nationelle* or the proper (*das Eigene*).[14] On the basis of a formulation

that might well capture the essence of what Heidegger meant by "anticipatory resoluteness" in *Being and Time,* and yet do so in a way that
presupposes a radical transformation of the project initially developed in
the 1927 *magnum opus,* it is, for Heidegger, a matter of designating the
conditions under which a free relation to one's own historical Dasein
might occur.

'We"

We recall how, in his rectoral address, Heidegger repeatedly referred to
a "we" that remained unproblematized: beside the "we" of the scientists,
the "we" of the community of professors and students, lay the "we" of
the *Volksgemeinschaft,* of a community bound by its forces of blood and
soil. In a way, one can read the whole of the 1934/5 lecture course as
an attempt to launch this question of the We anew, of turning it into a
real *question,* of problematizing it. In the lecture course, the "we" is no
longer a fact, but a question and a quest, the context of which has become
the poetic saying of Hölderlin. In the *Beiträge,* also, one finds a section
devoted to the question "Who are we?" – a question that is itself raised
in the shadow of the Hölderlinian theme of the flight of the gods, even
though that theme is itself subordinated to the fundamental question
concerning the truth of being.[15] Now the question is: why poetry? Why
does poetry allow for an entry into the question of the "we" that would
otherwise not be accessible? Because poetry, by instituting a relation to
the truth of beings, by disclosing the whole of being to man, and by situating man within this original opening, clears the fundamental domain in
which a community comes to constitute itself as such. Why Hölderlin?
Because Hölderlin is the poet of the Germans, that is, the poet in the
poetry of whom the German people is situated in its historical time, but
also granted with a new historical beginning and a freer relation to its
ownmost essence.

If, as we suggested earlier, politics indeed begins with the utterance of
a "we," this most familiar and yet enigmatic pronoun, to ask, as Heidegger
does, "who are we?" is to take a step back from politics in order to
reveal the question which politics would have always already answered.
It is even to ask whether this "we" that is commonly referred to actually *is,* whether, in other words, we are sufficiently in relation to that
which constitutes us as a We in order to be able to say "we." "We." We
who? We "here" and "now"? But where and when do "here" and "now"
begin? Where and when do they end? How are "here" and "now" given?
We "men," perhaps? But who is man? We, the people. What people? The
German people, perhaps. But do we know what "German" means? How
do we go about answering such a question, even about raising it, at a
time (1934–5) when everyone knows what it means to be German, to

belong to a *Volksgemeinschaft* and a *Geschlecht*, a race that has become the object of an absolutely rigorous science? Heidegger seeks his answer amidst the least expected terrains of all: poetry. Indeed, what can possibly be more "subjective" than the voice of the poet? What is more alien to the "we" of politics than the "I" of the poet? It is this paradox that Heidegger wishes to investigate, by way of a reversal of the commonly accepted state of affairs: the I that is bespoken in Hölderlin's poems is an I that speaks from the depths of the German being and, because of that, is an I that speaks the essence of the German being. It is an I, then, that is far more historical and decisive than the I of those who daily speak in the name of the German *Volk*, an I in which the reality and the future of the German nation has come to settle. It is an I which, despite its apparent solitude and isolation, or rather precisely because of it, is addressed to all of those who might be able to hear it. It does not address itself directly to the German people; it does not say: "Germans!" Such is the address of the politician, or of the late *Rektor* Heidegger, not that of the poet. For he, the poet, knows that only language as *Sprache* has the power to bring a people together under a common destiny. This I that is more binding than all the blood of the *Volksgemeinschaft*, this I in which the destiny of the West has come to crystallize is now the true *Führer*, of whom Heidegger only a year before said that it "alone *is* the present and future German reality and its law."[16] Despite appearances, the I that speaks in *Germanien* is not the individual I of the poet, but the I in which the German essence comes to resonate. Such is the reason why, according to Heidegger, Hölderlin moves so freely between the use of the I and the use of the We in that same hymn.

It is of the utmost importance, then, to distinguish between the I that broaches the present and the future of a people, the I that speaks in the name of a We that remains to be founded, and the We that is so commonly used, and that refers to a present situation that is devoid of historical promise. The paradox is that, for Heidegger, the fate of a nation is not decided by a We that would gather the largest possible number of individual Is (of votes, for example), but by the solitary and adventurous creator who, transgressing the laws and the standards of his own time, broaches a new historical present and offers the people new values. In this time, which Heidegger designates as "the original time of the people," and which he contrasts with "the measurable time of the individual,"[17] something radically new, something "initial" (*anfänglich*), is instituted. The time of the origin is a time that originates: it is the emergence of a new beginning, an emergence that involves violence against the time of the today. In the emergence of the new beginning, history is exposed to the non-foundational foundation of its self-positing and broaches the measure of its own law. Such, then, is the contradiction with which the "creators" (*die Schaffenden*) are faced: insofar as they are founders, they set new standards and new laws for the future; and yet, this founding is always made at the cost of a transgression of a given time, of a violence produced against the law of the today. As a result, the creator is always ahead of his time, exceeding it, outside his time, transgressing it:

> But if someone audaciously thrusts high above his own time, the today of which is calculable, if, like the poet, he is forced to thrust and to come into the free, he must also become a stranger to those to whom he belongs in his lifetime. He never knows his people and is always a scandal to them. He questions true time for his own time, and each time places himself outside the time of the today.
>
> (GA 39, 50)

Thus the creator, amongst whom Heidegger includes not only the poet and the thinker, but also the state founder, is untimely and solitary. He is a creator, and yet his creation is brought about at the expense of an essential solitude – the solitude of those who have elevated themselves to the vertiginous height of the summits blown by the great cold winds and by the transparency of the skies. Because of his very nature, the creator cannot be at home in the time of his today. He is always beyond, in a time that negates and opposes the present time. Hence the situation of the creator is one of exile, of unfamiliarity, of *Unheimlichkeit*, even though his creation is precisely such as to contain the promise of a new and more proper dwelling for the historical Dasein. The very possibility of an authentic dwelling presupposes a thrownness out of the familiar into the vertiginous abyss of the uncanny. Such is the reason why, to his contemporaries, to the *Hierigen* and the *Jetzigen*, the creator himself appears to be *unheimisch* – strange, uncanny: monstrous. No doubt, Hitler once appeared to Heidegger as such a monster, as a tracer of historical paths. Yet is it still Hitler that is intended in the 1934–5 description of the state founder? Certain indications seem to confirm it.[18] Yet the description that is given here of the position of the creator with respect to the today and to the majority of the people does not match the situation in which Hitler found himself at the time. Did Heidegger have another *Führer* in mind? Was he still hoping for a turn within National Socialism itself? These purely speculative questions are of no importance. What matters, on the other hand, is the description Heidegger gives of the statesman as well as the retrospective understanding that this description gives us of his political choice. The statesman is, for Heidegger, an exceptional figure, a solitary figure that is endowed with a certain vision. Politics itself is viewed as a way of bringing this "vision" to life, of putting the truth of the future into a work. Yet if this definition agrees with the one Rimbaud gives of poetry ("il faut être *voyant*, se faire *voyant*"), is it not radically insufficient with respect to politics? Can the political be made entirely dependent upon the greatness of the statesman? Is the political not always and already mediated, in relation with material forces that run through the human and to a large extent exceed it? Can the state, the *polis*, the community ever be conceived simply as a work and the statesman best described as a creator, or an artist? Is there not a political danger in folding the political onto the artistic? Is this not the danger of the political itself? Is it not in the name of art itself, of politics as the total work of art, that the right-wing totalitarianisms, from the Napoleonic Empire to Hitler's Third Reich (and beyond) were justified? Is it not this *plastic* glorification of the great man that characterizes the fascisms of our time, a glorification to which Heidegger succumbed remarkably easily?[19] In any case, the very hierarchy that Heidegger now draws amongst the *Schaffenden* seems to suggest a certain distance taken with respect to the political – not only a personal distance from political activism, but also a relativization of the historical decisiveness of politics in general, yet one that does not call into question the fundamental model of genuine politics as the creation of an exceptional artist:

> The historical Dasein of a people – its rise, its peak, its fall – originates in poetry. From the latter [arises] authentic knowing, in the sense of philosophy. And from these two, the actualisation of the Dasein of a people as a people through the State – politics originates.
>
> (GA 39, 51)

Heidegger will not be long in calling these creators "the future ones" (*die Zukünftigen*), thus emphasizing ever more strongly the temporal aspect of their being. Yet when this happens, in the *Beiträge*, the state founders will no longer be designated amongst them. By 1937 or 1938, politics no longer seem to designate a genuine possibility of bringing about the historical transformation necessary for the rescuing of the essence of the West. It is no longer Hitler, or any statesman, but Hölderlin, who now fulfills the role of the historical hero as it was presented in *Being and Time*:[20]

> Those to come [*die Zu-künftigen*] are those future ones [*jene Künftigen*] toward whom, insofar as they await and hold back in the sacrificial restraint, the sign and the imminence of the remoteness or the proximity of the last god approaches.
>
> (GA 65, 395)

Neither men, nor gods, but demigods, the future ones are primarily designated as the poets. And the most futural of them all is Hölderlin: "Hölderlin is the most futural one [*der Zukünftigste*], because he comes from farthest and in this farness travels farthest and most transforms."[21] Because Hölderlin has stepped ahead of his time, transgressed it, so as to open the possibility of a new relation to the earth, to the gods and to history, because his time is that of a time to come, the one in which the earth again will provide the place for the coming of new gods, because Hölderlin's poetry is entirely driven by this event to come, an event which is already coming, already approaching, Hölderlin is the most promising of all poets, the poet in which the promise of a new historical beginning is sheltered. In the face of the vain and nervous agitation of the statesmen and the servants of technology, in the face of what, in the *Beiträge*, Heidegger begins to call the "machination" that has taken possession of the earth, poetry appears as the site of a different encounter with the earth and with history. The poet stands beyond and before this frantic activity, not because of some incapacity to act and to respond to the events of his time, but because of his conviction that, in Apollinaire's words, only those "who are founded in poetry" can "renew the world." Yet poetry only indicates this way and prepares the way for the coming of the new god. In no way can it summon them to present themselves. Man is left powerless in the face of his destiny, for destiny itself is a gift of history. The future does not belong to us; it is not ours. We cannot say when or even *if* the gods will visit anew. To say that Hölderlin's poetry is still ahead of us, that it awaits us as this word that shelters the promise of a "we," does not mean that this poetry can become the object of a political program, that it can be actualized and translated into the concrete world. It does not mean that it is to come in the sense of a *not yet* awaiting its *now*. Rather, his poetry *is* already, in the sense that it unfolds from the beyond into which it has already leapt. Commenting upon the opening line of Hölderlin's *der Ister* – a line that begins with "Now come, Fire!" – Heidegger says the following:

> For the "Now" of his poetry there is no calendar date. Neither
> is there any need for a date. For this called and self-calling
> "Now" is itself a date in an originary sense, that is – something
> given, a gift.
>
> (GA 53, 8)

The "now" of the time of rescuing (*Rettung*) does not call for a date. For it is itself a *datum*, a gift. It is something that gives itself, something that sends and destines itself. It is, literally, a present: something that *is* in the way of a gift, yet a gift of something that will perhaps never be ours. And thus a promise, the promise of a future, indefinitely promised. In the "now" of the poem, then, it is not a matter of defining a precise instant. Rather, it is a matter of seeing how both future and past are gathered in the present, in a kind of future anterior in which what is happening has long since been sent, and hence decided, and which thus opens up the future. Such would be the structure of the event:

> The "Now come" shines from out of the present to speak into the future. And yet it first speaks in what has already happened. "Now" – that means: something is already decided. And this precisely, that which has already occurred [*was sich schon "ereignet" hat*], alone sustains all the relations to what is coming. The "now" names an event [*Ereignis*].
>
> (GA 53, 8)

The National

The event that is here in question, the event that describes who "we" are, is the unfolding of this time of the between, this time that remains suspended and torn between the flight of the gods and the coming of the new gods. In this time of distress and destitution, the earth itself is revealed in a specific way: it is no longer the earth that is loved and cherished by the gods, no longer the earth that is inhabited by men in proximity to the presence of the divine, but the earth that is abandoned to what Heidegger, in his Nietzsche lectures, begins to call the "will to will," the will that culminates in the planetary domination of the technological. The earth that comes under the control of the will to power and is exposed to its "machination" is a world that is no longer inhabited, but simply subjugated. As such, the earth ceases to be the site of an encounter in which both men and gods are revealed in their essential relation to the truth of beings. The earth is no longer an abode, no longer the site of this originary dwelling in which beings find their proper place through poetic language. The land that is now revealed is not a homeland, not the land that can be inhabited, since genuine dwelling occurs only in the appropriation of the moment of disclosure of the whole of being. Being and the gods have abandoned the earth to its own dereliction, thus turning it into a planetary wasteland. What Heidegger sees in Hölderlin's poetry is a way of returning to the earth, of instituting a different relation to it, one whereby the earth will again become the site of an originary dwelling. Yet in this return, in this homecoming or *Heimkunft*, it is not a matter of returning to a point of lost origin, to a space-time that would have remained untouched by the abandonment of the gods and of being. Rather, it is a matter of creating the conditions for a free relation to the earth, of preparing the ground for the gods to come. Homecoming, then, does not mean to go back home, as if the home designated the site of a preserved and uncontaminated origin. Rather, homecoming points in the direction of an origin to come, of a primal leap or an originary source, beyond the devastation of the desacralized earth, beyond the space-time of destitution. Hölderlin is the poet who has leapt ahead of his time into the time of homecoming, the poet whose saying approaches and addresses us from afar, from the reality of a time to come, thus revealing the essence of his time as abandonment (*Verlassenheit*) or homelessness (*Heimatlosigkeit*). And if man today is homeless, if he is without a home or a homeland that corresponds to his essence, it is not because of the loss of his national identity, a loss that can be seen as the result of military invasions, or of a cultural and economical homogenization of the planet as a whole. Rather, it is because of the abandonment of being that is now threatening man's very essence as the "there" of the unfolding of being. In other words, this is a "double homelessness" insofar as we are not even at home with – and that is to say, we do not even recognize – our own homelessness.

At stake, then, in Hölderlin's *Dichtung*, are the conditions of an authentic dwelling on earth, of what, in the most essential sense, this poetry calls the *Heimat*, the homeland. This alone should suffice to indicate that the national that is here in question is one that has already exceeded any nationalism and any nationalistic politics, that the dwelling that is here at stake does not concern Germany as a geo-politically and, least of all, racially constituted entity, but as the place in which the essence of the time is endured. But even this is not to say enough. For what is at stake in this thinking of the national is not even Germany or Germanness (*das Deutsche*) as such, but the destiny of the West as a whole. To a patriotic discourse that would sing of the homeland in the horizon of a national egoism, that would be grounded in a metaphysical and historiographical concept of the political, Heidegger wishes to oppose a discourse that would point to the essence of the homeland as grounded in the historical-destinal essence of being. To a homeland conceived in terms of "a mere space delimited by external borders, a natural region, a place as the possible scene on which this or that event would take place,"[22] Heidegger opposes a conception of the homeland as the site in which man's essential relation to the truth of being – this fundamental event that Heidegger designates as the event of the mutual appropriation of man and being: *Er-eignis* – is brought about. Heidegger's view concerning the national is perhaps most clearly expressed in the following passage from the 1946 *Letter on Humanism*:

> The word ["homeland"] is thought here in an essential sense, not patriotically or nationalistically, but in terms of the history of being. The essence of the homeland, however, is also mentioned with the intention of thinking the homelessness [*Heimatlosigkeit*] of contemporary man from the essence of Being's history. ... When Hölderlin writes "Homecoming" he is concerned that his "countrymen" [*Landesleute*] find their essence

in it. He does not at all seek that essence in an egoism of his nation [*seines Volkes*]. He sees it rather in the context of a belongingness to the destiny of the West.

(Wm 334–5/217–18)

Is the nation or the homeland "the West," then? Is the homeland to which Hölderlin is referring actually the sum of the nations that are normally characterized as "European"? Is Hölderlin a "European" before his time? Yet is "the West" the same as this conglomerate of nations – whether united or at war, whether geographically, economically, politically or racially defined – commonly referred to as "Europe"? Do we know where, when and with what the West begins and ends, do we even know whether it has begun or whether it has already ended? The passage from the *Letter* continues, in a series of statements that turn the question of the national into one of immense complexity:

But even the West is not thought regionally as the Occident in contrast to the Orient, not merely as Europe, but rather world-historically out of nearness to the source. We have still scarcely begun to think of the mysterious relations to the East which found expression in Hölderlin's poetry. "German" [*das "Deutsche"*: not the German idiom, the language that one possesses or learns, but Germanness, or the German (essence) in the sense of "the national"] is not spoken to the world so that the world might be reformed through the German essence; rather, it is spoken to the Germans so that from a fateful belongingness to the nations [*Völkern*] they might become world-historical along with them. The homeland of this historical dwelling is nearness to being.

(Wm 335/218)

Such, then, would be the paradox: Hölderlin, the poet of the Germans, is, for that precise matter, the poet of the West; yet in poeticizing the West, Hölderlin poeticizes more than just the destiny of Europe: he actually poeticizes the essence of world-history. But is not that the most blatant type of cultural imperialism, the most obvious sign of Heidegger's Euro-Germano-centrism? Is Heidegger not simply deriving world-history from a purely European experience? Is he not simply replacing nationalism with a concept of "the West" that is as imperialistic and totalizing as the politics he is attempting to move away from? Or, on the contrary, is he suggesting that the essence of the destiny of the West is in itself not specifically and exclusively Western? This essence, which Heidegger designates as the origin, and the proximity to which Hölderlin situates himself, might indeed be seen as an origin that exceeds its Western appropriation:

the origin is none other than the truth of being, a truth that might very well be more essentially experienced, better preserved and more genuinely understood in the East, an origin that might very well be alive and actual in the East. The East, perhaps, has found a homeland on this earth, a way to dwell on earth, and not simply to rule over it. Hölderlin, in that respect, insofar as he himself dwells near the source, might be closer to the distant East than to the homelessness that characterizes the time of the West, even though, of course, his homecoming is itself the experience of the West's essential homelessness. From out of this nearness to the source, Hölderlin's *Dichtung* might echo distant voices (Eastern, perhaps), either past, present or future, that also spring from out of this very nearness. There is, perhaps, after all, a secret communication between summits and heights, a communication that bypasses the traditional constructions of cultural identities and historical ensembles. The time and the space of world history (of the history of being) allow perhaps for what, with Baudelaire, we could call secret *correspondances*, the absolute proximity of voices and destinies despite infinite distances.

The homeland, then, is nearness to being. Yet what does nearness mean? How is this proximity brought about? Nearness to the origin or the source is not a given: the nearness itself is not originary. Rather, nearness is a nearing, a movement of approach in which what is most foreign is appropriated and through which a historical Dasein enters the sphere of its essence. The homeland, therefore, is not simply given from the start, but affirmed in the very movement of becoming at home (*Heimischwerden*) or homecoming (*Heimkunft*). Every homeland is a coming home as a coming into the proper, but in such a way that the coming into the proper presupposes the ap-propriation of that which is most foreign: to be at home is to return beyond the experience of the foreign (*das Fremde*), which is an experience of the *Unheimisch* or the unhomelike. This suggests that this movement of return is not a movement of returning to something that was originally, but that the origin itself is constituted through this movement of return. In the return, one does return to some properness that would have remained untouched by the movement of exile or encounter with the most foreign. Rather, it is precisely in the movement of exile that the proximity to the source comes to be. Proximity, then, or nearness, is to be understood as an approach, as a coming close: not as that which is given from the start, but as that which comes to be in the very movement of that return. The departure that takes place in the journey (in)to the proper does not simply leave the origin behind; rather, the departure away from what is simply given and into the unhomeliness of the alien is itself the movement of return to the proper in which the homeland comes to be experienced as such. This, of course, presupposes that, from the start and for the most part, man is not at home in the world, but simply wanders forgetfully at the surface of the earth, that the world is not immediately the home of

man, but that man comes to be at home in the world by way of a relation
to what is most alien to him, by way of a journey through the alien. This,
according to Heidegger, is the way to understand Hölderlin's sojourn in the
south-west of France, where the poet came to experience what the actualization of a truly German essence lacked most, and through the experience
of which that essence was first revealed:

> The love of not being at home with a view to becoming at home
> in the Proper is the law of essence of the destiny through which
> the poet is destined in the founding of the history of the
> "Fatherland."
>
> (EHD 83)

Hölderlin's poetry is the founding word of the German nation, because,
as Heidegger puts it in the 1942 lecture course on Hölderlin's *"der Ister,"*
"coming to dwell in the proper is the only concern of Hölderlin's
poetry."[23] The proper is nothing other than the national itself, nothing
other, that is, than the ability to dwell and be at home in proximity to
the earth. This, according to Heidegger, is what Hölderlin's "river poems"
(*Stromdichtungen*) achieve: they are not a representation of the proper,
or of the movement of coming into the proximity of the proper, but are
the very movement of homecoming, the very movement whereby *das
Deutsche* comes to enter the domain of its essence. The singing of the
Danube or of the Rhine in Hölderlin are not metaphors for the *Heimat*,
but they are the very movement of ap-propriation of the origin whereby
the German Dasein as a whole comes to dwell in proximity to the earth
and in the homeliness of the homeland.

But what is this element of foreignness through the ap-propriation of
which the German essence comes to constitute itself in its proper-ness?
What is the other of Germanness, in the relation to which Germanness
comes to enter the sphere of its own essence? And what is closest or most
natural – what is simply *given* – to the German Dasein? The answer to
this question lies in the famous letter to Böhlendorf dated 12 December
1801, in which Hölderlin writes the following:

> We learn nothing with greater difficulty than to use the national
> freely. And the way I see it, the clarity of representation is as
> original to us as the fire from heaven was original to the Greeks.
> Yet the proper itself must be learnt, as much so as the alien [*das
> Fremde*]. For that reason the Greeks are to us indispensable.
> Now in our proper [*unserm Eigenen*], our nationell [*Nationellen*],
> we shall precisely not follow up on the Greeks, because, as I
> have already said, the free use of the proper is what is most
> difficult [*das Schwerste*].[24]

If Heidegger refers to this precise passage on several occasions,[25] it is because it captures the very essence of what it means and takes for man to dwell historically on earth or to have a homeland. The passage reveals the fundamental chiasma-structure of history understood according to its essence: for a people to have a history, and not something that is simply immediately given to it as its historical heritage (the national), it is of the utmost necessity for that people to relate to that which is most alien and foreign to it. This is the most difficult task, and the reason why Hölderlin calls the homeland "the most forbidden fruit." Whether the national, or what is given from the start, be the ability to be struck by the fire from heaven or the power of being, as in the case of Ancient Greece, or whether it be the ability to grasp clearly and represent, as in the case of the Germans, the truly historical occurs only when the national is able to struggle so as to gain for itself that which is least natural for it. History, then, happens only in this coming together of the two historical extremes, which Heidegger designates as "a conflicting harmony" [eine widerstreitende Innigkeit] between "heritage" [das Mitgegebene] and "task" [das Aufgegebene]. The question is: does Heidegger frame history in such a way that it appears as essentially Greco-German? Are the two extremes or historical possibilities mentioned by Hölderlin interpreted in such a way that the whole of Western history seems to be echoing a voice that emanated from ancient Greece some two thousand years ago and to which, on the basis of some unquestioned metaphysical privilege, the German ear would be particularly attuned?[26] Or are "Greece" and "Germany" here names for an asymmetrical relation, where Greece stands for the model of a relation to the foreign or the alien, a model that remains actual only in that respect, that is, as an ability to relate to otherness, and where Germany stands as an historical task, as something to be achieved, and thus not as something that is quite yet historical? Isn't the difference between Greece and Germany, then, that Germany is still to come, that it has not yet begun, and that it can begin only by repeating that which marked the beginning of the history of the West, namely the ability to relate to what is most alien to it in such a way that what is closest to it becomes its own? Isn't this what Heidegger meant when he wrote that, "insofar as we fight the struggle of the Greeks, but in an inverted front, we do not become Greeks, but Germans?"[27] The law of history is such that it is only in the inversion of the struggle by which ancient Greece emerged as a historically and destinally decisive configuration that Germany can happen as a repetition of that initial moment. But whether Germany will be able to awaken itself to its opposite, to wander into the site of the unhomely, and thus to freely use its national, is something that remains absolutely undecided. Whether Germany will become the site of an encounter with the new gods, whether it will be able to place itself under the light or the truth of being, or whether it will drift ever further into the homelessness of contemporary man and continue to devastate the earth is precisely the point around which the very possibility of another beginning hinges; yet it is something that can neither be predicted nor simply declared.

In the letter to Böhlendorf, then, it is not so much a question of affirming some secret, transhistorical and privileged relation between the Germans and the Greeks, as if this relation were *de facto* given, as if "Greece" and "Germany" were themselves simply given. Rather, it is a question of acknowledging that what is most lacking in Germany in order for it to become the site of a historical dwelling is what was most immediately accessible to the Greeks, of acknowledging an infinite distance, then, between the two, yet a distance which is precisely and paradoxically the condition of possibility of a repetition of the Greek moment: it is only in the affirmation of this distance, which presupposes the journey to the site of the otherness of the other, that the proper of Germany can be freely appropriated and can thus become truly historical. What is most lacking in the German soul, what makes it unable to become a fate, is "the fire from heaven," the proximity to the gods and thus the ability to be struck by the godly power of heaven; what is closest to it, on the other hand, is the "clarity of representation" and the power of conception. In this opposition one recognizes what Nietzsche later identified as the synthetic and essentially tragic opposition of the Dionysian and the Apollonian, an opposition that characterized the Greek destiny as a whole. Specifically, this destiny consisted in gaining a free relation to its Dionysian essence by way of an appropriation of the Apollonian which it originally lacked. Only through the difficult conquest of the Apollonian were the Greeks able to bring the fire of heaven into the sheen of creative representation. From out of the rigorous shaping of the poet, of the thinker and of the artist, the gods, the mortals and all the other beings came into existence and were made to bear on the destiny of the Greek people, thus ordering it into a nation. As for the German situation, it seems to be the exact reversal of the Greek one: what is most immediately proper or natural to the Germans, and yet most difficult to use freely, is the clarity of representation:

> The ability to conceive, the art of the project, the construction of scaffoldings and enclosures, the placing of frames and compartments, the carving up and the regrouping – this is what carries the Germans along. Yet this natural trait of the Germans is not what is genuinely proper to them so long as this ability to conceive is not faced with the necessity to conceive the inconceivable and, in the face of the inconceivable, to bring itself into its own "constitution."

> (EHD 84)

In order to use this gift freely, the German task and only possibility of historical salvation from its homelessness – the only way for it to be a homeland – is to appropriate the fire from heaven. For only this fire, this exposure to the power of the divine and the holy can provide a Dasein with a destiny. Without this double movement, there can be no future for the German people, for, in Hölderlin's own words, "the absence of destiny, the *dysmoron* is our weakness."[28] The historical task, through which the German Dasein becomes a nation and gains a homeland is entirely contained in this formulation: to learn the free use of the proper. This learning to use the proper freely is precisely that which presupposes the jouney abroad, the appropriation of the most alien and distant, the counter-essence. Freedom, then, as well as national identity, presuppose a relation to the absolute other, an other which is other and uncanny, but which is also the other of ourselves, and through the relation to which our own properness is revealed and appropriated. It is only in the encounter with the unfamiliar and the alien, only in the experience of essential otherness in exile that the movement of appropriation of the proper is made possible. Such is the historical stake of Hölderlin's poetry and of his own experience of the alien in the south of France, which he recounts in the following verses:

> The Northeast wind blows,
> The loveliest amongst winds
> To me, for it promises to the navigators
> Firing Spirit and farewell.
>   ("Andenken," I, v. 1–4)

On their way to the far-off country, the poets are those navigators led by the north-east wind, the wind that blows in the direction of the south-west and that clears the skies, thus bringing a new light on earth, the wind that is the promise of the encounter with the fire from heaven in the foreign country. It is only by living under the skies thus disclosed that the poet can experience what is most proper to him and appropriate this proper. It is only by being exposed to the otherness of the other that he can return to his proper in a movement that is itself a founding of the homeland. If the poet can withstand the test of the burning fire, he will be ready to return home and found a new historical beginning at the site where the clarity of representation is preserved.

What is at stake in Heidegger's reading of Hölderlin is not simply the quest for a *Heimat* that would not be a *Volksgemeinschaft*, not simply a way to redefine national identity that would bypass nationalism, but the sketch of the necessary conditions for an historical dwelling on earth. At stake, then, is the fate of the West as a whole, the basic structure of which is here revealed in the Dionysian-Greek/Apollonian-German chiasma. This chiasmic structure would exhaust the historical fate of the West. Put differently: the fate of the West, both past and future, would be entirely contained in this chiasma. Is this a reductive reading of the historical possibilities of the West? In other words, do art, thought, religion, politics really emerge from out of this basic structure? Or must "Greece" and "Germany" be heard as two names or landmarks that would designate something that has always and already exceeded them, in such a way that those names could only function as reference points, as points on the map of a historical-destinal configuration? In other words, can "Germany" and "Greece" be seen as ways of appropriating historical extremes, the Dionysian and the Apollonian, the daimonic, excessive, manic aspect of the human with the more controlled, world-shaping and channeling faculty of representation? If such were the case, then the homeland, or the *polis*, would become the way in which these two antagonistic forces would be brought into a harmony; it would become the way in which the forces of creation (of poetry, art and thought) would come to be liberated, and the manner in which a new mode of inhabiting the earth would be freed for historical man.

5
Before Politics

Toward the end of the "political" failure of 1933–4, whilst deploying an effort of thought in the direction of the national on the basis of a sustained reading of Hölderlin, Heidegger also comes to question the contemporary concept and practice of the "political" in the light of the ancient *polis*. Thus, Heidegger can be seen to be engaged in a double gesture: on the one hand, he thinks the possibility of a use of the national that would be free from nationalism as well as from the form of the nation-state; on the other hand, he re-evaluates this latter and distinctively modern form of political organization, that is the nation-state – this very state which in effect is the vehicle and the most effective servant of technology – by way of a reflection on its forgotten essence, namely the *polis*:

> The basic modern form, in which the specifically modern and self-positing self-consciousness of man orders the whole of being, is the state. Such is the reason why the "political" becomes the normative self-certainty of historical consciousness. The political determines itself on the basis of history conceived in terms of consciousness, and this means experienced technologically. The "political" is the completion of history. Because the political is thus the technological-historical certainty underlying all doing, the "political" is characterised by the unconditional lack of questioning [*Fraglosigkeit*] with respect to itself. The lack of questioning of the "political" and its totality belong together. Yet the reason for this belonging together and the existence of it do not lie, as some naïve minds believe, in the free will of dictators. Rather, it is founded in the metaphysical essence of modern actuality in general. Yet the latter is fundamentally different from the being, in which and out of which Greekness was historical. For the Greeks, the *polis* is that which is

absolutely question-worthy. For modern consciousness, the "political" is the necessary and unconditional lack of questioning.
(GA 53, 117–18)

What distinguishes the modern experience of the "political" from the ancient *polis* is thus a certain lack of questioning with respect to itself, and this means with respect to its own essence. This lack of questioning is evident in that the state is but the political configuration best adapted to the essentially technological demands of modern consciousness. What characterizes this modern consciousness is that it is self-consciousness, a consciousness so conscious of itself that it has become absolutely certain of itself. In the movement of its absolutization, it has become world-consciousness. This consciousness is all encompassing and all mighty, because it is self-positing: its essence or its being is not derived from anything outside of it, but is its own foundation. As such, it is absolutely *fraglosig*. No doubt, this reading of modernity sees the culmination of an historical process as it is metaphysically described in Hegel's thought. The political, its state-organization and its technological domination, is itself the result of this process which culminates in the exposition of the history whereby consciousness becomes ab-solute by becoming free from its own presuppositions and positing itself as the only ground of its becoming. This is what Heidegger means by an "unconditional lack of questioning": a lack of questioning with respect to the forgotten ground of being, forgotten and shut off in the self-positing of man as absolute spirit. In this sense, the "political" represents the end or the completion of history, if it is true that history is the process whereby consciousness posits its own relation to the world as a relation of absolute freedom. But to speak of the end or the closure of history is not to acknowledge a terminal point (today? tomorrow? or was it yesterday?) at which history would cease. Rather, it is a matter of acknowledging how, with the political, history is now gathered into its most extreme possibilities. It is a matter of acknowledging how the total and global presence of beings, and that is the negation of the essentially withdrawing and concealing dimension of being, is at the same time the very condition of possibility for the over-whelming and totalitarian presence of the political. The "totality" and the "totalitarianism" of the political, which seem so specific to moder-nity, are thus to be accounted for not on the basis of the fortuitous will of some individuals once called tyrants, and today best labeled as "dicta-tors," but on the basis of what Heidegger describes as the history of the essence of truth, a history which, in effect, is the unfolding of the forgot-tenness of – and the increasing lack of questioning with respect to – the truth of being. In other words, the total penetration of the political – that is, its totalitarian presence – is not the deed of Hitler, Mussolini or Stalin. It is not a question of names and individuals, but a question of destiny or *Geschick*: the "decision" was made long ago; the fear and trembling that continues to animate our century could be heard long before the actual events. The events were long since destined, not as a fate or a fatality, but as a metaphysically extreme possibility. And what Heidegger designates under the word "political" marks perhaps this most extreme possibility, the possibility in which and as which metaphysics exhausts itself. The political today will have marked an end with airs of a funerary mask, of fire and ashes. Such is the reason why, ultimately, Heidegger is able to encompass under a single diagnosis the liberal democracy of America and the Workers' State of the Soviet Union.[1] All political organizations are merely a response to the challenge of the actuality of modern consciousness, which he designates as technology, and the sole demand of which is the total organization, manipulation and appropriation of the whole of being, which has become a pure *Bestand* or "standing-reserve." One can wonder as to whether Heidegger was right to suggest, as he did in the *der Spiegel* interview, that democracy is perhaps not the most adequate response to technology. With the collapse of fascism and of soviet communism, the liberal model has proven to be the most effective and powerful vehicle of the global spread of technology, which has become increasingly indistinguishable from the forces of Capital.

At the other extreme of the lack of questioning of the political with respect to its forgotten essence, the Greek *polis* is characterized by its question-worthiness. The fundamental goal of Heidegger's interpretation of the Greek *polis* is to show how it remained open to the founding abyss of the truth of being, thereby rendering its own closure impossible and escaping the modern conceptions and demands of the "political." Thus, to think the *polis* is tantamount to wresting it from the sphere of the political and the domain of political philosophy in order to bring it back to the site of its essence, which in itself is nothing political: it is to think something that is older than and prior to our concept of the "political" and of what has come to be practised under the word "politics." With a view to what? To calling for a return to the ancient *polis*? Or to opening a freer relation to the modern political?

Before one even begins to answer such questions, and look into the various interpretations Heidegger gives of the *polis*, it is perhaps necessary to say a few words concerning the contexts and modes of treatment of that question. The following remarks aim to illuminate the stakes of this discussion by situating it both chronologically and textually.

Roughly speaking, Heidegger devotes two series of texts to the interpretation of the Greek *polis*: the first discussion occurs soon after his resignation from the rectorship, in the 1935 *Introduction to Metaphysics*, and the second occurs in a series of texts from 1942–3.[2] As regards the latter, we can only note the striking continuity and homogeneity of its analyses: it indeed consists of three lecture courses in a row. This insistence can only suggest that something major was at stake for Heidegger in that question. Given the temporal sequence, it is also not surprising to find a great unity of style, emphasis and concern throughout those lecture courses. We need to wonder, however, whether there are significant differences with respect to the first interpretation of 1935, and whether Heidegger's interpretation of the *polis* matches the evolution of his thought in general.

As regards the types of sources which Heidegger decides to consult and interpret, there is a striking similarity throughout. The sources are Greek, naturally, but not directly "political" (Heidegger does not draw on political treatises, on constitutional documents or historical accounts and testimonies) and, in the most significant cases (in *Introduction to Metaphysics* and Hölderlin's "*der Ister*"), not even "philosophical." Heidegger's approach to the Greek *polis* is therefore not primarily informed by philosophy, that is, by what metaphysics has had to say about the *polis* and about politics, nor by history, by law or by what Heidegger would regard as any anthropology. By what, then? What is Heidegger's angle on the *polis*, that angle that will allow him to reveal the *polis* in its truth? To put it abruptly: the poetic, or the mythic. To be more specific: *Introduction to Metaphysics* and the *Ister* lecture course address the question of the *polis* on the basis of a reading of the famous second chorus from Sophocles' *Antigone*; the *Parmenides* volume, while referring to that same chorus, focuses on the two *muthoi* that are told toward the middle and the very end of Plato's *Politeia*; finally, the *Heraclitus* lecture course envisages the question on the basis of two anecdotes concerning the master. Not only does Heidegger ignore the political literature of Ancient Greece; he also very carefully avoids the founding philosophical texts: Aristotle's *Politics* and his two *Ethics*, as well as the major part of Plato's *Politeia*.

All of this is to indicate that Heidegger wishes to think the *polis* prepolitically and pre-philosophically: mytho-logically – as if the truth and the essence of what came to be experienced under the word *polis* remained secured in the very margins of the metaphysical text, in a saying whose mode of *aletheuein* remained more truth-ful than the truth of philosophy, or of any anthropology:

> The knowledge of primordial history [*Ur-geschichte*] is not a ferreting out of the Primitive or a collecting of bones. It is neither half nor whole natural science, but, if it is anything at all, mythology.
>
> (EM 119/155)

Muthoi remain truer to the essence of that which they name, because their mode of truth is itself closer to the essence of truth than the truth of metaphysics, which is merely *veritas* and *adequatio*:

> *Muthos* is the Greek for the word that expresses what is to be
> said before all else. The essence of *muthos* is thus determined
> on the basis of *aletheia*. It is *muthos* that reveals, discloses and
> lets be seen; specifically, it lets be seen what shows itself in
> advance and in everything as that which presences in all "pres-
> ence." Only where the essence of the word is grounded in
> *aletheia*, hence among the Greeks, only where the word so
> grounded as pre-eminent legend pervades all poetry and thinking,
> hence among the Greeks, and only where poetry and thinking
> are the ground for the primordial relation to the concealed, hence
> among the Greeks, only there do we find what bears the Greek
> name *muthos*, "myth."
>
> (GA 54, 89/60)

It is only by looking at certain *muthoi*, then, that one ought to be able
to grasp the essence and the truth of the Greek *polis*. Specifically, it is a
matter of understanding that the *polis* does not above all designate a
space, be it geometrical, political, economic, cultural or even philosophical, even though it does designate such a space *also*, but primarily names
the place or the site in which man comes to dwell in a historical-ontological manner. To say that the *polis* is primarily the site of a historical
dwelling is to say that its decisive character lies not so much in the
conjunction and the organization of essential needs, necessities or even
desires, but in an originary relation to the truth of beings. The difficulty
that Heidegger faces thus consists in thinking the essence of the *polis* prior
to its appropriation by the various discourses of anthropology, prior to
the historiographical, political, social and economic thematization of its
essence. The thinking of essence necessarily questions beyond any anthropology into the truth of *anthropos* as the being who always and from the
very start is ap-propriated by the essential and historical unfolding of
being. Speaking of the chorus from Sophocles' *Antigone*, as a poetic piece
that speaks prior to any such anthropology and that therefore names the
essence of man, Heidegger warns us against a misinterpretation of the
whole poem,

> a misinterpretation to which modern man readily inclines and
> which is indeed frequent. We have already pointed out that this
> is no description and exposition of the activities and fields of
> activity of man, a being among other beings, but a poetic outline
> of his being, drawn from its extreme possibilities and limits. This
> in itself precludes the interpretation of the chorus as a narrative
> of man's development from the savage hunter and the primitive
> sailor to the civilised builder of cities. These are representations
> that belong to ethnology and to the psychology of the primitive.

They stem from the unwarranted application of a natural science
– and a false one at that – to man's being.

(EM 118–19/154–5)

If myth constitutes indeed a point of entry into the truth of the *polis*, it is
an entry of an entirely different sort than the ones favored by the social sciences. Such sciences, for whom myth is one source of "information"
amongst many, and for whom myth itself can even become an object of
concrete investigation, a mytho-logy, nonetheless remain closed off from
the essence of the myth, for they question it on the basis of a preconstituted
logos the essence of which is precisely to have delineated the myth in such
a way as to assign it to a specific and determined region, that of "mythology" as it is commonly understood, that is, as the whole of "narratives"
recounting the origin of the cosmos and of the earth, the coming into beings
of the gods and their relation to humans, the heroic and founding deeds of
past generations, and so on. So long as the myth is seen in terms of a mode
of understanding that precedes the discovery and the progression of the sciences, so long as myth finds its place assigned and defined by this *logos* that
defines itself precisely in terms of a twisting free from myth, or rather, so
long as we continue to believe in this other myth according to which the
world coined by rational *logos* is truer than that of the early Greeks, a myth
which is itself Greek and, even more than Platonic, as Heidegger himself
saw, perhaps Aristotelian, so long as we continue to embrace metaphysics'
own myth, as an effort to liberate itself from myth and posit itself in itself
on the basis of itself – the myth of auto-foundation – we shall forever remain
sealed off from the truth of myth, which is precisely truth itself, or the
essence of truth as the play of concealment and unconcealment whereby
"there is," whereby presence occurs and beings find their own site – and
not only their "space" – in the midst of truth.[3] Thus, in the case of the
polis, it is a question of thinking beyond – that is, prior to, yet in accordance with a priority that is itself not chronological and with an order of
precedence that is not that of the *logos* of metaphysics – the (metaphysical)
thought of the *polis*, beyond this thought into the unthought of the *polis*.
It is, therefore, a question of becoming more Greek than the Greeks themselves, of thinking a *polis* that perhaps never *was*, never actually took place,
even though Heidegger will come to designate it as the place of being.
Should this be surprising? If being is such that it is never actually there,
neither *qua* being, nor *qua* substance, nor as this or that particular being-
present-at-hand, how could the *polis* itself, as the place of the unfolding of
the essence of being, be simply present? How could it *be* otherwise than in
the movement of its effacement? This, perhaps, is the point at which to
think prior to metaphysics becomes tantamount to thinking beyond metaphysics – if this is at all possible. To be sure, Heidegger will have his own
doubts: there perhaps never was a *polis* that was pre-metaphysical, a *polis*

in which and for which a certain metaphysical conception of *logos* and of truth was not already in place. The *polis*, insofar as it is, falls within the realm of presence and metaphysics. To think beyond its evidence into the truth of its essence is not to think another *polis*, or a more originary *polis*. It is perhaps to free the possibility of another *polis*, in what would amount to a turning or a shift within history. Is this not the point at which Heidegger's thought breaks with archaic thinking, and becomes an-archic? In the end, one can wonder whether Heidegger's *polis* is not Greek only by name, whether it resembles in any way this ancient *polis* we have become familiar with through the research of the scientific community. This suspicion is actually at work in Heidegger's own text, working it and shaping it from within, to the point where, having developed a first extended analysis of the *polis* in 1935, Heidegger feels the necessity to launch yet another series of interpretations in 1942–3.

The First Interpretation (1935)

Polis. This is a word that cannot be translated. To be sure, Heidegger will provide detailed interpretations of the meaning and the stakes underlying that word. Yet the word itself will remain untranslated. If that word resists translation, it is not for a lack of words and lexical resources, it is not because of some insufficiency on the part of those languages other than Greek. It cannot be translated idiomatically for it has already translated itself historically. Every attempt to translate the *polis* today is an attempt to translate it on the basis of a historical translation that has already taken place and that defines the very nature of the today. Thus, the historical translation of the *polis* is indeed its transformation into the city-state or the nation-state. Yet to translate *polis* idiomatically by state or nation is, from the very start, to close off the very possibility of grasping that which is at issue in the word *polis*. It is to translate a world into another world, an epoch into another epoch. Thus, if, as Heidegger claims, a world or an epoch is indeed defined in terms of its relation to truth, it is also to translate one experience of truth into another one. Yet since that originary experience of truth is fundamentally what is at issue for Heidegger in our relation to the Greeks, it is to lose any possibility of a genuine dialogue with the Greek world. In the move to the nation or the state, that is, in the move to the modern conception of the political, it is precisely this experience of the *polis* as the site of a relation to truth that is lost. This, however, does not mean that the state is no longer a happening of truth; yet it is a happening of this mode of truth or of *aletheuein* which consists in the uttermost covering up of the happening itself. It is that mode of truth characterized by the most extreme forgetfulness of truth. Such is the *Gestell*: the happening of truth as untruth or the domination of the counter-essence of truth. In other words: the age of absolute visibility and pure transparency, the epoch of unreserved patency and total presence where everything has become evident, "in your face" as it were, and where this all too visible reality has reached a point of irreversible saturation, a point where it feels the necessity to make itself virtual and invent for itself another space (cyberspace).[4] We must therefore exercise caution when confronted with the word *polis*, a word that has become so familiar under the guise of "politics" and the "political" that it goes simply unquestioned. By leaving the word untranslated, Heidegger restores questioning to the word, and hopes that it will thus open the way to the thought of its essence. There is no problem of the political outside of its translation from out of the Greek *polis*. We shall therefore never quite leave this question of translation, to which we shall be forced to return later.

Heidegger's first thematization of the *polis* arises out of the commentary of the chorus from Sophocles' *Antigone* that he provides in the section of *Introduction to Metaphysics* entitled "Being and Thinking." To be more specific, Heidegger derives the meaning of the Greek *polis* from the third strophe of the chorus (line 370), where, according to Heidegger, one finds the third and last essential determination of the Greek man as *hypsipolis apolis*, which Heidegger translates as "Rising high above the place, he is excluded from the place." In Heidegger's translation, the strophe as a whole reads like this:

> Clever indeed, mastering
> the ways of skill beyond all hope,
> he sometimes succumbs to malice,
> sometimes is prone to valiance.
> He wends his way between the laws of the earth
> and the adjured order of the gods.
> Rising high above the place, he is excluded from the place
> he who for the sake of adventure always
> takes the non-being for being.[5]

The traditional translation of *polis* by "city" is thus dismissed, and replaced by *Stätte*, place. This is how Heidegger justifies his translation:

> *Polis* is usually translated as city or city-state. This does not capture the full meaning. *Polis* means rather the place, the there, wherein and as which the being-there [*das Da-sein*] is as historical. The *polis* is the historical place, the there *in* which, *out of* which and for which history happens [*die Geschichte geschieht*]. To this place and site of history belong the gods, the temples, the priests, the festivals, the games, the poets, the thinkers, the ruler, the council of elders, the assembly of the people, the army and the fleet.
>
> (EM 117/152)

The *polis* is thus the place or the site of history, that is, the very way in which the historical essence of man is *there*. The *polis* is the site in which the encounter with history happens. It is only insofar as the *polis* is the site of such a specific encounter that to the *polis* belong features such as gods, temples, festivals, poets, etc. What needs to be addressed, then, and grasped, is the very nature of history itself, if it is such that it alone can account for the very existence of the *polis*. What is history? How does history occur? This question is decisive, for the answer that it is given in 1935 is significantly different from that of 1942–3. In *Introduction to Metaphysics*, Heidegger sees history, along with the *polis* as the site of its unfolding, as the happening of a conflict or a confrontation between man, essentially determined on the basis of *technè*, and the whole of being (or *phusis*), essentially determined as *dikè*. This twofold determination follows from Heidegger's interpretation of the opening verses from the chorus, in which man is designated as *to deinotaton*, the uncanniest, strangest and most unfamiliar of all beings: *das Unheimlichste*. The *deinon*, which serves to designate the essence of beings as a whole, points in the direction of both the overpowering power (*das Überwältigende Walten*) of *phusis*, and to the violence (*Gewalt-tätigkeit*) of man. The verses read as follows:

> There is much that is unfamiliar, but nothing
> that surpasses man in unfamiliarity.

To think the *polis*, it is therefore necessary to understand how everything – the whole of being – is best interpreted as *to deinon*, and how, from within this *deinon*, man emerges as the *to deinotaton*, the most *deinon* of all beings. Specifically, it is a question of understanding the *polis* as the happening of the uncanny strife between man and world, between *technè* and *dikè*.

To Deinon, das Unheimliche thus serves to designate "the many," all of those things that are. It is, therefore, the whole of being that is *unheimlich*: strange, uncanny, unfamiliar, uncomfortable, at once aweful and awesome, dreadful and colossal, frightening and overwhelming. Why is the whole of being *unheimlich*? Simply because it *is*, because "there is." There is something awe-inspiring about the world, and that is the very fact that it is, the very fact that there is something rather than nothing. The sheer facticity of the world, its overwhelming presence is sufficient for the chorus to proclaim: "Many is the unfamiliar." Yet not everything is *unheimlich* in the same way. There is, first of all, the overpowering domination of nature, there is the force of the sea and of the winds, of the seasons, and of the earth, there is the burning sun and the biting cold. All of this is awesome: overpowering and inescapable. And yet, over against this power rises the no less uncanny violence of man who, in the midst of this *deinon*, navigates the sea and ploughs the earth, catches the beasts of the skies, of the sea and of the earth, tames the wildest animals and the most hostile of all rivers. Man dwells in the world in such a way that he is most exposed to its power. Because he is most exposed to this power, and therefore most vulnerable, this world can become the site of his abode only by way of the most violent of all gestures, only by way of the unleashing of a certain violence against the ruling of nature. Yet this unleashing only serves to reveal and expose the overpowering power of *phusis* further. Because man is the violent one, the one who surges forth amidst nature and stands erect therein, he is also the one who gathers the dominating and brings it into the Open. Such is the reason why, ultimately, man is the uncanniest of all beings: not at home in the world, without a place, man becomes even more unfamiliar, monstrous as it were, through the unleashing of this violence whereby the earth is turned into the site of his dwelling, and yet gathered in its inescapable domination.

This confrontation between man and nature Heidegger designates further as the opposition between *technè* and *dikè*, which is the twofold essence of the *deinon*. Could the *deinon* be an early word for *Ereignis*, for the event through which man and being are brought together and reciprocally ap-propriated? Let us look more closely at this essential opposition.

As we recall from the previous chapters, *technè* is a motif that began to occupy an absolutely decisive position in the economy of Heidegger's thought in 1933, where it was made to designate the essence of knowledge, and was identified with the greatness of the Greek beginning, the repetition of which was to open the way to a new historical configuration. It should not be surprising, then, to see it here put to work in a way that is no less decisive. While retaining the fundamental identification with *Wissen* or *Fragen* as the most fundamental and history-making comportment, Heidegger decides to retrieve yet another sense of knowledge, which he designates as *Machenschaft*. Knowledge, then, this most human and unfamiliar of all activities, this mode of standing in the midst of the whole of being that is proper to man (this stance which, from the outset, Heidegger identified with existence itself – ek-sistance) is now "machination." This new determination is striking for, as we recall, it is the very determination which, in the *Beiträge*, serves to designate not *technè* in the originary sense, but rather the essentially nihilistic becoming of metaphysics, which culminates in planetary technology. Thus, if one ought not to be misled by the occurrence of this philosophem in the context of the discussion of the chorus, the essential connection between *technè* and *technology* is nonetheless affirmed further: if, as "The Question concerning Technology" will later assert, technology as we know it today is rooted in *technè*, if, in other words, the complete and utter covering up of the essence of truth is itself rooted in this truth and is a mode of truth, similarly, *technè*, as the origin and counter-essence of technology, remains sheltered in it, in such a way that it constitutes the hinge around which history will come to turn anew. This connection is asserted all the more strongly, that the word *Machenschaft*, when applied to ancient Greece, far from designating an experience of the machinic and the mechanical, refers to art, and particularly to this conception, developed at length in "The Origin of the Work of Art," according to which art is the putting into work of truth, the *ins-Werk-setzen der Wahrheit*:

> Knowledge is the ability to put into work [*das Ins-Werk-setzen-können*] being as this or that being. The Greeks called art in the true sense and the art work *technè*, because art is what most immediately brings being, that is, the appearing that stands there in itself, to stand [in something present (in the work)]. The work of art is a work not primarily because it is wrought [*gewirkt*], made, but because it brings about [*er-wirkt*] being in a being. To bring about means here to bring into the work, in which the dominating surging forth [*das waltende Aufgehen*], *phusis*, comes to shine [*zum Scheinen kommt*] as the appearance [or the shining forth: *Erscheinen*]. It is through the work of art as a being that is [*als seiende seiend*] that everything else that appears and is to be found is first confirmed and made accessible, explicable and understandable *as being* or non-being [als Seiendes *oder aber* Unseiendes].
>
> (EM 122/159)

The word *technè*, then, does not primarily refer to the various *technai* or techniques – whether agricultural, industrial, military, etc. – of the Greeks, but to this specific relation to being that consists in a putting being to work into a work. *Technè* is to be understood primarily in terms of a relation between a work and being, or, as "The Origin of the Work of Art" makes clear, between work and truth. It is on the basis of this very relation that one can come to understand not only the Greek conception of art, but the essential complicity between the work of art and those other modes of production generally referred to as technological.[6] In both cases, what is at stake in the production of the work is a relation to the truth of beings – to *phusis* – whereby *phusis* comes to be gathered in itself and exposed in its overpowering power. *Technè*, whether as art or as technology, reveals a relation to *phusis*, in which *phusis* does not appear as an object of mastery and possession, but as an ultimately unmaster-able order to which man is irreversibly attached. In the work, whether in the temple or in the plough, whether in language or in city-creating, it is the very power of the whole of *phusis* that is gathered and brought to its most complete manifestation.

What is thus perhaps most significant with respect to the previous thematizations of *technè* is the emphasis on the "making" (*machen*) or the productive dimension of what now seems to be an activity that is not primarily linked to *theoria* as the highest form of *energeia*. If *technè* does indeed include the poietic activity of the poet, the thinker and the statesman, it also includes those other poietic activities ordinarily referred to as "practical," such as the building of houses and ships, such as hunting and fishing, such as breeding and cultivating. *Technè*, in the context of *Introduction to Metaphysics*, refers to the activities of man in general. There is no opposition between *theoria* and *poiesis*, no transformation of the concept of *technè*. *Technè* as machination still "means" knowledge, yet knowledge does not exclusively mean theory or philosophy. It does mean, however, this ability to put being into a work on the basis of man's transcendence. *Technè* still refers to the transcendence of man, and it is as such that it provides an entry into the meta-physical essence of man and into meta-physics proper.

As for *dikè*, normally identified with justice, whether human or divine, it is here translated as *Fug*, a word which is all the more difficult to translate in English – or in any other language, for that matter – that it does not occur in modern literary German, except, as Manheim notes,[7] in the expression "*mit Fug und Recht*" – "with *Fug* and justice," where the expression, beyond its ordinary meaning of "with complete justification," suggests "proper order" or "fitness." Heidegger stresses that the word be understood first in the sense of joint (*Fuge*) and structure or framework (*Gefüge*). By this, we need to understand that *Fug* is not primarily a juridical or ethical determination, but a metaphysical one: at stake, in *dikè*, is above all a way for things to be joined together according to a certain order and structure; *dikè* refers to the jointure whereby things come together so as to reveal a common ordering. It is only then that it can be understood as a decree, a dispensation or a directive to which such things – beings as a whole, including man – must comply. Far from designating the traditional realm of the ethico-juridico-political, *Fug* designates the originary power of assemblage and gathering of being.

We can now better understand why man is characterized as the most *deinon* of all beings: man's own *deinon*, *technè*, consists in bringing the *deinon* of *dikè* into a work; it consists in surging forth in the midst of *phusis* in a violent gesture against it, which, paradoxically, brings the overpowering power of nature to its highest achievement and manifestation. Man is the uncanniest of all beings because in his very opposition to the overwhelming ruling of nature he brings the uncanniness of nature to stand and shine forth in the work. At the point at which man comes to posit himself in the midst of beings, in what appears like a triumphant stand, the very power of nature comes to be exposed in its irreducible unmasterability. At the very point at which man seems to have found his way amidst beings as whole, he is thrown out of the way and exposed to the world as to the site of his own homelessness. At the point at which man, in the most violent of all gestures, rises against the might of nature, his violence shatters against the power of being:

> The knowing man [*der Wissende*] sails into the very middle of the dominant order [*Fug*]; he cracks being open into beings [in the "rift"] [*reißt im <Riß> das Sein in das Seiende*]; yet he can never master the overpowering. Hence he is tossed back and forth between order and disorder, between the evil and the noble. Every violent bending of the powerful is either victory or defeat. Both, each in a different way, fling him out of the familiar [*aus dem Heimischen heraus*], and thus, each in a different way, unfold the dangerousness of achieved or lost being.
>
> (EM 123/161)

Man is designated as *to deinotaton* or as the *Unheimlicheres*, the uncanniest of all beings, because, in this uncanny world, always at the mercy of the overwhelming and colossal power of nature, he is not at home in it, feels the irremediable impulse to oppose his own freedom and transcendence to the incommensurable force of nature, to transform it and find in it the site of his abode; and yet it is precisely in this titanic effort, in the unleashing of *technè*, that he also unleashes the ordering power of nature, exposes it and reveals it in its unfamiliarity and frightful prodigiousness, as much as he is revealed in his own finitude:

> For the poet, the assault of *technè* against *dikè* is this happening, whereby man becomes not-at-home [*unheimisch*]. In his exile from the homely, the homely is first disclosed as such. But in one with it and only thus, the alien [*das Befremdliche*], the overpowering [*das Überwältigende*] is disclosed as such. Through the event of unfamiliarity [*Unheimlichkeit*] the whole of being is disclosed. This disclosure is the happening of unconcealment. But this is nothing other than the happening of unfamiliarity.
>
> (EM 127/167)

The *polis* is the site of the happening of this unfamiliarity. It is the site where the twofold and strifely nature of the *deinon* unfolds. The site of man's dwelling, his historical abode is such that it is also and at once the site of his homelessness. Man dwells historically by dwelling homelessly. It is only because man is without a home that there is history, it is only because man creates the space of this homelessness that there is a *polis*. If the *polis* designates a home, it is only the home of man's essential homelessness. If it designates a site or a place, it is only the site or the place of man's essential placelessness. If it is historical, it is only because history emerges from out of the essential strife between *technè* and *dikè*, only because history emerges as the happening of the unfamiliar. Now if the *polis* is indeed the site of this strifely encounter between two conflictual forces, between *technè* and *dikè*, between the quasi-demonic violence of knowledge and the no less excessive and overpowering power of nature, or between freedom and necessity, then the very structure of the *polis*, its very appearance must testify to the way in which this strife actually takes place. Although we do not have the space to sketch what could be called an onto-urbanism, we can only speculate as to what it might look like. Thus, the walls, the streets, the temples and the *agora*, the fields, the forests and the sea of the *polis*, as much as the speeches, the statues or the festivals would reveal man's ongoing confrontation with the whole of being, the very inscription of man's becoming (not) at home in the face and in the midst of *phusis*. One can only imagine how such an onto-urbanism, prior to the anthropological interpretation of the *polis*, particularly to its designation as the site of an essentially political – isonomic – construction, a construction that would respond to questions of distribution of power and representation of the population as a whole, would point in the direction of the *polis* as a happening of truth, as that very strifely and violent happening in which man and being would come to be revealed as such. If the *polis* is indeed this place where the confrontation between *technè* and *dikè* occurs, the site at which the whole of beings comes to be gathered in its most irreducible power by being brought into the works of language, of art, of architecture and of technology, then it becomes easier to understand why Heidegger wishes to leave the word untranslated: the *polis* indeed designates this place that is not only and primarily political, but that emerges as the site of a strifely encounter between man and nature, between violence and power. The *polis* is the site at which history appears. It cannot be translated, because its inter-lingual translation is also inter-epochal: the nation and the state are precisely the transformation of this originary relation between *technè* and *dikè*, this transformation whereby the encounter no longer occurs as the violent creation through which being comes to shine forth in its over-powering power, but as the ordering and mastery of the whole of being through planetary technology. With technology, the overpowering power of *phusis* ceases to be disclosed, is itself overpowered, and gives way to the domination of hyper-violence. The question, though, is to know whether it is still violence in the sense described by Heidegger that is at play in contemporary technology, or whether the total domination of tech-nology marks the step beyond human violence into nihilism, a nihilism so utterly completed that it can contemplate the possibility of a global annihilation. The question, with respect to the modern Political and its state apparatus, is to know whether it is still violence that characterizes man, or something beyond violence, whether there is not a hitherto unimaginable danger that has taken possession of the whole of being, that of the loss of originary and creative violence.

At stake, then, in the discussion of the *polis*, and in a way that will remain programmatic for the second series of analyses, is none other than what we have already thematized under the motif of the national and the native in relation to Hölderlin. This connection with Hölderlin will be made quite explicit in the 1942 *Ister* lecture course. Yet if such a connection is made possible, it is because the point of departure in both instances is that of the historical abode of man, that of the possibility of an authentic dwelling on earth. Underlying the discussion of the *polis* as well as of the national is thus the economic determination of the home, of the shelter or the abode. Yet it is essential to note that such a determination is always thought in metaphysical or ontological terms, that is, on the basis of man's relation to the truth of beings. And it is because of such an ontological interpretation that the question of the home is inseparable from that of an originary homelessness and unfamiliarity. The question, we shall have to ask, is to know whether the motif of the home can indeed be ontologized in such a way, or whether it does not carry with it a residual economy that comes to haunt ontology itself. To be more precise: it will be a matter of asking whether any thought of the abode, of the shelter, and, by extension, of the national or the native must not open itself to the sphere of economy, which always and already has oriented dwelling in a particular way. In other words: is our relation to the world, our very way of inhabiting the world not ultimately dependent upon material conditions of existence? And are such conditions not decisive for the way in which thinking itself comes to unfold?

The Second Interpretation (1942–3)

In 1942, Heidegger launches a new series of analyses devoted to the question of the *polis*. More strikingly perhaps, these analyses are deployed on the basis of the very same chorus from Sophocles' *Antigone* Heidegger interpreted in 1935. The point, of course, is to reveal the necessity underlying this renewed reading of Sophocle's *Antigone*. Why, in other words, turn to the question of the *polis* again, and to that same text in particular? To put it abruptly, and for the sake of clarity: so as to gain a more originary understanding of the *polis*, and by originary I do not mean more faithful to the Greek conception of the *polis* – whatever such conception may be – but more Greek than that of the Greeks themselves: archi-Greek. This, I believe, is the specificity of the analysis from 1942 to 1943, one that matches perhaps an evolution in Heidegger's thought with respect to the Greek beginning, at least as it was envisaged in 1935, itself different from the way it was approached in 1927, that is, an evolution whereby the task of thinking is no longer subordinated to the repetition of a question, or of a comportment, but to the step back beyond the beginning into the domain of an *archè*-beginning. This, as we suggested earlier, is perhaps the point at which thinking becomes an-archic.

As far as the detail of Heidegger's analysis goes, we can note the following: first, that what constituted the central axis of the interpretation of the *polis* in 1935, namely the strifely belonging-together of *technè* and *dikè*, is no longer the focus of the 1942 intepretation, but is replaced and reconstituted as it were by the more originary dyad *polis–pelein*; second, and as a result of the first transformation, that the violence that was inherent to the *polis* is not simply dismissed in favour of a more peaceful or less antagonistic conception of the space of originary politics, but is ontologized further and fully integrated into the very structure and logic of the truth of being. The passage from the 1935 to the 1942 analysis of the *polis* is none other than the passage from a consideration still based on the truth of beings, thus still metaphysical – and in 1935 the analysis was indeed to serve as an introduction into metaphysics itself – to a more originary interpretation based on the truth of being itself; third, and still as a consequence of the recentering of the primordial analysis, the political nature of man is yet further subordinated to this truth.

Just as in the interpretation of *Introduction to Metaphysics*, the *deinon* serves as the *Grundwort* of the chorus, and of the Greek Dasein as a whole. Yet whereas the 1935 interpretation, while accounting for the *unheimisch* dimension of the Greek man, insisted on its violent aspect, that very violence that allowed for the overpowering to be gathered and revealed in the work of *technè*, and while the *unheimsich* dimension itself was linked to a natural tendency to transgress and step beyond the familiar into the unfamilar, the 1942 interpretation, while retaining the aspects of *Furcht* and *Gewalt*, insists that the *Unheimlichkeit* or strangeness of man be thought primarily in terms of his essential *Unheimischsein* or being homeless:

> Now insofar as in the *deinon* lie also the powerful and the violent we are able to say that the *deinotaton* means as much as: man is the most violent being in the sense of the cunning animal, which Nietzsche calls "the blond beast" and the "predator." Yet this predatory strangeness of the historical man is a remote variation and a consequence of that concealed strangeness which is grounded in unfamiliarity [*Unheimischkeit*], an unfamiliarity which itself has its own concealed ground in the reversible relation [*gegenwendigen Bezug*] between being and man.
>
> (GA 53, 112)

The strangeness and uncanniness of man is now entirely identified with its *Unheimischkeit*: man is the unfamiliar being, because he is essentially not at home, essentially not at home in and with the familiar (*nicht daheim – nicht im Heimischen heimisch ist*).[8] Man is the uncanniest of all beings because he dwells in the un-familiar. This unfamiliarity is itself grounded in the relation between being and man. It is this not-at-homeness, along with its essential and grounding connection with being that requires a full and thorough interpretation. What needs to be thought, then, is how the *deinon* comes to be characterized on the basis of man's relation to being. What needs to be accounted for, is how being, and man's relation to it, is seen as playing the decisive role in the poem as a whole, and in the Greek Dasein in particular. Furthermore, because the *Unheimlichkeit* is now decisively and essentially reoriented in the direction of a founding *Unheimichsein*, itself rooted in man's essential and destinal relation to being, it is also a question of understanding how the *Heimischwerden*, the becoming-at-home and the becoming native, comes to constitute the very task of the chorus:

> The word of Sophocles, according to which man is the most unfamiliar being thus means that man is, in a unique sense, not at home and that the becoming-at-home [*das Heimischwerden*] is his concern.

> (GA 53, 87)

Such, then, is the threefold reworking of the designation of man as *to deinotaton*: man is the most unfamiliar of all beings, because he is essentially *unheimische*, not at home. This not-at-homeness is essentially ontological, or rooted in man's relation to being. Because man is not at home, the becoming-at-home is the historical task of man, the task through the completion of which man becomes historical and gains a homeland. Finally, and as a consequence of this threefold designation, the *polis* appears as the site or the place of this *Heimischwerden*. What distinguishes this interpretation is thus the introduction of the *Unheimischsein* and the *Heimischwerden* as the explicit essence and concern of the Greek man, as well as the complete ontologization of this thematic of the *Heim*. This transformation is due to the convergence of the thinking of being and of the sustained reading of Hölderlin. It is perhaps necessary, at this point, to note that the discussion of Sophocles appears as the middle section of a lecture course otherwise devoted to Hölderlin, and that it is only with a view to clarifying the fundamental stakes of Hölderlin's poeticizing that Heidegger turns to the ancient poet. The Sophocles that is presented to us in this lecture course is therefore in conversation with Hölderlin, and secretly governed by the thematic of the native and the national one finds in Hölderlin. If there is a secret dialogue between Hölderlin and Sophocles, if the Hölderlinian hymns, and specifically the river hymns, echo the chorus from Sophocles' *Antigone*, it is because what

comes to be decided in both poems is the homeliness and the homelessness of the Western man. At stake, then, in this secret encounter, is nothing
less than the historical destiny of the West. And if one can locate
Heidegger's concern for the political, and by that we mean the possibility
for Western man of a genuinely historical dwelling, of a becoming native
and a becoming at home, it is as much in this decisive orientation of the
deinotaton in the direction of the homelessness of man as it is in the
apparently more explicitly "political" discussion of the *polis*. Or rather,
to be more specific, the discussion of the *polis* is itself entirely derived
from the way in which the *deinon* comes to be thematized anew.

Heidegger finds the justification for this new interpretation in the way
in which the verb *pelein* comes to bear on the characterization of the
deinon. Yet there again, Hölderlin will be in the background, secretly
governing the interpretation. In the 1935 analysis, the verb *pelein* was
made to signify *ragend sich regen*, to be in a sort of towering motion, to
rise above and thus perhaps to surpass or stand beyond. While the verb
pelein does stress the idea of being in motion, Heidegger made it a little
more specific by characterizing this motion or mobility as one of *ragen*,
of rising and of towering. In the context of the analysis of 1935, this
interpretation fitted well with the overall sense of the destiny of man as
being caught in a strifely and violent encounter with the overwhelming
force of the whole of being. In 1942, *pelein* still "means" *ragend sich
regt*. The translation is left unaltered. *Pelein* means *sich regen*, to be in
motion, and this motion is further defined in terms of a *Ragen*. Yet the
Ragen itself does not refer so much to a rising above and a surpassing,
as to a *Hervorkommen*, a coming forth or a bursting out. Into what?
Into the Open, into presence. Thus *pelein* points in the direction of the
presencing whereby every being breaks into the Open, finds its place and
holds its position within presence. *Pelein* is thus synonymous with *einai*,
with being in the sense of presencing: "*Pelein*: to appear out of oneself
into the fore and thus to be [present] [*anwesen*]."[9] The move that is
enacted in the interpretation of 1942 seems to be from an understanding
of *pelein* as a specific kind of motion to that originary motion that
is presupposed in every motion. *Pelein*, in the chorus, would refer to
that primordial *Regen*, to motion in the most originary sense: to being
as *Hervorkommen* or presencing. *Pelein* points to the constance behind
change, to the tranquillity and the motionlessness underneath the storming
sea of becoming, of presencing and absencing. Thus *pelein* is not mere
Vorhandenheit; it is not sheer being in the metaphysical sense, being in
the sense that has come to prevail from Plato to Nietzsche. But to say
that being is the originary movement that allows for every presencing and
absencing to be, that allows for the coming into being and the fading of
every being is to recognize that it itself is not a being, that it itself does
not respond to the law of presence. Being, in other words, is never as

this or that being, is never simply present, nor simply absent, but is only as this withdrawal that allows for beings to be, only as this absencing from out of which beings take place and lose their place. Beyond or rather before the movement of coming into being and vanishing, before beings come to be identified with change and movement, there is an originary movement of presencing which, as such, is never present, a movement whose only mode of being is absencing. In presence, what comes to the fore is not presencing as such, but always this or that being, the essence of which never is present, but always is or rules and unfolds as this constant absence. The law of presence is such that what it presents is only its counter-essence; presence happens only in the covering up of its essence. It is in that sense that the strange can be said to rule in beings as a whole. Strange, indeed, are beings, because they only present the non-essential face of their essence. Strange, indeed, are beings, because their familiarity is deceiving, because their very presence is only the covering up of their essence, of their originary site and abode. It is not surprising that the abode itself, or the hearth the chorus speaks of in the last strophe, will come to signify being itself for Heidegger: the concealed site and the original dwelling of all things. Now if amongst such uncanniness, man appears as the most uncanny and least familiar of all beings, it is because he alone is the being who, when relating to beings, does not only relate to their non-essence or their sheer presence, but also to the movement of their presencing. In his encounter with beings, man does not solely encounter such beings, but being as such. Man is thus the being for whom this very uncanniness is a question, this very being for whom, in his being, this uncanninness is at issue. Man is the *Unheimlichste* because he not only is governed by the law of his essence, but because he also *dwells* within it, and this means relates to it. This, perhaps, is the way we ought to understand the reinscription of the *ragen* in the way of a *Hervor-ragen*: man's coming forth in the midst of beings is a bursting forth and above, a breaking into the open, not (anymore) in the sense of a violent rising against the earth, at least not primordially, but in the sense of an emergence beyond the mere familiarity of the world into the unfamiliar, beyond the mere presence of things into the movement of their presencing and absencing. Man is the being for whom the whole of being is the site of his own homelessness, the being whose abode is the unfamiliar. Thrown into the world as in the site of his dwelling, man is nowhere at home in the world, for in being in the world he is essentially beyond the world, on the verge of its abyssal foundation and disclosure. If *pelein* means being, man is the *Unheimlichste* because this "is," that designates the *Unheimlich* in everything that is, is for man a question and an issue, something to which man, insofar as he himself is, relates. In this sense, man "is" more (uncanny) than all beings, for the very uncanniness of being becomes an issue for it and is revealed as such in his very being.

This relation to the unfamiliarity of being is revealed in a twofold way in the chorus. First of all, man is said to be *pantoporos* and *aporos*: all over the place, finding ways and tracing paths in the midst of beings, and yet without a place, always faced with dead ends, with paths that lead nowhere. Everywhere is man at home in the midst of beings, working his way through it, encountering beings. The world is his domain, his way: *poros*. And yet, whenever he comes across something, he comes across the nothing, for he clings to this being and fails to grasp its being and essence. This nothing to which man comes is that which excludes man from being, that which makes him, literally, aporetic. Man reaches the site of his essence only when this familiarity with beings as a whole is suspended, that is, when the *Unheimlichkeit* that is proper to him, namely the *Unheimischkeit* through which man relates to beings *qua* beings is brought into play. For even when man comes under the awesome, violent and uncanny power of the forces of nature (*die Mächte und Kräfte der Natur*), he is still not experiencing the unfamiliarity that is proper to his essence. This unfamiliarity is, once again, no longer identified with the violence exposed in *Introduction to Metaphysics*, but with man's ability to relate to beings as such, and that is to the being of such beings. Yet because man dwells amidst beings to such an extent, immersed in his relation with beings, he is most inclined to lose sight of being itself, to forget it and thereby become *aporos*. It is in the very familiarity with beings that man becomes oblivious of being and therefore is confronted with the nothing: *Heimischkeit* alone is the site of man's abandonment in the midst of beings, the site of absolute evidence, the site of man's destitution and dereliction. The *polis*, and of, course, the political itself must be reinterpreted in terms of this presence or absence of a relation to being: the *polis*, insofar as it remains question-worthy, that is, insofar as it remains the site of man's relation to the truth of beings, or to the being of beings, constitutes the place in which man unfolds according to his essential unfamiliarity and not-at-homeness; yet insofar as the *polis* is translated into the modern state, it is the overwhelming evidence of beings that comes to rule, in such a way that man is only confronted with the nothing, thus transforming the political into the site of global nihilism. This is perhaps best captured in the following passage:

> This mode of *Unheimlichkeit*, namely the *Unheimischkeit*, is available to man only, for he alone relates to beings as such and thereby understands being. And because he understands being, he alone can also forget being. Such is the reason why the *Unheimlichkeit* in the sense of the *Unheimischkeit* infinitely, that is, in essence, surpasses all other modes of the *Unheimlich*. Strictly speaking, the *Unheimischkeit* is altogether not one mode of the *Unheimlich* alongside the other modes. Rather, it

is essentially "above" them, which is what the poet expresses by calling man the *Unheimlichste*. The most violent "catastrophes" in nature and in the cosmos are nothing in the order of unfamiliarity [*Unheimlichkeit*], in comparison with that *Unheimlichkeit* which man is in himself, and which, insofar as man is placed in the midst of beings as such and stands for beings, consists in forgetting being, so that for him the homely [*Heimische*] becomes an empty erring, which he fills up with his dealings. The *Unheimlichkeit* of the *Unheimischkeit* lies in that man, in his very essence, is a *katastrophe* – a reversal that turns him away from the genuine essence. Man is the only catastrophe in the midst of beings.

(GA 53, 94)

The first determination of man as the uncanniest of all beings is thus entirely dependent upon his essence as the being who, in relating to beings, is confronted with being as such, and yet who, because of the depth of his involvement with beings, is always about to forget being. Such is the double bind of being the being who understands being. In Sophoclean terms: *pantoporos–aporos*.

Should it come as a surprise that the second determination be articulated along the same ontological priority? That it respond to the same ontological double bind? The antithetical "*hypsipolis–apolis*" of the second antistrophe is indeed a repetition of the *pantoporos–aporos* of the first strophe: "In this word combination the *pantoporos–aporos* is taken up again".[10] In what way? In other words: what is the relation between the *poros* or the way that is spoken of in the first instance – that way that leads to something or nothing – and the *polis* that is at stake in the second opposition? The relation is one of specificity: the *polis* designates more specifically that which remained undetermined in the *poros*, in other words "a particular region of the *poros* and a field of its concrete realisation".[11] *Polis*, then, would further serve to designate the way (*poros*). Let us be cautious, therefore, Heidegger warns, and not assume that the word *polis* is essentially about politics, and that everything in Ancient Greece was "political." Particularly, let us not assume that the Greeks were, for that reason, the pure and originary National Socialists (this, by the way, would not only be anachronistic: it would also do National Socialism "a favour that it does not actually need").[12] Let us leave this kind of talk to the community of airheads (*Dummköpfe*) that calls itself "scientific."[13] Let us not assume outright that the *polis* is a "political" concept and that it is best determined "politically." Let us even consider the founding "political" texts, or rather, those texts that have come to be considered as foundational for the political history of the West and in which the essence of the *polis* would be exposed, in the most cautious way. Let us wonder whether Plato's *Politeia* and Aristotle's *Politics* indeed question in the direction of such an essence, or whether, in talking politically about the *polis*, they have not already lost sight of its essence, while retaining something of it at the same time. And if such is the case, then "we need to become more Greeks than the Greeks themselves"[14] when questioning about the essence of the *polis*. But how does one go about such a difficult task? Where does one begin, and what does one hold on to? What is to serve as an access to the unthought truth of the Greek *polis*? The chorus itself, of course. Yet insofar as this chorus is only poetic, the unthought still remains in need of its own interpretation. This enterprise can only be tentative and hazardous. Such is the reason why Heidegger prefaces every determination of the *polis* with a prudent "perhaps," as if offering an interpretation to which no empirical verification could correspond:

> Perhaps the word *polis* is the name for the domain that became increasingly and continually questionable and remained question-worthy.
>
> (GA 53, 99)

> Perhaps the *polis* is the place and the domain around which revolves everything that is question-worthy and unfamiliar in a distinctive sense.
>
> (GA 53, 100)

Tentatively, cautiously, the *polis* begins to unfold as a place (*Ort*), a domain (*Bereich*), in which, around which things are made manifest in their question-worthiness, that is, in their unfamiliarity. The *polis* itself is thus an uncertain site, the site of questioning. But if it is the site of questioning, it is because it is directed toward and also exposes things in their question-worthiness. For there to be questioning, there must be things – beings – that are made manifest as being question-worthy. The question-worthiness of beings lies in the fact that there is more to their being than their sheer beingness. In other words, questioning begins when beings are held in view on the basis of their being, and this means on the basis of being itself, as that which is most worthy of questioning. This is precisely the point at which the modern experience of the political comes to be distinguished from the ancient *polis*: where the ancient *polis* appears as the place of the unfolding of beings in their questionableness, and this means in their originary belonging to a truth that is not their own deed, and least of all the deed of man, the modern conception of the nation and the State appears as the site of the most extreme questionlessness of beings with respect to their being, and this means as the site where man posits himself as the measure of truth and rules over beings as a whole.

Like the *poros* of which the chorus speaks, the *polis* that is in question here is the site of an ontological unfolding, one that is characterized by its ability to reveal the *deinon* or the *Unheimlich* in which man comes to dwell historically:

> The polis is *polos*, that is, the pole, the whirl in which and around which everything revolves. Both words name what is essential, what in the second verse of the chorus the verb *pelein* designates as the constant and the changing. The essential "polarity" of the *polis* is a matter for the whole of being. The polarity concerns the beings in which, around which it, beings as the manifest, revolve. Thus man is related to this pole in a distinctive sense, to the extent that man, in understanding being, stands in the midst of beings and there necessarily always has a "status," a stance [*Stand*] with its circum-stances [*Umständen und Zuständen*].[15]
>
> (GA 53, 100)

It is only insofar as man relates to beings in such a way that there comes to be history, that history happens in a distinctive sense, and that the *polis* takes shape in its concreteness. As in 1935, *polis* still "means" *die Stätte*, the place, the site or the scene of the historical happening of man, yet history is here more specifically determined as man's encounter with the truth of beings as a whole, and not so much as the happening of this particular conflict between the ordering power of *phusis* and the violence of machination. More than the scene of a titanic and indeed tragic conflict between opposing forces, the *polis* is now seen as the *polos*, the pole (*der Pol*), the whirl (*der Wirbel*))or the hinge around which everything – beings as a whole – revolves. There is now something intrinsically pivotal about the *polis*: it is no longer a matrix, a scene, the point at which the paths of man and nature meet in an originary *polemos*; it is more a hinge that pivots on its own axis, thus attracting beings and organizing them in a specific configuration, a constellation or a *cosmos*. In the *polis*, beings as such are disclosed, and brought together so as to constitute a world, with its laws, its gods, its architecture and its festivals. Yet if beings as a whole can be disclosed, it is essentially because man is the being who understands being, that very being for whom, in its very being, being as such is at issue. The *polis* is the site or the there in which this understanding happens historically. Neither state (*Staat*) nor city (*Stadt*), the *polis* is

> the place [*die Stätte*] of the historical abode of man in the midst of beings. This, however, does not mean that the political takes precedence, that the essential lies in the *polis* understood politically and that the *polis* is itself the essential. Rather, it means that

the essential in the historical abode of man lies in the pole-like [*polhaften*] relatedness of everything to the site of the abode, and this means of the being-at-home [of man] in the midst of beings as whole. From this place or site springs what is allowed and what is not, what is order [*Fug*] and what is disorder [*Unfug*], what is fitting and what is not. For what is fitting [*das Schickliche*] determines destiny [*das Geschick*], and the latter determines history [*die Geschichte*]. ... The pre-political essence of the *polis*, that very essence that first allows for everything to become political both in the original and derivative sense lies in that it is the open site of the sending, from which all relations of man to beings, and that is always primarily the relations of beings to man, determine themselves. Thus the essence of the *polis* appears as the way in which beings as such and in general step into unconcealment.

(GA 53, 101–2)

What is decisive and absolutely distinctive about the *polis*, therefore, is its pre-political, that is, ontological, essence. Only insofar as the *polis* is viewed as the there in which beings are made manifest to man is the *polis* authentically political. For in being thus viewed, it is envisaged on the basis of its essence. What is expressed here is the essential connection between the *polis* and the unconcealment or the truth of beings. Yet this connection is possible only insofar as the *polis* is itself grounded in the truth of being, only insofar as it itself is a happening of truth: "The *polis* is grounded in the truth and the essence of being, out of which everything that is comes to be determined."[16]

Finally, the *polis* is similar to the *poros* in that in it a twofold and opposite possibility rules: much in the same way in which man, as the most unfamiliar of all beings, was declared to be *pantoporos–aporos*, he is also declared to be *hypsipolis–apolis*, always exceeding the place, always in danger of losing the place. If the *polis* is the site of man's unfamiliarity, it is essentially because man has the twofold tendency to look beyond his place into the place of being, thus opening up his own place as the place of an essential belonging-together with being, as much as to overlook such a place, and thus to dwell in such a way that the whole of being becomes the most familiar and the most obvious:

Man is placed in the place of his historical abode, in the *polis*, because he and he alone relates to beings as beings, to beings in their concealment and unconcealment and keeps an eye on the being of beings and, from time to time, that is always in the furthest regions of this place, must be misled in being, so that he takes non-being for being and being for non-being.

(GA 53, 108)

The *polis* is thus governed by a certain reversibility (*Gegenwendigkeit*), since the unconcealment that takes place in it is at once the risk of the concealment of that very movement. As a result, the historical abode of man is torn between two extremes, always open to the play of its strifely and reversible essence. Ultimately, then, the *polis* functions like the site in which being comes to be for man as this most questionable and fragile gift, always in danger of losing its questionability, always running the risk of falling into the realm of evidence. The *polis* is the site of this questioning, the locus of this understanding relation. It is the site where man becomes at home in his own homelessness, the site where man's essential unfamiliarity or not-at-homeness is made the very center or pole around which everyday life comes to whirl. It is thus the site of the questionability of man, the site that reveals the originary relation between man and being. Man can dwell and become at home in the world only insofar as being has opened itself up to man, only insofar as being is the Open. To be able to see this Open as such, and not only to be sucked into it and be ruled by it, is the specificity of man. Man is this being who can relate to or understand being as such, being in its truth or openness. If man is the uncanniest of all beings, it is precisely because of this ability to look into the abyssal – incommensurable, colossal, dreadful and overwhelming – openness of being, his ability to withstand it and find his own stance within it. The risk – *polma* – the greatest risk that man runs is to mistake being for non-being, and vice versa, that is, to mistake mere presence for the truth of being, to respond to the law of the essential unfolding of being by covering up the essence.

This extreme ontologization of the chorus is further confirmed and accentuated in the interpretation that Heidegger gives of the *hestia*, ordinarily thought to serve a social and political function. Yet such a function, which roughly describes the situation of classical Greece, seems to derive from a perhaps more cosmological and physical conception of the *hestia*, one which, at times, seems remarkably close to that (purely hermeneutical) of Heidegger.

In section 19 of the *Ister* lecture course, Heidegger recounts the *muthos* of the cosmic procession of the twelve gods, led by Zeus through the immensity of the skies, as it appears in Plato's *Phaedrus*. Hestia, alone, stays behind in the gods' abode:

> There in the heaven Zeus, mighty leader, drives his winged team. First of the host of gods and daemons he proceeds, ordering all things and caring therefor, and the host follows after him, marshaled in eleven companies. For Hestia abides alone in the gods' dwelling place, but for the rest, all such as are ranked in the number of the twelve as ruler gods lead their several companies, each according to his rank.
>
> (246e–7a)

It is thus that the goddess Hestia comes to be associated not only with the home, in the very center of which she sits enthroned, but with the earth, to which the home is attached. This connection between home and earth is retained in the way in which, in the Mycenaean house, the circular hearth, identified with the home as such, and with the divinity protecting it, is actually fixed to the ground, as if it were the *omphalos* or "the belly button that roots the house into the earth."[17] Because the hearth is the fixed point or center on the basis of which the dwelling space orients and organizes itself, it is identified with the earth, immobile and stable in the very center of the universe, at an equal distance from the most extreme points of the universe, thus enjoying a privileged position within it. Such, at least, was Anaximander's conception of the *cosmos*, a conception that found echoes in domains that extended far beyond those of cosmology (in conceptions of ethics and politics in particular). One understands how Plato, in the *Cratylus*, is then able to offer a twofold and seemingly irreconcilable etymology of Hestia: for some, he says, it must be related to *ousia* or *essia*, that is, to the fixed and unchanged essence, while for others it must be related to *osia*, for they believe that all things that are are in motion.[18] Does Hestia not then become another name for being or presence itself, whether in the sense of the being that is in the way of being, or the being that is by way of becoming? Is Heidegger not ultimately right to assimilate the hearth with being itself? Is Hestia not the goddess of permanence and change, of being and becoming, of fixity and mobility? Should it be read with the *pelein* after all? What Heidegger says concerning the *polis* as the pole around which everything revolves, as the center and the axis in the proximity to which things find their place appears in fact as an accurate description of the *hestia*: following up on Deroy's analyses,[19] Vernant suggests that the *hestia* or the hearth of the Greek home be compared to the mast of a ship, solidly anchored in the deck, yet standing up straight and pointing toward the sky, much in the same way in which, while deeply rooted in the earth, the flame of the hearth elevates itself toward the highest spheres of the cosmos through a hole in the roof of the home, thus establishing a communication and a continuity between the terrestrial abode and the world of the gods, thus bringing sky and earth together in a single gesture.[20] It is in this sense that, with Heidegger,[21] we could read the famous anecdote, recounted by Aristotle,[22] according to which, one day, as he was receiving guests by the fire of a baking oven, Heraclitus declared to his bemused and benumbed visitors: "Here too the gods are present." In other words, it is not only in temples that the gods can become present, and that man can experience the unity of his being with that of the divine, but in the home as such, if the home is understood originarily, that is, precisely in terms of man's essential ability to dwell amidst the unfamiliarity of being.[23] Such, therefore, is the image of the *hestia* that Plato inherits from the oldest religious traditions in Greece:[24] immobile, yet in control of the movements that gravitate around it, central, but in the way of an axis that runs through a machine and keeps its various parts together. Heidegger's interpretation seems all the more probable, that to the emergence of the Greek *polis* between the time of Hesiod and that of Anaximander also corresponds the re-placing of the *hestia* at the very heart of the then newly conceived *agora*, that open and central space in which communal matters are debated publicly, that space that belongs to everyone and no one in particular and in which the community as a whole comes to gather itself. The hearth that now sits enthroned in the *agora* no longer belongs to a single family or a single *oikos*, but to the political community as a whole: it is the hearth of the city, the common hearth, the *hestia koinè*. There now is a center that is more central than that of the *oikos*, there now is a law that is more common than that of the family and the home – a law that is nonetheless not identical with that of the priest or the king, the law that comes from on high, but a law that is the deed and the expression of the community of *oikoi*. Yet whereas for Vernant this transformation designates a specifically political phenomenon, for Heidegger, the emergence of the *polis* in the re-centering of the *hestia* designates the openness to being itself, the originary openness out of which the *polis* comes to exist as such, the pole or the center that gathers humans around an originary opening to the essentially aletheic nature of being. Whereas Vernant sees this transformation as a horizontalization of the relations between men – the *hestia* no longer serves to establish a contact between the various cosmic levels, but now designates the horizontal space in which the equality and exchangeability of citizens is revealed through *logos* as the absolutely common value – Heidegger would see the centrality of the open space as confirmation of the founding and inescapable power of being. No doubt, Heidegger would interpret the *agora* primarily in ontological terms: it is the open space that belongs to everyone, the Open in which beings come to be revealed in their truth and men come to be revealed as the beings for whom this truth is of historical importance. The political, what Vernant identifies as the sharing and exposition of power amongst the various groups of the *polis* would be interpreted as an effect of this originary disclosure. In a way, Heidegger's discussion of the *polis* in terms of a pole around which everything comes to whirl, and the connection he draws between this pole and the *pelein* from the chorus, which he equates with being, already confirms this suspicion. The *agora* could itself be seen as the pole around which the matters of the *polis* come to revolve. It could even be seen like the clearing in which such matters come to be revealed for the first time, the clearing through which the *polis* comes to exist as such. But it is the identification of the *hestia* itself with being that is most striking, both in the *Ister* lecture course as well as in the *Heraclitus* lecture course:[25] the true hearth, the true homeland is being itself, what the Greeks called *phusis*, with respect to which man can be homeless or can become at home: homeless, when he forgets his home, being, becoming native when he becomes alive to his essential belonging to being. Antigone is the very incarnation of this authentic homelessness – as opposed to the inauthentic homelessness, the "issueless busyness in the midst of beings"[26] – the fate that consists in the unreserved embracing of the *deinon*. Antigone is the heroine of the becoming at home in homelessness. For Heidegger, then, *hestia* is neither the ancient purely domestic hearth nor the religious center, nor even the *hestia koinè*, the central (political) hearth, symbol of a center and a medium and of shared power; rather, it designates the Open and the originary law of being, that of concealment and unconcealment.

What can we say with respect to this second round of analyses devoted to the *polis*? How different is it from the 1935 interpretation? The translation of the chorus from *Antigone*, which constitutes Heidegger's major source of interpretation, remains identical to that of 1935. What changes is the interpretation proper. Not that translation would not already be interpretation: on the contrary, Heidegger insists at length that translation is not simply the passage from one idiom to another, but operates at the very heart of each idiom.[27] Thus, Heidegger says, it is not enough to translate a Greek word by a corresponding German word, as if translation were a simple case of transposition or equation; rather, it is only in translating the Greek into German in such a way as to move the Greek word itself toward its unthought that one genuinely translates, and in so doing, becomes more Greek than the Greeks. The passage through the other-than-Greek is necessary and productive, not in its equating the Greek and the German, and thereby losing all that was irreducibly Greek in the original, but in its bringing the Greek itself back to the site of its unthought. To be more Greek than the Greeks through translating is not to play by the rules of scientific translation, of philology and etymology. The so-called etymologies of Heidegger in no way constitute a science; they neither confirm nor condemn the work of specialists. Rather, if they seem to embrace or reject this or that standard etymology or translation, it is never in the name of science, but in the name of that which, in language (*Sprache*), holds itself in reserve and opens onto the recessive domain of the comprehension of being. It matters little, then, in the end, that *to deinon* does not "mean" *das Unheimliche*, if this is the direction in which it points. It is primarily a matter of knowing what must be understood by *Sinn*: *Bedeutung* or *Richtung*, meaning or direction. Likewise, it matters little that, in the eyes of classical philologists, the translation of *polis* by "place," its connection with the verb *pelein*, and the interpretation of the latter by means of a poem by Hölderlin, seem dubious, if not erroneous or even fanciful. It is a matter of something altogether different than the correct (*richtig*) – it is a matter of the true.

By truth, one must here understand that which speaks in language independently of any intention. It is from this perspective alone that the comprehension of a hymn by Hölderlin can enable one to *hear* a saying of Sophocles. This is not an anachronism: history is not the linear unfolding of time, but the unequal sequence of resonances of a power of beginning (*archè*). It is thus that Hölderlin's saying echoes that of Sophocles, that, despite the "time" which separates them, the two sayings resonate from out of an identical site. Chronological time is not the time of being. History is not *Geschichte*: if the former retains the true semblance or the correct as its sole criterion, the latter, on the other hand, responds to that of truth alone. It is thus the truth of the *deinon* or the truth of the *polis* that Heidegger tries to delimit. And if it is of the very nature of truth to always remain somewhat veiled in its manifestation, if this manifestation itself takes place only on the basis of an originary concealment, then it is this obscure part which thought must go in search of, it is this obscure region, older than light, that philosophy must plunge itself into. To think the *polis* as it manifests itself in the chorus from *Antigone* is to think it in accordance with its truth or its essence, to think it, in other words, from out of the unthought and as if withdrawn site of its unfolding. To think the *polis* in its withdrawal is not to think the *polis* as that which withdraws, but is to think it as that which takes place only in the retreat of its essence. And it is perhaps here, in the movement beyond the *polis* in the direction of the unthought site of its essence, in the leap beyond the Greeks, that the slender but nonetheless decisive difference between the first interpretation of the *Introduction to Metaphysics* and the second series of interpretations dating from 1942 and 1943 is played out. I would not say that the 1942 interpretation calls the reading of 1935 into question, that it runs counter to it, and that it is as if Heidegger had changed his mind as regards what constituted the kernel of his first interpretation, namely the conflict between *technè* and *dikè*; rather, I would say that Heidegger is now in search of a more originary interpretation: not more a faithful interpretation, but one yet more Greek and that is to say, paradoxically, one yet more Hölderlinian. Between 1935 and 1942 the in-depth reading of Hölderlin took place, a reading which by and large amounted to a progressive demarcation of Hölderlin's poetry from Nietzsche's thought as from metaphysics in its totality. What is new in 1942 is the questioning of the *polis* in the light of the truth of being and not simply in the light of *phusis*, which would remain the experience of the truth of beings. Such is the reason why the analysis that the 1942 lecture course on the goddess Truth in Parmenides' poem devotes to the *polis* comes as no surprise.[28] I do not believe, then, as has been recently argued,[29] that the essential difference between the two interpretations is played out around an evolution marking the progressive elimination of the conflictual and of violence from the political sphere, and this in favour of the awaiting of what is question-worthy. Heidegger retains the determinations of violence, of insurrection, of monstrosity even, which would characterize the man of the *polis* in his opposition and his submission to the power of *phusis*. Only this conflict is now clarified in the light of the truth of being itself, which henceforth supports the full weight of the analysis. There is, in other words, a movement from one truth to another, from a truth of beings to a truth of being. Both are, in themselves, strifely, and are deployed only in terms of the opposition between an essence and a non- or counter-essence. The question that bears on the truth of being is the most question-worthy of all questions, and it is only insofar as the *polis* presupposes such a truth that it is itself question-worthy. Put simply, and a little inadequately, the reading that Heidegger provides is yet more "ontological" than that of 1935, which still suffered from onticity. This was due to the fact that the chorus is an attempt to speak the essence of man by describing him in his opposition to *phusis*. But the essence of man is nothing human, and that of *phusis* nothing natural. To put this more clearly: if the interpretation of 1935 managed to describe the *polis* as the gathering site of the truth of beings for man, it did not manage to think the *polis* from out of the truth of being, and thus wrest it from all metaphysics. After all, the reading of 1935 served as an introduction *into* metaphysics, whereas, in the 1940s, it is for Heidegger a matter of thinking before and beyond metaphysics: a matter of leaving metaphysics.

Throughout, Heidegger will have thought the *polis*, of which the modern state is the historical translation, as a place or a site – the site of a historical relation to the truth of beings. The attempt thus consisted in wresting the *polis* from the hands of the various specialized discourses in which it was traditionally placed. Relentlessly, Heidegger insists that the *polis* is not primarily a space – whether geographical, urban, social, economic or political – but a "place," an *Ort*. The difference between space and place lies in the fact that the place refers to the very possibility from out of which anything like a constituted social, economic and political space might arise. This possibility is that which Heidegger designates as a dwelling or an abode, which is always *geschichtlich*: to dwell historically means to relate to the whole of being in such a way that what comes to be experienced and understood in the relation is not just beings, but the truth or the being of such beings. The specificity of the human dwelling is captured under the motif of the *Unheimischkeit*: the abode of man, his *Heim* or his *polis*, is first and foremost the experience of the unfamiliarity of beings and of his essential homelessness. Man can truly be at home in the world, and thus create his own abode, only when he is faced with his fundamental not-at-homeness. The apparent familiarity, the peculiar obviousness and in effect the mastery of the world which modern man experiences, and in which he recognizes his own freedom, is actually only the latest and most complete expression of his alienation. Ultimately, then, the possibility of an authentic historical dwelling amidst beings, the possibility of the *polis* is entirely subordinated to the law of being. And if the *polis* does indeed mark the site of a reworking of spatiality as place, this spatiality is itself to be understood ontologically. For those, then, who approach Heidegger's analysis of the *polis* with the secret hope that it will reveal some decisive clues regarding the status and the practice of politics in general, the disappointment will be very strong.

Yet one can wonder to what extent Heidegger's ontologization of the *polis* is successful, independently of the twisting and the bending of the sources on which he draws, mainly the chorus from Sophocles' *Antigone*. Specifically, one can wonder as to the extent to which the question of the abode and the dwelling is purely a matter of truth (of being), or whether, to use a vocabulary that is perhaps inadequate even from a late Heideggerian perspective, there is not something irreducibly ontic about it. What would such onticity consist in? It would consist in certain material elements, always in play and already at work, that would determine the mode of historical dwelling in its specificity. If such elements are indeed already in place, the discourse on dwelling which Heidegger subjects the discussion of the *polis* (but also of the national) to will itself be materially determined, if not overdetermined. I wish to suggest, at the outcome of this chapter, that Heidegger's conception of the *polis*, of the national, and by extension, of politics itself remains economically overdetermined. Striking, indeed, about Heidegger's entire vocabulary when addressing this question of the *polis*, of the historical dwelling and what we have come to call the national is the domestic economy to which it remains riveted, that is, the law of the *oikos*, of the home, the hearth and the house to which it is ultimately submitted. The *Heim* remains the standard, the ultimate value in the light of which the very possibility of a historical dwelling and the very possibility of the nation come to be measured. But there is no sense of this decisive move that takes place in the installation of the *polis*, the move of the hestia from the sphere of domestic economy to that of a political economy.[30] Our historical dwelling is one that can no longer be thought along the lines of a domestic economy: it is now entirely mediated by the laws of political economy, today of global economy, laws which in themselves cannot be brought back to the economy they have superseded and to the central model they once were made to correspond to. The political itself, and this includes the very viability of notions such as the nation and the national, is now the reflection of this essentially dis-located economy. By becoming global, this economy has exceeded the boundaries of national thinking. It is no longer even attached to a political center, or to any center for that matter: it is trans-national, fluid, a-centered, multiple. It operates horizontally, not vertically, not from a single centralized force but from a disseminated plurality of points of intensity. It has a dynamic of its own, it stabilizes itself in a multiplicity of micro-centers, yet it increasingly rules over the planet as whole. "We" are the products of this dynamic, the effect of post-industrial capitalism. By refusing to think economically, by subordinating the economic, and the political, to the ontological, Heidegger does not simply bypass and surpass this decisive question. His thinking regarding the national and the historical, his thinking as such, I would maintain, is stamped by a certain domestic economy, without ever considering the possibility of that economy being already overcome, already transformed and absorbed into a much larger sphere, that sphere that mediates our relation to things, to others and to the very possibility of feeling at home or not in this world. And if our world is indeed that of homelessness, it is perhaps not as a result of some ontological alienation (the forgottenness and/or abandonment of being), but as a result of the essentially global nature of a material process which in no way can be measured on the basis of the sole law of the *oikos*.

Heidegger's thought is ultimately submitted to the possibility of retrieving and preserving a sphere of life and a mode of relation to the world that is in effect always and already mediated by a larger economy. We cannot pose the question of our mode of inhabiting as if this capitalistic processor did not exist; we cannot raise the question of an authentic or proper mode of dwelling with the *Eigene* conceived in terms of the *Heim* or the *oikos* – even if such a *Heim* is, as in Heidegger, indissociable from an originary *Unheimischkeit*. We cannot abstract from these processes which on a daily basis inform the very way in which things become manifest. We cannot abstract from the question of value, from the way in which money comes to bear on those very questions concerning modes of historical and national dwelling. Technology itself cannot be abstracted from such an economic process, and reduced to a process of representation derived from the forgottenness of the question of being. In the thinking of being, things are considered independently of the way in which the introduction of value comes to modify the way in which we relate to them and in the way they come to appear. Everything happens as if, for Heidegger, things were devoid of value, as if this determination were of no consequence on the way in which we come to perceive them. It is striking to see how National Socialism was able to draw on the fantasy of this pre-capitalistic economy, on a conception of labor equally distributed and geared toward use-value. This is where I find the strongest attunement between Heidegger and Nazism: more than his nationalism, it is perhaps his lack of economic understanding, his refusal to consider that element as decisive that played a key role in his support for Nazism.

6
And into Silence . . .

'Speak to me. Why do you never speak? Speak.
'What are you thinking of? What thinking? What?
'I never know what you are thinking. Think.'

I could not
Speak, and my eyes failed, I was neither
Living nor dead and I knew nothing,
Looking into the heart of light, the silence.

T. S. Eliot, *The Waste Land*

Heidegger will have kept silent. He will not have spoken a single word against the event that is for ever associated with Nazi barbarity. He will have never responded, whether in speech or in deed, to that event. He will not have left language find its way through the disaster. He will not have allowed thought to open onto the deadly and savage today. He, the thinker of remembrance, will not have provided a space for the memory and the mourning of those millions gone up in smoke. He never will have turned his gaze to the immense cloud of cinders hanging over the German soil. To those who, like Celan or Jaspers, approached him in the hope of a word, a sign, a movement of the eye, he will have remained inmovable. Not even a tear will have blurred the surface of his gaze. For when it has become impossible to speak, when words remain smothered, as though strangled at the back of one's throat, when, petrified and shocked, the voice cannot echo the pain, tears can yet come to water the gaze and bring one back to light. Tears are hungry for words, and yet they express nothing but the impossibility to speak, for in them speech drowns. Response without a response, sheer exposition, absolute nudity, tears bear testimony to the unspeakable trace of the Other, to the ineluctability of responsibility. Those tears could have bespoken grief, they could have wept for those millions of eyes that went closed forever without having had a chance to cry. Heidegger could have dipped his quill into his teary eyes, he could have written with his tears.

Heidegger's silence speaks as an open wound. This silence casts a dark and almost unbearable shadow on Heidegger's thought. Such is the reason why this chapter is the most painful to write, the chapter that brings pain into thinking, the chapter that penetrates the wound and exposes it in its unsuturable gaping. We must now learn to think with pain.

But how does one bespeak silence?

Before such silence is associated with a failure of thinking, with the most absolute of all derelictions, one would wish, perhaps, to think this silence as a response, indeed as the only response capable of harboring the event. One might even wish to think this silence as responsibility, and argue for an ethics of silence and passivity. Or even for a responsibility beyond ethics and a silence beyond language. A silence, then, such as the one to which Abraham is condemned when asked to sacrifice his own son. This is how Kierkegaard describes the scene:

> When his heart is moved, when his words would provide blessed comfort to the whole world, he dares not to offer comfort, for would not Sarah, would not Eliezer, would not Isaac say to him, "Why do you want to do it, then? After all, you can abstain." And if in his distress he wanted to unburden himself and clasp to himself all that he held dear before he proceeded to the end, the terrible consequence might be that Sarah, Eliezer and Isaac would take offense at him and believe him to be a hypocrite. Speak he cannot; he speaks no human language. And even if he understood all the languages of the world, even if those he loved also understood them, he still could not speak – he speaks in a divine language, he speaks in tongues.[1]

And a few lines down, Kierkegaard adds: "Abraham cannot speak, because he cannot say that which would explain everything (that is, so it is understandable): that it is an ordeal such that, please note, the ethical is the temptation."[2] The temptation, our temptation, perhaps, with respect to Heidegger, would be to understand his silence as the expression of what cannot be understood, as the absolutely singular response to the event which cannot be universalized, as the sacrifice of ethics. He did not speak because he could not speak, might we not want to argue? Words are still lacking to speak the event, language itself is inadequate, too universal, too public, too *economical*. Is it not the same irreducible singularity of the event that Levinas himself expresses when he writes that "The pain of the antisemitic persecution can be told only in the language of the victim: it is transmitted through signs that are not interchangeable"?[3] Might we not even be tempted to read Heidegger's silence with Blanchot, who writes: "If you listen to our epoch [*"l'époque"*], you will learn that it is telling you, quietly, not to speak in its name, but to keep silent in its name."[4] And is it not at this precise point that, as Celan's poetry as well as his *Bremen Address* reveal, silence can emerge as the site whence language becomes richer for being imbued with silence? With Jabès, can we not wonder whether the language of silence is the language that refuses language, or whether it is the language of the memory of the first word?[5]

Yet, most importantly perhaps, one might wish to evoke and mobilize those texts that run through the whole of Heidegger's itinerary, from the early *Schweigen* and *Verschwiegenheit* of *Being and Time* to the *Erschweigen* and the *Erschweigung* of the *Contributions to Philosophy*, all the way to the *Geläut der Stille* and the whole problematic of poetic language in *Underway to Language*, where silence is presented as the origin and ground of language, as speech in the most proper sense. One would want to murmur to oneself: "He kept silent because he could only keep silent, because keeping silent was the only way to respond to the event that will have shattered language and revealed its irreducible lack. By keeping silent he kept silence itself, safekept it, that is, guarded it, shepherded it. By keeping silent he remained faithful to the silenced voice of the Other as well as to the task of thinking." "That is correct," one might hear in response, as if inhabited by Heidegger's *daimon*. "Yes, yes, now you understand why I had to remain silent. Do you recall section 34 of *Being and Time*, where I allude to silence as the voice of the friend that each Dasein carries alongside itself, as well as sections 56 and 57, where the entire discussion of the phenomenon of 'conscience' revolves around the possibility of a 'call' or a 'voice' that must remain silent? Could I refer you to those sections?"

And indeed, one cannot but be struck by the fact that, if Heidegger remained silent about the Holocaust, he did not remain silent about silence. From the very beginning, silence seems to occupy a specific and indeed privileged situation in Heidegger's writings. In section 34 of *Being and Time*, for example, silence (*Schweigen*) is presented as an essential possibility of discourse (*Rede*), along with hearing (*Hören*), with which, as we shall see, it is profoundly attuned. Silence is not muteness. It is neither a negation nor a privation. It is not an impossibility, namely the impossibility of speaking. Nor is it a negative possibility, namely the possibility of not speaking. Rather, it is a positive possibility, indeed speech in the most proper sense. For to keep silent, to be able to keep silent, Dasein must have something to say. Like discourse, of which it is an instance, silence is essentially *Mitteilung*, communicating and sharing. Thus silence is a way – indeed the most proper way – of being-with-one-another: in discretion (*Verschwiegenheit*), one is most able to hear and listen to the Other, one is most turned to the Other, open onto the Other:

As a mode of discourse, discretion articulates the intelligibility of Dasein in so originary a manner that it gives rise to a potentiality-for-hearing [*Hörenkönnen*] which is genuine, and to a being-with-one-another which is transparent.

(SZ 165/208)

It is in silence that Dasein is most attuned to the other, that it is closest to it, genuinely open onto the alterity of the Other. In silence, Dasein has an ear for the Other, it is "all ears," as it were. Through hearing and listening, Dasein is essentially open to otherness. And Heidegger goes as far as to suggest that such otherness or alterity does not presuppose the physical presence of the Other, for Dasein carries such otherness with and alongside itself (*bei sich*), in the mode of a voice, a purely phonic presence. Furthermore, Dasein's capacity to hear and listen is identified with Dasein's aperture to its ownmost self:

Indeed, hearing constitutes the primary and proper [*eigentliche*] aperture of Dasein for its ownmost can-be [*für sein eigenstes Seinkönnen*] – as in hearing the voice of the friend whom every Dasein carries along with it [*den jedes Dasein bei sich trägt*]

(SZ 163/206)

Through hearing, then, Dasein is open, disclosed to itself, to the world and to others in the most authentic way. Dasein is, or rather exists, *hearingly*. To say this is not to call into question the privilege of the *hand* that the analytic of Dasein established in the context of Dasein's everyday dealings with the world. For the ear that is spoken of here is not an organ; it is not the ear which perceives the sounds of the motorcycle outside. Rather, it is the ear of and for one's self, the ear that one would be tempted to define as turned inward, if the inwardness of Dasein properly understood were not its very outwardness or disclosedness, its very ek-sistence. And what does that inoutward ear hear? When Dasein is "all ears," attentive to its ownmost existential possibilities, tuned in existence *qua* existence, what does it hear? Not the busy buzzing of everyday life, not the chatter of pub conversations and academic conferences, but the silent voice of the friend that every Dasein *bei sich trägt*. When properly tuned in, then, Dasein hears a voice, a voice that is *another* voice, yet a voice that does not come from outside, but that resonates within Dasein itself, as if it were Dasein's ownmost voice. That voice does not *belong* to Dasein, since it is the voice of another. And yet, that voice belongs essentially *in* Dasein and is what matters most to Dasein. If such a voice is at once what is closest to Dasein (every Dasein carries it *along*) and what cannot be simply appropriated by Dasein, what is both inside and outside, mine and not mine, should we be surprised to see Heidegger define it further as the voice *of* the "friend"? Is the voice not a metonymy for what seems to be a very traditional concept of friendship, in the same way in which Dasein's ear is a metonymy for existence as understanding (*Verstehen*)? Yet if Heidegger seems to reinscribe a fairly traditional conception of friendship in the context of the analytic of Dasein, he does so only by way of a displacement, the effects of which are vertiginous: for the friend is not an actual friend, but the very trace of alterity within Dasein itself. Dasein is itself only by being other than itself, by being stamped by alterity, prior to any actual encounter (whether friendly or antagonistic) with an other Dasein. My relation to the Other, when understood *properly*, and this means when *understood* through *hearing*, is a relation of friendship. The Other is my friend. As such, as trace or purely phonic presence, the friend says nothing to Dasein: the voice of the friend is silent. It says nothing, delivers no message – yet delivers me to otherness in its very silencing. It sounds like nothing, and yet in it the whole of existence resonates. It is not because the voice of the friend has nothing to say that it is silent. It is not a vacuous voice. It is a voice whose silencing reveals existence to itself, a call that can be heard only in the withdrawal of language. Dasein's relation to the Other is one of familiarity and hospitality, where the Other is at once closest and yet still Other, other in its very proximity. Such is the reason why Heidegger identifies this structure with that of friendship, even though the otherness that is at stake in such structure does not presuppose an actual relation with an embodied Other, least of all with what is usually thought of as "a friend." Here, prior to any psychology, anthropology, ethics or politics, and, most importantly perhaps, outside or in the margin of phenomenology itself, it is a matter of acknowledging the presence, indeed the *absent* presence of the Other in Dasein. Otherness is inscribed in the very structure of Dasein. Dasein carries with it the trace of the Other in the mode of a voice. The voice is that of the Other, yet it resonates within me: it does not come from an outside me, from an exteriority that would be assimilated, interiorized, not only because the friend whose voice I hear is not an embodied friend, but also because Dasein itself is nothing but exteriority. Whence does that voice speak, then, if it is neither the voice of an actual exteriority nor the inner voice of self-consciousness? And how does it speak, since it cannot actually speak? That voice, whose origin is untraceable and whose voicing is silent, that voice which is neither inside nor outside, can it still resonate within language? It can only resonate silently, within the inner ear of Dasein, which does not mean *through* its ear (and such would be the reason why a deaf Dasein would still be a Dasein, still attuned to the voice of the Other). The hearing silence of Dasein echoes the silent voice of the friend. In silence, Dasein is so close to the Other that the Other has always left its trace within me from the start, its inscription allowing for my very silence, for my very hearkening.

This is indeed a remarkable passage, one that has only recently started to draw some attention.[6] Its remarkable character comes from the fact that, by developing what one could call an ontology of friendship or an ontophilology, Heidegger seems to provide a space for a rethinking of ethics. In that respect, this short passage seems to contradict what has come to be considered as a profound lack in *Being and Time* and seems to work against the analyses of the being-with-one-another that reveal the public sphere as the anonymity and the dictatorship of the One, thereby threatening the very possibility of an ethics. Yet Heidegger's remarks become even more remarkable if we are to pay particular attention to the connection he draws between the listening to the voice of the friend and Dasein's ownmost can-be. For this connection seems to run counter-stream to what has thus far been understood, and to what Heidegger himself suggests, namely that Dasein's relation to its ownmost possibility of existence is a process of singularization. In Dasein's confrontation with its ownmost can-be it would be a matter of coming face to face with itself, and not with the Other or the Other's face. Is Heidegger suggesting, then, that even in the moment of absolute solitude, when, confronted with its own death as with its ownmost and uttermost possibility, Dasein is no longer in relation with others, Dasein still carries the silent voice of the friend along with it? Must we understand that even in the process whereby Dasein becomes its own self and thus gains its authenticity, it still bears within it the trace or the mark of the Other? Might we even go further and suggest that Dasein can become itself only by listening to the voice of the friend?

One can find confirmation of this suspicion in the vocabulary used in sections 56 and 57, where Heidegger finds the existentiell attestation of the *Sein-zum-Tode* in the phenomenon of conscience. Where in section 34, within the context of understanding and language, Heidegger simply alludes to Dasein's ability to relate to its ownmost can-be through a "hearing", "as in hearing the voice of the friend," sections 56 and 57 are much more explicit as to the relation between the "hearing" and the ownmost possibility of existence, since such possibility has now been explicitly thematized as being-towards-death. Yet the "call" (*Ruf*) that resonates within Dasein, and that says nothing but only voices silence, is no longer assimilated with the voice of the friend. It is now the call of "conscience" (*Gewissen*). Yet conscience is Dasein itself: not self-consciousness, but conscience to and for one's self. In conscience, Dasein calls itself to itself, but not out of will or decision. Dasein is rather called by conscience, and summoned to confront its ownmost possibilities of existence. Conscience, then, is not something that Dasein possesses, an attribute of some kind, to which it could relate and have recourse. But neither is it something that comes from the outside, a call coming from afar. Like the voice of the friend, it is neither in Dasein nor outside of it. Such is the reason why we can only say that "It" calls:

> "It" calls, against our expectations and even against our will.
> On the other hand, the call undoubtedly does not come from
> someone else who is with me in the world. The call comes from
> me and yet from over me and beyond me.
>
> (SZ 275/320)

The call is not made by me, it is not made by someone else (another
Dasein), and yet, according to Heidegger, nothing justifies "seeking the
caller in some being with a character other than that of Dasein" (God,
for example).[7] Is this sufficient to identify the "It" of the calling with the
silent voice of the friend? Is it the friend, whose silent voice is neither in
me nor outside of me, who is at once closest to me and most foreign
to me, who does the calling? Or, to put it the other way around, does
conscience, as that which calls myself to myself, have the figure of alterity?
Is this not the way to understand Heidegger when he defines the voice
of conscience as "something like an alien voice"? Is Heidegger not
suggesting that Dasein is fundamentally alien to itself, unknown and
uncanny to itself, and that, in a way, what is at once closest to itself and
farthest to itself is its own self or what is most its own? The friend, in
that sense, would be otherness inside Dasein, yet the becoming-Other of
Dasein would take place in the movement of appropriation of itself. Thus
the friend would be nothing but the other self that one always carries
with oneself, that self which is ordinarily neglected and abandoned, that
friend which is fundamentally one's best and only friend, and which is
nonetheless perceived as alien because of its uncanniness, because of the
nullity and the nothing which it serves to reveal: guilt and death. In that
respect, the friend would be the mark of existence as difference, it would
reveal existence as the very locus of this difference, as the differing in the
spacing of which existence would come to *be*. Thus, it would be the trace
of the ontological difference *per se*, the *dia* or the gaping in which existence would come to bear or carry – *pherein* – its own being. To say this
is not to say that friendship is another name for being, that difference is
alterity and that ontology is ethics. Heidegger does not speak of "friendship," he does not offer a theory of friendship, nor even a conceptual
thematization of "the friend." Rather, he suggests that we think of otherness in Dasein itself, an alterity that is so close to Dasein that it becomes
one with the figure – or rather the voice – of the friend. This voice
resonates within Dasein and calls Dasein forth. In the depths of Dasein's
ear, "It" calls – like the discreet trembling of a friendly voice.

One might wish, then, to hear the silent voice of Heidegger sympa-
thetically, as if echoing the almost imperceptible moan of the victims. One
would like to understand this silence as memory and mourning, as if
language, wounded and bruised, had found refuge only in the inner ear
of thinking. Yet the meaning of Heidegger's silence lies elsewhere: not in

memory, not in mourning, but in a lack and a failure of thinking itself. For, to begin with, he will not have remained entirely silent. On a few occasions, which are now widely known and extensively commented upon, he will have broken his silence, only to reveal the extent to which the Holocaust remained for him an event amongst others, only to expose the blindness of the thinking of being.

Let me refer here to three such occasions. The first and by far most controversial statement appears in the context of a discussion concerning technology. As such, it is the most philosophically significant of all three statements. On 1 December 1949, in a lecture entitled "Das Ge-stell" ("The En-framing"), Heidegger said the following:

> Agriculture is now a motorized food-industry – in essence, the same as the manufacturing of corpses in gas chambers and exter- mination camps, the same as the blockading and starving of nations, the same as the manufacture of hydrogen bombs.[8]

The second statement is dated 20 January 1948, and is a response to the letter of his former student, Herbert Marcuse, who had asked (almost begged) Heidegger for a "long awaited statement that would clearly and finally free you from such identification [with the Nazi regime], a state- ment that honestly expresses your current attitude about the events that have occurred."[9] Heidegger's response consists of six points, the last of which addresses the question of the organized murder of millions of Jews:

> To the serious legitimate charges that you express "about a regime that murdered millions of Jews, that made terror into an everyday phenomenon, and that turned everything that pertains to the ideas of spirit, freedom, and truth into its bloody opposite," I can merely add that if instead of "Jews" you had written "East Germans", then the same holds true for one of the allies, with the difference that everything that has occurred since 1945 has become public knowledge, while the bloody terror of the Nazis in point of fact had been kept a secret from the German people.[10]

The third and final statement I shall be considering is relevant not so much in what it says as in what it does not say, in what it refuses to say in a context that would have allowed for words concerning the Holocaust. At the opening of his lecture, on 20 June 1952, Heidegger addressed his students in a way that is strikingly reminiscent of the passage of *Being and Time* on the silent voice of the friend:

> Ladies and Gentlemen!
>   Today, the exhibit "Prisoners of War Speak" opened in Freiburg.

I invite you to go and see it, so as to hear this silent voice [*diese lautlose Stimme*] and never let it come out of your inner ear [*aus dem inneren Ohr*].

Thinking is commemorating [*Denken ist Andenken*]. Yet commemorating is something other than the fugitive making-present of that which is past.

(WHD 159)

I wish to organize my remarks concerning these statements by Heidegger around three poles:

1. What is perhaps most evidently striking and common about these three statements is that they resist treating the Holocaust as a specific and irreducible event. In other words, what is deeply puzzling about Heidegger's references to the Extermination is that they always occur in a larger context, as if exemplifying it, as if subsumed under an ontological law and governed by a common historical fate. Heidegger's silence is bewildering because it is only partial: Heidegger did not refuse to mention the Holocaust, yet he did refuse to single it out as an event that would call for another thinking, a rethinking of the very nature of the event and the historical. Heidegger's silence is thus more the result of a certain *philosophical* indifference to the Extermination than the symptom of either a rampant antisemitism or, to consider another extreme, the very piety of thinking. And therein lies the scandal. Heidegger's silence is scandalous not because it impedes a moral judgment with respect to the murderous outcome of Nazism (as he states himself in the letter to Marcuse dated 20 January 1948, this will have been easy, perhaps too easy, and yet perhaps not), although such condemnation would have been necessary, but because it reveals an inability to think and question on the basis of the event, an impossibility to let *thinking* be affected by the death of those millions of Jews (and non-Jews). The failure, then, is a failure of thinking itself, insofar as it can think the Extermination only by integrating it into a chain of events (mechanized agriculture, the hydrogen bomb, the Berlin blockade, the fate of the East Germans, etc.), as if the Holocaust had not forced thinking outside of itself, as if thinking had not been exceeded by that which it cannot simply contain and which it must nevertheless think, as if, before the magnitude of what took place, thinking could remain otherwise than distraught and dazed, as if, after Auschwitz, thinking could dispense with questioning anew, as if it could remain intact in the precedence of the event, as if it could ignore this gap in history, this black hole from which we must learn to rethink light and reinvent the day.

Heidegger's silence is indeed the silence of his thought, that is, the moment at which the thinking of being can no longer speak, the point at which it can only come to a halt. By silence, then, we not only mean an inability to speak, a lack of words, but we also have in mind those few words that Heidegger did pronounce and that are even more damaging than his very silence. For even when referring to the great massacres, Heidegger lacks an ear to hear the voice that continues to resonate from the now deserted camps: not the voice of technology, which perhaps made the whole enterprise *technically* possible, but the voice of the Other, the friend, whose death without death or without mourning is still awaiting remembrance and whose moan is still in search of new words.

2. What lies at the origin of Heidegger's silence, then, a certain bad faith or presumption notwithstanding, is thinking itself. In what sense can we say that Heidegger's thinking remained blind to the murderous reality of Nazism? On what basis can the Holocaust be thought together with mechanized agriculture or the Berlin blockade? Heidegger provides an answer in the spoken version of the lecture, "*Das Ge-stell*," quoted earlier. I wish to focus on Heidegger's use of the words "essence" and "the same" in the context of that lecture. Such a task should lead us into a close reading not only of "The Question Concerning Technology," but also of "On the Essence of Truth," where one can find Heidegger's most thorough treatment of the notion of essence. In the context of this chapter, my remarks will have to remain programmatic and, to a certain extent, peremptory. The passage from the 1949 lecture reveals that Heidegger is not interested in thinking the state of contemporary agriculture or the gas chambers in themselves, but with respect to their *essence*.[11] To be more specific, philosophical thinking would start to operate precisely when engaging with the essence of that which is made manifest. In that respect, to think something, whether a work of art, an historical event or even truth, would be to raise the question of its *essence*. For Heidegger, the essence of a thing, that which allows it to *be* in the way in which it *is*, does not belong to the thing itself. Rather, the thing belongs to its essence and is a manifestation of it. Yet the essence unfolds and manifests itself in many different ways. Such is the reason why the essence is one (in essence), although it is plural in its manifestations, and why, according to their essence, two things can be said to be "the same." Thus, according to Heidegger, the essence of mechanized agriculture is nothing "agricultural," the essence of the extermination camps is nothing "architectural," etc. What, then, is the essence on the basis of which mechanized agriculture and death camps can be said to be "the same"? The answer is: technology (*Technik*). But what is technology? Does technology itself have an essence, one that would not simply point to its machinality and its instrumentality? In other words, is our epoch the epoch of technology because we use and develop various technologies that range from high-performance agricultural machines to sophisticated means of extermination, or do we create such technologies on the basis of an historical situation (an epoch)

governed by the unfolding of its essence? And what might such essence be? Heidegger calls the essence of technology "*das Ge-stell*." Technology, as a practice, is a way of making things manifest. As such, it is a mode of truth. Yet, as a revealing, it is governed by an essence that provokes it to reveal reality in a particular way. How can that way be described? What is the specific mode of truth that one finds in technology? It is a revealing where reality as a whole is summoned or challenged to reveal itself as standing-reserve (*Bestand*), as sheer availability and manipulability, where beings, including human beings, stand there, ready to be used and transformed, where everything is from the outset envisaged as potential energy and resource.

Now, to mention the "manufacturing of corpses in gas chambers and extermination camps" in that context is not only insensitive. It is also profoundly inadequate and radically insufficient from a philosophical perspective, even in the very context sketched out by Heidegger himself (which itself can be called into question). Indeed, the questions that immediately come to mind when reading Heidegger's statement are the following: did the extermination of millions of people have anything to do with a manufacturing or a producing, albeit in the sense of a "challenging" (*Herausfordern*)? In other words, is exterminating a mode of truth, in the same way in which "unlocking, transforming, storing, distributing, and switching about" are said to be "ways of revealing"?[12] Can the vocabulary of the *Bestand*, of the standing-reserve and the resource, be applied to the victims of Hitler's mania? When Heidegger defines the enframing as "the supreme danger" (*die höchste Gefahr*) on the basis of the fact that under its reign man "himself will have to be taken as standing-reserve",[13] we must wonder whether the death of the victim in the extermination camp does not represent a danger that is other and perhaps greater than the one anticipated in the enframing. Has the victim not moved beyond the status of the standing reserve? Does it not fall outside that logic, outside what Heidegger identifies as the fundamental trait, the *essence* of our epoch? In what sense can the victim be said to have formed part of an economy, of a technological strategy aimed at maximizing and storing, when it is now a well-known fact that the final solution represented, on the part of Germany's struggle for world hegemony, a waste of financial, natural and human resources, a radically *aneconomical* gesture? The unbelievable and unacceptable character of the Holocaust has to do with the fact that National Socialism revealed its "essence" or "inner truth" not, as Heidegger claimed, in the "encounter between global technology and modern man," but in a figure that escapes and exceeds the mere boundaries of technology, a figure that cannot be assimilated with that of total mobilization – I mean the figure of evil as the *positive* possibility of existence that marks the annihilation of the very possibility of existence or of freedom.[14]

3. When, twenty-five years after the publication of *Being and Time* and only a few years after the liberation of the death camps, Heidegger publicly mobilizes the silent voice of the friend safekept in his *magnum opus*, hope arises anew. For now, in the general historical context and the more specific context of the 1952 lecture course, the somewhat marginal sentence of *Being and Time* resonates in an unprecedented and indeed most promising way. The emphasis has shifted from a project of fundamental ontology and a conception of thinking as questioning to a meditation on history and a conception of thinking as remembrance, commemoration and mourning. The very task of thinking and the very possibility of freedom are now attached to the listening and the harboring of the silent voice of history. Without such attunement, without hearing the voice of the friend resonating in one's inner ear, there can be no historical today. The whole of the later Heidegger's meditation revolves around the possibility of a listening, of an openness to and an affirmation of what is destined. In "*die Sprache im Gedicht*," reading Trakl's poem "To a Young Diseased," Heidegger thematizes further his conception of thinking as *the crying shadow in the funeral dance*. Yet the silent voice of the friend, whether in *What is Called Thinking?* or in *On the Way to Language* is not the voice of the Other. It is the voice of the friendly friend, or the voice of the fellow citizen. It is the voice of the *Geschlecht* – of the *Heim*, the *Heimat* and the *Vaterland*, of the earth and of Spirit. But it is not the passive voice of the savagely silenced victim.

It is not as if Heidegger could have spoken and yet chose not to do so. It is not as if his responsibility were primarily ethical, or even political. He did not speak because he could not speak. This means that his language – the language of being as *Ereignis* – was not in a position to provide a space for a thinking of the death camps. Rather, the only space available was the one provided by being itself in its destining, and that is by the problematic of technology. The question is: can one – is it both feasible and legitimate – to think the Holocaust within this horizon? Or does the event exceed and extend beyond the limits of technology? What thinking might be in a position to greet the ungreetable and contain the uncontainable? What happens to thinking when it opens itself onto that which overflows it? What conception of the event and of history must it invent, if it is to make sense of senselessness? "How can thought be made to be the guardian of the Holocaust, where everything was lost, including the thought that guards?"[15] Must it not cease to be guardian, shepherd or keeper, whether house or brother's, so as to become fountain, if the fountain indeed overflows with what it cannot contain and if it can contain only by overflowing? What if thought were to deploy its essence anew on the basis of such an excess? What if history were to find another beginning, other than "the other beginning" (*der andere Anfang*), in the very happening of the disaster?

Three Concluding Questions

If not by way of conclusion, at least by way of gathering some of the recurrent motifs and stakes of these pages, let me formulate three questions or, shall we say, three irreducible reservations that I wish simply to mark. To a large extent, these questions remain programmatic and will no doubt need to find their own space of articulation in due time.

1. The first question has to do with the centrality of the motif of the *Heim* for the question of politics. This question, as I have already suggested, touches on what I have designated as an economical overdetermination of Heidegger's thought. To economy proper – that of labor and of the Worker, that of production in the age of technology – Heidegger wished to oppose or liberate another economy, which he never acknowledged as such, not even as an aneconomy: it is the law of the *oikos*, of the home and the hearth, the law of the proper, of the national and the native. This law is not the effect of labor and production, but that of (the) work (of art) and the poet. It arises out of the necessity to articulate the *Da* of *Sein*, to delimit the space or the place of being. In other words, it is an economy of being, or, as Schürmann has shown, of presence.[1] As soon as the question and the thinking concerning being is dependent upon that of the "there," of its presentation and its donation, the path is laid, as it were, for the introduction of the thematics of the abode, of the site and of the place: in short, of the *topos*. Ontology is an onto-topology. Must we conclude that phenomenology, insofar as it remains attached and subordinated to a problematic of presence and of donation is, from the start and forever, oriented toward a certain economy, toward a certain predilection for the home and the abode, for the shelter and the hearth? Can we – and this seems to take place as early as section 12 of *Being and Time* – inquire into the topology of being without being driven into a thematic of the sojourn and the dwelling? Are the *topoi*

bound to be thought as *oikoi*? Not necessarily. I would want to suggest that if the spatiality of Dasein as being-in-the-world does indeed presuppose a certain mode of dwelling, it does not necessarily imply that mode of dwelling that became central to Heidegger's thought in the 1930s, and to which the political engagement of 1933–4, as well as the subsequent confrontation with this engagement, remained indebted: the national and the native, the *Heimatliche* and the *Heimische*. True, Heidegger must be recognized as forever having rendered the thematic of the proper, of the abode and of the nation problematic: the abode is never simply given, the proper is never accessed or appropriated without the most extreme experience of the improper, the national itself is always an experience of the fundamental unfamiliarity of being. A thinking of the nation might even benefit from working its way through the complexities of its Heideggerian thematization. Nonetheless, we can wonder as to whether this thinking of the proper is altogether inevitable. We can wonder as to whether thinking, poetry and art, while retaining some essential connection with this dwelling spatiality of being, must ultimately be pushed in the direction of a domestic topology. Instead of conceiving of language as this space where being comes to find and appropriate itself as in its own shelter, could we not conceive of language as the open plain (or plane) at the surface of which presence would sketch its own lines of flight? Rather than submitting language – poetry, literature – to a logic of translation and appropriation, could we not inhabit language as the land of our errancy, in quest of our own foreignness? Why, in other words, should we not become strangers in our own language? Beckett, or Joyce, might here become paradigms. This, to be sure, is infinitely close to what Heidegger suggests in certain places. Yet, ultimately, Heidegger's conception of thinking, of language and of history remains subordinated to the exigency of the return (*Heimkunft*), of the becoming native (*Heimischwerden*), of the proper and of the home. Ultimately, the space of the abode – whether as existence, as language or as *Volk* – remains bound to a domestic economy, in a gesture that excludes the appropriation and the translation of such an economy by the laws of a larger economy, that of Capital. Ultimately, then, it would be a matter of wondering whether thinking must not be wrested from propriety altogether, whether dwelling has not entered a mode that is irreducibly transnational and translinguistic, always mediated by the absolute exchangeability and fluidity of an absolutely common value (money), thus forcing thinking into a different economy. Let it be clear: it is not henceforth a question of simply validating the effects of global capitalism on the contemporary mode of historical dwelling, much in the same way in which it cannot be a matter of embracing or rejecting technology as the dominant mode of presencing. But it is a matter of acknowledging the extent to which these material processes bind thinking to a new critical becoming. Thinking, if it is to remain critical, cannot abstract from such processes. Would the task, then, not become to think the destinal and the material together, to think the economy of presence as the presence of a global and hegemonic economy, that is, as the presence of Capital?

2. Wanting always to hand the essence of politics over to something which would not be political (namely: being, presence), does Heidegger not simply miss what constitutes the specificity of this sphere, does he not refuse it any existence outside of that which is imposed upon it by the unveiling of being? And does not this specificity have to do, precisely, with a certain impossibility of essentialization? If politics indeed grows not out of the soil of being, but between men, if its site is indeed that of the between, then does it not designate that which resists every unifying and essentializing appropriation? Is it not irreducibly horizonal? Does not every attempt to draw politics back to a place other than that of this between in which it plays itself out in its entirety, henceforth signify its annihilation? Such, at least, would be our hypothesis here: if Heidegger never managed to recognize the autonomous existence of the political, then this is insofar as it is, from the start, measured by the yardstick of something which signifies its own annihilation; wanting to anchor the political in the folds of presence alone, what sees itself closed off is its irreducible horizonality and multiplicity. What is the political, then, if not a way in which presence comes to unfold? We must here leave this fundamental question hanging. At stake, however, is this space of the between, this irreducibly flat space in which the humanity of man is played out, this space where the ancient name of justice comes to be articulated. "There is" politics, properly speaking, from the moment that justice becomes a question: not the *dikè* that Heidegger always traced back to being, but the justice which Aristotle says constitutes the ultimate goal of all activity and the last stake of *praxis*. Politics is born from this indelible "fact" which enjoins us to think away from being. Politics is this place where a difference other than the one which separates being from beings, and being from non-being, is played out: the difference through which everyone comes to be related to an Other. Politics is only the expression of this differential relation which is always a relation of power and desire. It lives and produces itself in this gap; it negotiates itself there, in this critical space, this space of crisis and incision, this space of decision, this space where it is always a matter of cutting into the flesh of the matter. This space, in other words, of justice. Totalitarianism designates the closure of this space, the will to resolve everything or the desire to have done with justice. Nothing, in the thought of being, rises up against such a desire. On the contrary. This thought went so far as to serve as a relay for this desire.

3. Finally, there is the question of myth, which is still in need of its own deconstruction,[2] the closure of which Heidegger experienced without ever being able to think it through. If Heidegger's conception of myth remains bound to a metaphysical logic that can be traced back to early German Romanticism, and specifically to the "new mythology" called for by Hegel in "The Oldest Systematic Programme of German Idealism,"[3] it is first and foremost in the essential complicity that links the possibility of a historical beginning with the power of myth. In Heidegger's sense, myth is primarily the saying through which the relation to the origin is asserted. Only secondarily, and to a lesser extent, perhaps, does Heidegger also retain the traditional social function of myth, that function whereby a community gathers, commmunicates and perpetuates itself through the repetition of the founding myth. In the sharing of myth, then, it is a question of bridging the gap that separates us from the origin, of recapturing the lost or forgotten *archè*. Only in this appropriation of the origin is history made possible; only in the becoming-present to the founding moment does the possibility of a future arise, and with it the sense of destiny and community. Despite the tensions and complexities of Heidegger's relation to the *archè* and to the Greek *muthoi*, whether Sophoclean or Platonic, his attitude toward them seems to echo this basic logic of myth. As for his reading of Hölderlin, which can be seen as operating at the very limit of myth, insofar as, in a time of distress marked by the absence of the gods, poetry can only free the space for the hypothetical coming of a new god, it nonetheless subordinates the political and the whole of Western history to the return of the divine and the problematic of salvation. Salvation, as always, can only come from a god. But is salvation what is at issue? Or must we not finally free (save?) ourselves from salvation, from all gods and ideals, at least when thinking politics? Is the death of god not also the death of the theologico-political, or of mytho-politics? Is the closure of metaphysics not also that of myth?

In the end, the mythology Heidegger calls for has perhaps very little to do with "the Nazi myth," at least that myth that sings the superiority and historical destiny of the Aryan race. Yet Heidegger never quite put himself in a position to identify this myth as such and to deconstruct the political logic that is attached to it. He only diagnosed it as the cheapest metaphysics and offered a counter-myth in return. His move toward the mytho-poetic, and toward art in general, is indeed a move away from the Nazi myth, yet it is also a further inscription of the political sphere in that of mythology. It is a move into the "truly" or "authentically" mythic. Admittedly the privilege of a language (the German one) and of a *muthos* (Hölderlin's) is radically different from the Nazi myth. Yet it is this very primacy of a language and of the historical situation of a people that governed Heidegger's nationalism, even in its Hölderlinian form. Ultimately, nationalism remains bound and subordinated to mythology, which provides it with its heroes and its gods. Together, they mark the end and closure of politics. After Heidegger, and in the wake of this century's destructive myths, it is a question of marking the closure of mytho-politics, a question of abandoning myth to myth itself. It is, in other words, a question of acknowledging the fact that the very appeal to myth as the founding moment of a people is itself a myth, a fiction that is doomed to the most catastrophic outcome. Indeed, to *will* to live under the power of myth is already to announce the closure of the space of politics. To appeal to the political and historical power of myth, to put myth to work, is to attach the space of the between of politics to the grounding and univocal voice of a single narrative. As soon as the mythic appears as a "solution" to a historical "crisis," it can no longer operate as myth. Myth indeed *works*, or worked, in that it was historically productive, yet it cannot be put to work. If myth cannot work without a work (of art, of poetry), the work itself cannot be (politically, historically) put to work. Myth is essentially paradoxical in that its utterance always designates the absence of that which it names, and yet it is in the name of this absence that actuality is transformed, and that politics is brought to an end. There is no hope in myth. There can be no new mythology. Myth cannot be made to replace the space of politics, that space for which we wish to reiterate the ancient name of justice.

Notes

Preface

1   Victor Farias, *Heidegger et le Nazisme*, translated from the Spanish and
    German by Myriam Benarroch and Jean-Baptiste Grasset, with a preface by
    Christian Jambet (Lagrasse: Verdier, 1987). The revised and longer German
    edition appeared as *Heidegger und der Nationalsozialismus* (Frankfurt:
    Fischer, 1989), translated from the Spanish and French by Klaus Laermann,
    with an important preface by Jürgen Habermas, "Heidegger: Werk und
    Weltanschauung." The English edition, *Heidegger and Nazism* (Philadelphia,
    Temple University Press, 1989), edited, with a foreword, by Joseph Margolis
    and Tom Rockmore, was translated from the French and the German
    editions, without, unfortunately, incorporating all the corrections made in
    the latter. Despite these late corrections, Farias' book remains highly contro-
    versial. Amongst the many responses to and reviews of Farias' book, I wish
    to point in particular to those provided by Philippe Lacoue-Labarthe at the
    end of *La fiction du politique* (Paris: Christian Bourgois, 1987), pp. 175–88;
    by Pierre Aubenque, Gérard Granel and Michel Deguy in *le débat*, 48,
    January-February 1988; and by Thomas Sheehan in "Heidegger and the
    Nazis," *The New York Review of Books*, June 16, 1988, pp. 38–47.

2   These are the works I would include in the first category: Reiner Schürmann,
    Les Principes de l'anarchie: Heidegger et la question de l'agir (Paris: Seuil,
    1982). English translation by Christine-Marie Gros, in collaboration with the
    author, *Heidegger on Being and Acting: From Principles to Anarchy*
    (Bloomington: Indiana University Press, 1987). Philippe Lacoue-Labarthe,
    "La transcendence finie/t dans la politique" (1981) and "Poétique et poli-
    tique" (1984) in *L'imitation des Modernes (Typographies II)* (Paris: Galilée,
    1986); *La fiction du politique*, op. cit. I owe to Lacoue-Labarthe the neces-
    sity to take Heidegger's own political dereliction absolutely seriously. It is
    also Lacoue-Labarthe who, almost despite himself, led me to expose the limi-
    tations of a purely immanent reading of Heidegger's politics. In one way or
    another, Lacoue-Labarthe's work is behind every chapter of this book.

Jacques Derrida, *De l'esprit – Heidegger et la question* (Paris: Galilée, 1987). Dominique Janicaud, *L'ombre de cette pensée – Heidegger et la question politique* (Grenoble: Jérôme Millon, 1990). Annemarie Gethmann-Siefert and Otto Pöggeler, eds, *Heidegger und die praktische Philosophie* (Frankfurt: Suhrkamp, 1989).

3   There are, however, some notable exceptions: see, for example, *The Graduate Faculty Philosophy Journal* (New School for Social Research), vol. 14, no. 2 and vol. 15, no. 1, edited by Marcus Brainard et al., published as a double volume in 1991). David Farrell Krell, *Daimon Life* (Bloomington: Indiana University Press, 1992), particularly chapters 4–6. Michael E. Zimmerman, *Heidegger's Confrontation with Modernity: Technology, Politics and Art* (Bloomington: Indiana University Press, 1990). Fred Dallmayr, *The Other Heidegger* (Ithaca: Cornell University Press, 1993).

Introduction

1   Theodor W. Adorno, in an open letter to the Frankfurt student journal *Diskus*, January 1963. Reprinted in the editorial Afterword to volumes V and VI of Adorno's *Musikalische Schriften* (Frankfurt am Main: Suhrkamp, 1976), pp. 637–8.

2   US 37/159.

3   Chapter 2 of this book, "Archaic Politics," does not consider *archè* in the sense that Heidegger identifies in Aristotle's *Physics* (see Wm 244 ff.), not, in other words, in the metaphysical sense of a secure and unique origin and ground, but in the sense of a power of beginning, which he also and most of all sees at work in poetry.

Bordering on Politics

1   Karl Löwith was the first to formulate his concerns in "Les implications politiques de la philosophie de l'existence chez Heidegger", *Les Temps Modernes*, 14 (1946). English translation by R. Wolin in *The Heidegger Controversy* (Cambridge: The MIT Press, 1993), ed. Richard Wolin, pp. 167–85. Theodor W. Adorno's *Jargon der Eigentlichkeit. Zur deutschen Ideologie* (Frankfurt: Suhrkamp Verlag, 1964) and Pierre Bourdieu's *L'ontologie politique de Martin Heidegger* (Paris: Minuit, 1988), originally published in 1975 in *Actes de la recherche en sciences sociales*, are two further significant examples of a "political" reading of *Being and Time*. More recently, although not in direct connection with *Being and Time*, but rather with the 1929/30 lecture course entitled *The Basic Concepts of Metaphysics* (GA 29/30), see Winfried Franzen, "Die Sehnsucht nach Härte und Schwere," in *Heidegger und die praktische Philosophie* (Frankfurt: Suhrkamp, 1989), eds Annemarie Gethmann-Siefert and Otto Pöggeler, pp. 78–92.

2   This new wave of attack was triggered by the publication of Victor Farias' *Heidegger et le Nazisme* (Lagrasse: Verdier, 1987), originally published in France, and much discussed there, but now enjoying a lively career in the United States.

3   SZ 18/40; my emphasis.

4   Aristotle, *Politics*, 1253 a 3.

5   This is an implicit reference to the beginning of the "Letter on Humanism," where Heidegger expresses doubts as to the possibility of corresponding to the task of thinking when operating within the framework of traditional onto-theology. Even though there is no explicit reference to the concept of the political as being in need of its own deconstruction, I believe that the overall context of the Letter is political. Furthermore, as I shall attempt to show, such deconstruction is carried out in other texts written under the rule of National Socialism.

6   Cited by Heinrich W. Petzet in his preface to Martin Heidegger–Erhart Kästner, *Briefwechsel* (Frankfurt: Insel Verlag, 1986), p. 10.

7   The question of whether *Being and Time* opened the way to Heidegger's support of Nazism in 1933 out of of a lack of definite political orientations and fundamental guidelines, or of whether Heidegger's *magnum opus* already provided its author with a vocabulary and a construal of collective life that was compatible with the Nazi ideology, is obviously crucial. For Janicaud, it is the absence of the political in *Being and Time* that was at the origin of Heidegger's political misadventure. For us, and in a way that owes nothing to the analyses of Adorno, Löwith, Habermas, Bourdieu or Farias, the clues to Heidegger's political support for Nazism can only be found in positive elements contained in the "early" Heidegger.

8   Karl Löwith, *Mein Leben in Deutschland vor und nach 1933* (Stuttgart: Metzler, 1986), p. 57.

9   In a terse statement, Lacoue-Labarthe declares: "And as for politics in general, that is to say, as for History, most of what is proclaimed in 1933 was already stated in *Sein und Zeit*, if only one refers to Division Two, Chapter V" (*La fiction du politique* [Paris: Christian Bourgois, 1987], p. 35). While fully subscribing to Lacoue-Labarthe's declaration, I would argue that what needs to be thought is precisely the connection between the concepts of history (as determined by Heidegger) and politics. In others words, we need to know what is meant by "politics in general, that is to say ... History."

10 Let us simply note, at this point, and in a way which is reminiscent of the Heidegger of the late 1910s and the early 1920s, that it is the question of *life* which forces the analysis of temporality into a discussion of historicity. Dilthey and his *Lebensphilosophie* are already in the background of the discussion. For a detailed and illuminating discussion of the question of factical life in the early Heidegger, see David Farrell Krell's remarkable *Daimon Life. Heidegger and Life-Philosophy* (Bloomington: Indiana University Press, 1992), especially Chapters 1 and 2.

11 SZ 374/427.

12 How are we to translate the German *Geschehen*? The connection drawn here between *Geschehen* and *Geschichte* is fairly traditional and can be traced

back to Herder. Literally, *geschehen* means to happen, to take place, to occur. In that respect, history is a happening, a taking place, an event: ein *Geschehen*. Hence our "historical happening," which serves to designate Dasein as an event that unfolds historically. Yet it must immediately be made clear that the event that is spoken of here is not a point in time, and that the unfolding of Dasein is not linear. Rather, the event is ekstatic and the unfolding is a stretching.

13   In order to maintain a graphic difference between history as *Geschehen* and history as historiography, we shall translate *Geschichte* by History and *Historie* by history.

14   SZ 382/434.

15   *Das Leichte* is one of the four categories of factical life in motion identified in the 1921/2 lecture course on Aristotle (GA 61, 108–10). Factical life seeks to make things easy for itself (and even its worldly difficulties – How hard is my life! – are *Erleichterungen*) and craves for security: it reassures itself by falling away from itself, by turning a blind eye to itself, by masking itself and fooling itself. It flees itself by drawing the Difficult (the unifold) aside and by avoiding primal decision. For a further discussion of this motif and its resonance within the economy of the Heideggerian text, see Krell's remarks on "The Facts of Life" (especially, pp. 45–9), "The University of Life" (pp. 147–57) and "Shattering" (pp. 177–9) in *Daimon Life*, op. cit.

16   SZ 384/435.

17   This difficulty concerning the passage from singular destiny to communal fate has already been stressed by P. Ricœur in *Temps et récit* (Paris: Seuil, 1985), vol. III, p. 112.

18   Soon after *Being and Time*, Heidegger will start evoking the historical Dasein, and then the German Dasein. One can understand the use of such formulations only in the wake of the analyses developed in *Being and Time*. The sections on Dasein's history are precisely the turning point, where Heidegger moves from the exhibition of Dasein's structures as a singular existing being to the expositon of Dasein's commonality. And because the analyses of commonality were so negative to begin with, Heidegger has no choice but to forge the possibility of an authentic common existence on the basis of an exceptional – indeed heroic-tragic – vision of existence. This clearly comes through in the 1933 speech commemorating the tenth anniversary of the death of the Freiburg student Albert Leo Schlageter, who was shot for acts of sabotage against the French occupation army, and whom Heidegger refers to as "a young German hero who a decade ago died the most difficult and greatest death of all" (*Der Alemanne*, 27 May 1933, p. 6; "Schlageter," trans. William S. Lewis in *The Heidegger Controversy* [Cambridge, The MIT Press, 1993], ed. Richard Wolin, pp. 40–2).

19   In a passage from his 1934 lecture course on Hölderlin, Heidegger, commenting on the experience of the soldiers at the front (an experience which he himself never underwent), writes the following: "It is precisely the death

which every man must die for himself and which completely isolates every individual, it is this death, and the acceptance of the sacrifice it demands, that creates in the first place the space whence the community surges" (GA 39, 73). At this particular point, there is nothing that distinguishes Heidegger's sacrificial conception of the community from, say, Hegel's.

20 *Volksgemeinschaft* or "national community" was the term used by the Nazis to designate the true essence of the German nation: a community bound by forces of blood and earth.

21 Oswald Spengler, *Der Untergang des Abendlandes* (München: Beck, 1920). English translation by Charles F. Atkinson, *The Decline of the West* (London: George Allen & Unwin, 1926), vol. II, chapters XI–XIV. Max Weber, *Wirtschaft und Gesellschaft. Grundriss der verstehenden Soziologie* (Tübingen: J. C. B. Mohr [Paul Siebeck]), 1956). Translated in English under the supervision of Guenther Roth and Claus Wittich, eds, *Economy and Society* (New York: Bedminster Press, 1968), vol. I, pp. 40–3. Max Scheler, *Der Formalismus in der Ethik und die materiale Wertethik* (Bern: Francke, 1963), Gesammelte Werke, vol. 5, pp. 524–36.

22 Ferdinand Tönnies, *Gemeinschaft und Gesellschaft. Grundbegriffe der reinen Psychologie* (Darmstadt: Wissenschaftliche Buchgesellscahft, 1963). Translated by Charles P. Loomis as *Community and Association* (London: Routledge and Kegan Paul, 1955). Both the German version we refer to and the translation are based on the 8th edition of *Gemeinschaft und Gesellschaft*, published in Leipzig, 1935.

23 *Gemeinschaft und Gesellschaft*, 243/263.

24 Ibid., 251/270.

25 Oswald Spengler, *Jahre der Entscheidung* (München: Deutscher Taschenbuch Verlag, 1961) and *Der Untergang des Abendlandes*, op. cit.

26 Heidegger gave two lectures on Spengler at a "Scientific Week" in Wiesbaden in mid-April 1920, and praises Spengler's work in his lecture course of the summer of 1923 (see GA 63, 55–7).

27 *The Decline of the West*, vol. II, 58/48

28 Ibid., 127–8/107

29 If *Volk* and *Gemeinschaft* serve to identify the proper way of being-in-common for Dasein, would there be a way of identifying the improper or everyday way of being together with *Gesellschaft*? There are certainly indications of such a possibility in Heidegger's analysis, if only in the anonymity and the dictatorial dimension of *das Man*. Yet one should still bear in mind that Heidegger's purpose is not to develop a critique of society on the basis of a more authentic mode of social organization, but to articulate the ontological structure of human existence.

30 Max Müller, "Martin Heidegger. Ein Philosoph und die Politik," *Freiburger Universitätsblätter*, June 1986, pp. 13–31. Reprinted and translated by Lisa Harries as 'A philosopher and politics: A conversation' in *Martin Heidegger*

and National Socialism. Questions and Answers (New York: Paragon House, 1990), eds Günther Neske and Emil Kettering, pp. 175–95.

31   Hans Jonas, "Heidegger's Resoluteness and Resolve" in *Martin Heidegger and National Socialism*, op. cit., p. 200.

32   The communication that is spoken of here is to be connected with and yet distinguished from the average kind of communication referred to as *Gerede* (idle talk) in section 35. Here, Heidegger is referring to the possibility of an authentic communication, the authenticity of which would precisely unfold from the common resoluteness that constitutes the community as such.

33   For precise references regarding the use of this word in *Being and Time*, see Krell's *Daimon Life*, op. cit., p. 338, note 7.

34   For further discussion on the question of tradition as *Tradition and Überlieferung*, see Robert Bernasconi's "Repetition and Tradition: Heidegger's Destructuring of the Distinction Between Essence and Existence in *Basic Problems of Phenomenology*" in *Reading Heidegger from the Start* (Albany: SUNY, 1994), eds Theodore Kiesel and John Van Buren, pp. 123–36.

35   SZ 385/437.

36   SZ 385/436.

37   This semantic of the opposition, the struggle, the rejoinder will find new developments in the rectoral address. We refer to what Heidegger says concerning the *Widerstand* and the *Kampf* toward the end of the address.

38   In that respect, one can only agree with Derrida who sees in Heidegger's reference to the *Kampf* an anticipation of the later developments around the notion of *polemos* as ontological strife. See Jacques Derrida, *Politiques de l'amitié* (Paris: Galilée, 1994), pp. 359 ff.

39   Ten years after the publication of *Being and Time*, Heidegger will recapture his statements in the following way: "The properly temporal is the stirring, exciting, but at the same time conserving and preserving extension and stretch from the future into the past and from the latter into the former. In this extension, man as historical is in each case a "spread." The present is always later than the future; it is the last. It springs from the struggle of the future with the past" (GA 45, 42/40).

40   SZ 2/21; my emphasis.

41   Is it a coincidence if Heidegger punctuates the first two pages of *Being and Time* with references to the "today," as if, from the very start, the whole of that text were oriented toward a rethinking of the nature of the present? For further developments on Heidegger's use of the word "today" and its implications, see Andrew Benjamin, "Time and Task: Benjamin and Heidegger showing the Present" in *Walter Benjamin's Philosophy* (London: Routledge, 1993), eds Andrew Benjamin and Peter Osborne, pp. 216–50.

42   Should it be reminded that the "Heidegger affair" appeared very quickly to be directed at Heidegger's call for a deconstruction of the history of ontology, interpreted as an anti-humanistic (and hence anti-human, hence pro-Nazi)

crusade? And should it be made explicit that, most often, such attacks were really aimed at destabilizing the spiritual son of Heidegger, the apostle and leader of world-deconstruction, the bogy philosopher, Jacques Derrida? For a thorough and illuminating discussion of the dominant interpretation concerning the connection between Heidegger's alleged anti-humanism and his politics, see William V. Spanos, *Heidegger and Criticism. Retrieving the Cultural Politics of Destruction* (Minneapolis: The University of Minnesota Press, 1993), pp. 181–251. Although Spanos focuses on the American reception of this question, with specific attention paid to the debate that took place in the Winter 1989 issue of *Critical Inquiry*, he also analyses its French and German origins. Thus, along with the names of Arnold I. Davidson, Tom Rockmore and Richard Wolin, one also finds those of Jürgen Habermas, Luc Ferry and Alain Renaut, and Victor Farias. To this long list one might also wish to add Jean-Pierre Faye's recent *Le Piège. La philosophie heideggerienne et le Nazisme* (Paris: Balland, 1994), sections 21, 25, 29, and pp. 165–89, as well as Nicolas Tertulian's "Histoire de l'être et révolution politique," *Les Temps Modernes*, February 1990, no. 523, pp. 109–36.

43　The view according to which history itself is a fall away from a higher and brighter origin is itself of course a very traditional interpretation, one that runs from Hesiod or Genesis to Spengler. Yet the originality of Heidegger's thought lies in the fact that, for him, there is the possibility of what René Char would call a *"retour amont,"* a return that is not aimed at recapturing the lost origin, but at leaping back so as to leap forward, at leaping back *before* the origin so as to free a future. Implicit here is the complex structure of the step back, of the temporality underlying it and, ultimately, of the impossiblity of reducing Heidegger's view on history to a linear conception of time (one that is necessarily presupposed in the interpretations of history we have just suggested). And it is precisely this complex structure of temporality that ultimately impedes the assimilation of the Heidegerrian *Verfallen* with Spengler's "Decline of the West," despite the similarities that can be drawn from a confrontation between the two texts.

44　For a sustained treatment of the question of nihilism, see Chapter 3 of this book, "After Politics."

45　SZ 387/439.

46　What Heidegger enigmatically designates as "the essential sacrifice" in "The Origin of the Work of Art" (Hw 50/62) is perhaps best exemplified in the following passage from the 1934/5 lecture course on Hölderlin, where Heidegger tries to thematize the experience of the soldiers in the front:

> The comradery amongst soldiers in the front does not arise from a necessity to gather because one felt far from those who were missing; nor does it come from the fact that one first agreed upon a common enthusiasm. Rather, its most profound and only reason is that the proximity of death as sacrifice brought everyone to the same annulation, which became the source of an unconditional belonging to the others.
> (GA 39, 72–3)

47   From the unconditional support of the ongoing revolution expressed in 1933–4 to the call for a revolution with respect to being and to the language of metaphysics expressed in 1935, there seems to be an evolution of the motif of revolution, one that reveals an increasing discontent on Heidegger's part with respect to the outcome of Nazi politics.

Archaic Politics

1   Who would want to contest that, in the history of the twentieth century, from the Spanish Civil War to the Vietnam war, from May 1968 and the Prague Spring to Tian Anmen Square, the modern State lived some of its most decisive hours in the university and that this modern university played a role similar to that of the street or the factory?

2   See Heidegger's statements in the interview that he gave to *Der Spiegel* on 23 September 1966 and published after his death on 31 May 1976 under the title "Nur noch ein Gott kann uns retten". English translation by Lisa Harries in *Martin Heidegger and National Socialism. Questions and Answers* (New York: Paragon House, 1990), eds Günther Neske and Emil Kettering, pp. 41–66.

3   See *Der Streit der Facultäten* in Kant, *Werke*, Bd. VII (Berlin: Walter de Gruyter, 1968), *Zweiter Abschnitt*, section 7: "*Die Wahrsagende Geschichte der Menschheit*". In many respects, this text could be said to be Kant's own rectoral address. Kant addresses questions concerning the relation between thinking and governing, between the law of freedom and the laws of the State, between education and power. No doubt, a detailed confrontation of the two texts would be most fruitful. For a sustained treatment of Kant's text, see Jacques Derrida, "*Mochlos* – ou le conflit des facultés" in *Du droit à la philosophie* (Paris: Galilée, 1990), pp. 397–438.

4   See Friedrich Hölderlin's letter to Casimir Ulrich Böhlendorff, dated 4 December 1801 in Friedrich Hölderlin, *Sämtliche Werke* (Stuttgart: Verlag W. Kohlhammer, 1954), Bd. VI (*Briefe*), ed. Adolf Beck, pp. 425–8. English translation by Thomas Pfau in *Essays and Letters on Theory* (Albany: SUNY Press, 1988), ed. Thomas Pfau, pp. 149–51.

5   For a discussion of Heidegger's remarks on the Greek *polis*, see Chapter 5 of this book, "Before Politics".

6   See Schelling's 1802–3 ("Lectures on the Method of Academic Studies") "Vorlesungen über die Methode des akademischen Studiums" in F. W. Schelling, *Werke*, (München: Beck, 1927) ed. Manfred Schröter, Bd. III, 207–352.

7   Besides the Jena Lectures by Schelling already mentioned, we should also mention Fichte's "Deductive Plan for an Establishment of Higher Learning to be Founded in Berlin" ("Deducierter Plan einer zu Berlin zu errichtenden höheren Lehranstalt"), written in 1807 and published in 1817, in J. G. Fichte, *Sämtliche Werke*, Dritte Abtheilung, Bd. III, 97–204; Schleiermacher's response to Fichte in his "Occasional thoughts on universities in the German sense" ("Gelegentliche Gedanken über Universitäten in deutschem Sinn"), in F. Schleiermacher, *Sämtliche Werke*, Dritte Abtheilung, *Zur Philosophie*, Bd.

I, 535–644; von Humboldt's 1809 or 1810 "On the Internal and External Organisation of the Higher Scientific Establishments in Berlin" ("Über die innere und äußere Organisation der höheren wissenschaftlichen Anstalten in Berlin"), in W. von Humboldt, *Gesammelte Schriften*, Königlich-Preussische Akademie der Wissenschaften, Politische Denkschriften, Bd. I, 250–60; finally, Hegel's 1816 "On Teaching Philosophy at University" (Über den Vortrag der Philosophie auf Universitäten"), in G. W. F. Hegel, *Werke in zwanzig Bänden*, Bd. IV, *Nürnberger und Heidelberger Schriften*, 418–24. For an excellent presentation and systematic analysis of these contributions, to which my remarks are indebted, see L. Ferry, A. Renaut and J. P. Pesron, *Philosophies de l'université* (Paris: Payot, 1979).

8   Letter to Karl Löwith, 19 August 1921, first published in *Zur philosophischen Aktualität Heideggers: Symposium der Alexander von Humboldt-Stiftung vom 24–28 April in Bonn-Bad Godesberg*, vol. 2, eds Dietrich Papenfuss and Otto Pöggeler (Frankfurt: Klostermann, 1990).

9   See GA 61, 66.

10   "Heidegger in the University of Life" is the title of the fourth chapter of Krell's *Daimon Life*, where one can find the most illuminating discussion of the question of life in relation to that of the university.

11   GA 56/57, 4.

12   See GA 61, 62–76.

13   GA 61, 73–6.

14   Now published under the the title "Was ist Metaphysik?" in *Wegmarken* (Frankfurt-am-Main: Vittorio Klostermann, 1967), pp. 1–19. English translation by David Farrell Krell in *Basic Writings* (New York: Harper and Row, 1977), ed. D. F. Krell, pp. 95–112.

15   Hugo Ott, *Martin Heidegger. Unterwegs zu seiner Biographie* (Frankfurt: Campus Verlag, 1988).

16   One finds this *finis universitatum* (without the question-mark) inscribed in the diary of the Vice-Rector of the University of Freiburg, Josef Sauer, in an entry dated 22 August 1933.

17   See the telegram to Adolf Hitler dated 20 May 1933 and reproduced in Ott, op. cit. 187.

18   SA 208.

19   SA 210.

20   Sections 5 and 6 of the 1934/5 *Germanien* (GA 39) lecture course are devoted to this question of the "we" and to what looks like a problematization of a question that remained insufficiently thematized in 1933. Would Heidegger's politics have been in any way different had he become aware of the difficulties underlying his appeal to the "we" of the German nation constituted as *Volksgemeinschaft*? For a further discussion of Heidegger's first interpretations of Hölderlin, see Chapter 4 of this book.

21 SDU 10/30.

22 The *Aufstehen* and the *fragende Standhalten* that are here mentioned serve
to introduce the motif of the stance, which plays a decisive role throughout
the address and sheds a new light on the originary rectoral dimension of the
rectorship. The stance that is spoken of here is none other than what
Heidegger elsewhere (in *Being and Time*, of course, but also long after the
project of fundamental ontology had been abandoned) characterizes as the
ek-stasis or the *transcendence* of Dasein. To say that the stance proper to
Dasein is ek-static is to designate its mode of dwelling on earth – its being
in the world – as one of clearing and disclosedness, as a dynamic and ultimately temporal relation to its own being. If Dasein dwells on earth, it means
that Dasein is at home in the world. Yet Dasein dwells in the world in such
a way that it is driven toward the very limits of the world. Everywhere at
home, since the world is its home, Dasein is also nowhere at home, since it
is always thrown beyond itself. Dasein stands in the world as the
Unheimlichste or the uncanniest of all beings. Now when Heidegger identifies this basic existential-ontological mode of standing with original
questioning, it is clear that questioning, and along with it, "science," mean
something quite different from interrogation or raising questions with a view
to answering them. In an *archaic* sense, questioning refers to Dasein's own
transcendence, to the fact that, for it, its Being is always at issue for it, or
that it has always already understood its "to be." It is in the light of this
archaic meaning of questioning that one ought to (re)think the very possibility of the *Seinsfrage*: if being can become a question for us, it is because
it is always *in* question for us. This being in question or at issue points in
the direction of Dasein's specific stance or mode of dwelling, which is none
other than ek-static finitude. This connection between philosophy originarily
understood and dwelling is perhaps made most explicit in *The Basic Concepts
of Metaphysics* (GA 29/30, section 2), where, quoting from Novalis,
Heidegger identifies the *Grundstimmung* of philosophy with nostalgia or
homesickness (*Heimweh*). Heidegger writes:

> Let us remain with the issue and ask: what is all this talk about home-
> sickness? Novalis himself elucidates: "an urge to be everywhere at
> home. Philosophy can only be such an urge if we who philosophise
> are not at home everywhere.
>
> (GA 29/30: 7)

23 See in particular chapters II (*"Der Anklang"* – "The Resonance") and III
(*"Das Zuspiel"* – "The Interplay").

24 The essential belonging together of *technè* and technology is of the utmost
importance, for if *technè* can come to designate "the saving power", to use
Hölderlin's terms, it is precisely by way of its historical-destinal attachment
to technology. This attachment is what distinguishes Heidegger's conception
of history from redemption and messianism.

25 SDU 13/33.

26   The most sustained treatment of Plato's *thaumazein* (which Heidegger inter-
      prets as "wonder" and "amazement") as the basic disposition of the
      primordial thinking of the West is perhaps to be found in GA 45, sections
      36–8. There, Heidegger is careful to distinguish wonder from related kinds
      of marvelling, which include admiration.

27   Excerpt from an address presented by Heidegger at an election rally in Leipzig
      on 11 November 1933. Reproduced and translated in *The Heidegger
      Controversy* (Cambridge: The MIT Press, 1993), ed. R. Wolin, p. 51.

28   For a thorough and remarkable reading of the economy of spirit in
      Heidegger's address – and beyond – see J. Derrida's *De l'esprit. Heidegger
      et la question* (Paris: Galilée, 1987). English translation by Geoffrey
      Bennington and Rachel Bowlby, *Of Spirit. Heidegger and the Question*
      (Chicago: Chicago University Press, 1989).

29   SDU 15/34.

30   This pathetic rhetoric invades most of Heidegger's speeches and texts from
      the period of the rectorate. In a speech delivered to the Heidelberg students
      and dated 30 June 1933, Heidegger describes the "new courage" demanded
      of them in the following terms:

> *University study must become again a risk*, not a refuge for the
> cowardly. Whoever does not survive the battle, lies where he falls. The
> new courage must accustom itself to steadfastness, for the battle for
> the institutions where our leaders are educated will continue for a long
> time. It will be fought out of the strengths of the new *Reich* that
> Chancellor Hitler will bring to reality. A hard race [*Geschlecht*] with
> no thought of self must fight this battle. . .
>
> (*The Heidegger Controversy*, op, cit., pp. 45)

Elsewhere, in a series of appeals launched in support of the plebiscite of 12
November 1933, called by Hitler to sanction Germany's withdrawal from
the League of Nations and consolidate his power within the country,
Heidegger indulged in the most zealously Nazi bombast:

> Let your loyalty and your will to follow be daily and hourly strength-
> ened. Let your courage grow without ceasing so that you will be able
> to make the sacrifices necessary to save the essence of our people and
> to elevate its innermost strength in the State.
> Let no propositions and "ideas" be the rules of your Being.
> The *Führer* alone is the present and future German reality and its law.
>
> (Ibid., p. 47)

And again:

> It is not ambition, not desire for glory, not blind obstinacy, and not
> hunger for power that demands from the *Führer* that Germany with-
> draw from the League of Nations. It is only the clear will to

unconditional self-responsibility in suffering and mastering the fate of our people.

(Ibid., p. 50)

(Here again, the confrontation with Kant, for whom the finality of nature lies precisely in the elaboration of a League of Nations, would be most illuminating. See Immanuel Kant, "Idea for a Universal History with a Cosmopolitan Purpose," particularly the seventh proposition; English translation by H.B. Nisket in *Kant: Political Writings* (Ithaca: Cornell University Press, 1991), ed. Hans Reiss, pp. 41–53.

31 In a speech delivered on 30 June 1933 to the Heidelberg Student Association, and published in the *Heidelberger Neuste Nachrichten* on 1 July 1933, Heidegger said the following: "The warning cry has already been sounded: "*Wissenschaft* is endangered by the amount of time lost in martial sports and other such activities." But what does that mean, to lose time, when it is a question of fighting for the State! *Danger* comes not from *work* for the *State*. It comes only from indifference and resistance. For that reason, only true strength should have access to the right path, but not halfheartedness." (Reproduced, and translated in English by William S. Lewis, in *The Heidegger Controversy*, op. cit., p. 45) Does the excessively heroic pathos of this passage find its roots in Heidegger's own physiological halfheartedness, that very physiological defect that frustrated him from heroism in the First World War and turned him into a weatherman? Again, Nietzsche would have laughed at this poor constitution and at his desire for revenge.

32 For more details on this "scientific camp," see Ott, op. cit., pp. 214–23.

33 As John Sallis has so cautiously and convincingly demonstrated, this so-called model is far more complex and paradoxical than is usually thought. Heidegger himself would have benefited from taking this complexity more seriously. See John Sallis, *Being and Logos* (Atlantic Highlands: Humanities Press, 1975), pp. 346–401.

34 Specifically, in the second edition of *Introduction to Metaphysics*, 1953, where Heidegger decided to leave the statement from the 1935 original edition untouched, only adding in parenthesis, by way of a further – and of course retrospective – explanation, the following sentence: "(namely the encounter between technology determined globally and modern man)," (EM 152/199). For a sustained and illuminating dicussion of this passage, see Janicaud's *L'ombre de cette pensée* (Grenoble: Jérôme Millon, 1990), Chapter 4 ("La lettre volée"), pp. 77–96.

35 SZ 385/437.

36 SZ 386/438.

37 SDU 18/38.

38 SDU 18/37.

39 This motif of the *polemos*, first articulated in section 74 of *Being and Time*, begins to take its full measure in the rectoral address, but finds further

developments in subsequent texts, at which point it has become a leitmotiv. As already indicated in Chapter 1 of this book, on the question of the *polemos*, see Derrida's "L'oreille de Heidegger – Philopolémologie" in *Politiques de l'amitié* (Paris: Galilée, 1994), pp. 343–419.

After Politics

1   GA 2, 138/6.

2   SZ 396/448.

3   Martin Heidegger, letter to the Rector of the Freiburg University, 4 November 1995. Published and translated by Richard Wolin in *The Heidegger Controversy* (Cambridge: The MIT Press, 1993), p. 65.

4   It is Russia and America which, for Heidegger, designate the two poles and extremities of this global process which he designates as "technological nihilism":

> From a metaphysical point of view, Russia and America are the same; the same dreary technological frenzy, the same unrestricted organisation of the average man. At a time when the farthermost corner of the globe has been conquered by technology and opened to economic exploitation; when any incident whatever, regardless of where or when it occurs, can be communicated to the rest of the world at any desired speed ... when time has ceased to be anything other than velocity, instantaneousness, and simultaneity, and time as history has vanished from the lives of all peoples; when a boxer is regarded as a nation's great man; when mass meetings attended by millions are looked on as a triumph [would this critique apply to the Nazi rallies themselves?] – then, yes then, through all this turmoil a questions still haunts us like a specter: What for? – Whither? – And what then?
>
> (EM 28–9/37–8)

These comments, which can be seen as retaining a critical or philosophical – and, specifically, Nietzschean – edge, eventually indulge in a rhetoric of "spirit" virtually indistinguishable from that of Nazism. The "emasculation of the spirit," which originated in Europe, is now taken to an extreme in Russia and in America, which thus become figures of the demonic:

> In America and in Russia this development grew into a boundless etcetera of indifference and always-the-sameness – so much so that the quantity took on a quality of its own. Since then the domination in those countries of a cross section of the indifferent mass has become something more than a dreary accident. It has become an active onslaught that destroys all rank and every world-creating impulse of the spirit, and calls it a lie. This is the onslaught of what we call the demonic (in the sense of destructive evil).
>
> (EM 35/46)

5   Alfred Bauemler, *Nietzsche der Philosoph und Politiker* (Leipzig: P. Reclam, 1931).

6   SDU 13/33.

7   Should one have to be reminded that it is in this chapter that one finds Heidegger's famous statement, along with the parenthesis added in the 1953 edition (the lecture course was delivered in the summer semester of 1935), according to which "the works that are being peddled about nowadays as the philosophy of National Socialism but have nothing whatsoever to do with the inner truth and greatness of this movement (namely the encounter between technology determined planetarily and modern man) – have all been written by men fishing in the troubled waters of "values" and "totalities." (EM 152/199) For an exhaustive and illuminating discussion of the history and the implications of this statement, see Dominique Janicaud's *L'ombre de cette pensée* (Grenoble: Jérôme Millon, 1990), Chapter 4, "La lettre volée."

8   Heidegger often emphasizes that the verb *wesen*, from which the substantive *Wesen* (essence) is derived, is itself derived from the old high German *wesan*, to dwell, to sojourn, thus to happen, to unfold, to rule.

9   These are the texts that focus on the question of nihilism:
1936–46: "Overcoming Metaphysics" (essay, first published in VA).
1940: "European Nihilism" (a lecture course, GA 48; also published in N II).
1944–6: "Nihilism as Determined by the History of Being" (an essay published in N II).
1946–8: *Das Wesen des Nihilismus* (unpublished essay).
1955: "On 'The Line' " ("Über 'die Linie' "). Originally written and published as a contribution to a *Festschrift* for Ernst Jünger's 60th birthday, then reproduced as a book under the title *Zur Seinsfrage* (Frankfurt am Main: Vittorio Klostermann, 1956). Now included in Wm.

10   Ernst Jünger, "Die totale Mobilmachung," *Werke* Vol. V, *Essays I*. (Stuttgart: Ernst Klett Verlag, 1960).Originally published in 1930 in *Krieg und Krieger*, a collection of essays edited by Jünger himself.

11   Ernst Jünger, *Der Arbeiter* (1932), *Werke*, Vol. 6, *Essays II*, op. cit.

12   "On 'The Line'," Wm.

13   Oswald Spengler, *Der Mensch und die Technik* (München: Beck, 1931).

14   Ibid., 55.

15   One might also wonder the extent to which Heidegger's notion of *Machenschaft*, which appears in the mid- and late-30s, is indebted to the machinic and mechanical aspects of the modern age Spengler describes here. On *Machenschaft*, see below, "The essence of nihilism".

16   VA 91–7.

17   N I, 183/N I, 156–7.

18   N II, 38–9/N IV, 8.

19   N II, 48/N IV, 16

20   Martin Heidegger, GA 56/57, 13–78 and 140–68. These early writings consti-
      tute Heidegger's farewell to the neo-Kantianism of his youth and are directed
      against Rickert and Windelband, in whom Heidegger saw the true founder
      of the transcendental philosophy of values. Yet the key figure underlying
      the philosophy of values is not so much Kant as it is Fichte for Heidegger,
      so that this philosophy would best be defined as a "neo-Fichteanism" (GA
      56/57: 142)

21   "With a view to the other beginning nihilism must be grasped more funda-
      mentally as an essential consequence of the abandonment of being
      [*Seinsverlassenheit*]" (GA 65, 139).

22   See "The Question Concerning Technology," TK, 5–36/287–317.

23   See GA 65, II: "Der Anklang" (sections 50–80).

24   GA 65, 145.

25   GA 65, 149.

26   In the Webster's New World Dictionary, the word "might" comes with the
      following explanations:

          might (mit) n. [ME. mighte < OE miht, akin to G. macht < IE base
          *magh-, to be able: cf. MAY] 1. great or superior strength, power,
          force or vigor 2. strength or power of any degree.

      Like the German *Macht*, then, which constitutes the heart of the word
      Machenschaft, "might" suggests power in the twofold sense of *force* and
      capacity (as being able to).

27   That power (as might) presupposes will (as capacity), that will (as volition)
      implies power (as disposition), that, in other words, will is always *to* power
      and power *of* the will, is something that should be clear from the previous
      footnote.

28   GA 65, 127.

29   GA 65, 219.

30   Heidegger's critical engagement with Jünger's position is played out in "On
      'The Line'," Wm.

31   Wm 219/45.

32   N II, 373/N IV, 229. Heidegger's statement dates from 1944–6.

33   Hw 273/118; my emphasis.

34   TK 44.

35   In 1944–5, one might be surprised, if not utterly shocked, to see Heidegger
      so concerned with the destruction of the *essence* of man, when millions of
      men and women were *actually* being annihilated. I discuss Heidegger's inabil-
      ity to relate philosophically to the Holocaust in the last chapter of this book.

The Free Use of the National

1   GA 29/30, 7.

2   This engagement, which was to take place over nearly three decades, totalizing four lecture courses, a collection of essays and numerous references can
be chronologically gathered in the following three major periods:
1. Mid-1930s to the end of the 1930s:
Winter Semester 1934/5: a lecture course devoted to Hölderlin's hymns
Germanien and *der Rhein* (GA 39); "Hölderlin and the Essence of Poetry"
(1936), later published in *Erläuterungen zu Hölderlins Dichtung* (1951); "*Wie
wenn am Feiertage* ..." (1939), later published in EHD; but the presence of
Hölderlin is also overwhelming in the 1936–8 *Beiträge zur Philosophie (vom
Ereignis)* (GA 65).
2. Early 1940s:
Winter Semester 1941/2 (announced, but not delivered): in effect a dialogue
between Nietzsche and Hölderlin (GA 50); Winter Semester 1941/2: a lecture
course devoted to Hölderlin's hymn *Andenken* (GA 52); Summer Semester
1942: a lecture course devoted to Hölderlin's hymn *der Ister* (GA 53);
"*Heimkunft/An die Verwandten*" (1943) and "*Andenken*" (1943), both
published in EHD.
3. 1950s and 1960s:
"*Hölderlins Erde und Himmel*" (1959) and "*Das Gedicht*" (1968), both
included in the 1971 Klostermann edition of EHD; and while the second
part of *What is Called Thinking?* (1954) is largely devoted to an interpretation of Hölderlin, the poetry of Hölderlin continues to haunt many of the
commentaries of *On the Way to Language* (1959).

3   See J. G. Fichte' s *Addresses to the German Nation* (1807–8), *Sämtliche
Werke* (Berlin: Veit, 1845), Bd. VII.

4   This requires further explanation. By redeploying the question of national
identity on the basis of a certain reading of Hölderlin, he does not simply
displace the terrain of nationalism. Specifically, Heidegger does not simply
redefine nationalism in terms of a privileging of a certain idiom, as opposed
to the nationalism of blood and/or soil. As a matter of fact, this latter type
of nationalism is almost always complicitous with a certain idiocentrism,
which often serves as its metaphysical or ideological justification. Rather, by
rethinking national identity via Hölderlin's poetry, Heidegger subordinates
the German idiom to what he designates as *Sprache* or poetic language, that
is, as this language that is not instrumental but serves to designate the site
of a historical dwelling. In the move from the terrain of nationalism to that
of the nationell, what takes place is the abandonment of the terrain of the
territory and of its logic of territorialization in favour of a dwelling that is
essentially homeless. Whereas the nationalism of blood, of soil and of the
idiom is essentially territorializing (colonizing and imperialistic), the nationel-
lism of poetry is engaged in the most uncanny and dangerous of all activities,
and that is in the exposure to the homelessness of the human condition.
Despite the decisiveness of this move, Heidegger will regularly indulge in the
most virulent – and at times even comical – nationalistic rhetoric, often by

way of launching diatribes against the techno-practical imperative of the Anglo-American idiom (GA 53, 79–80), which culminate in broader attacks such as this:

> We know today that the Anglo-Saxon world of Americanism is determined to annihilate Europe, which is to say, its homeland and the beginning of the West. What is of the beginning cannot be destroyed. The entry of America into this planetary war is not the entry into history, but is already the final American act of American ahistoricity and self-devastation.
>
> (GA 53, 68)

More comical, perhaps, is Heidegger's burning desire to identify the *Brauen Frauen* or tanned women from Bordeaux in Hölderlin's *Andenken* with "the German women" (see EHD 108).

5   This is perhaps the point at which the most decisive break with the problematic of fundamental ontology occurs. One recalls how section 34 of *Being and Time* introduced the question of language (*Sprache*), yet in a way that made it entirely subordinate to its existential-ontological foundation, which Heidegger characterized as "discourse" or "talk" (*Rede*), and which served to designate the existential in which the intelligibility of something is articulated. Ultimately, then, the question of language was subordinated to the broader question of meaning, which marked the ultimate horizon of the treatise as a whole. In a unique reference to poetry, Heidegger also characterized "poetic discourse" as just one mode of expressedness (*Hinausgesprochenheit*) amongst many. Yet if Heidegger recognized the tool or ready-to-hand aspect of language, and even its present-at-handness, insofar as language appears as something that is encountered in the world, he also raised fundamental and puzzling questions that simply could not find an answer within the problematic defined in *Being and Time*, questions that, if pursued, would call the whole of the treatise into question, and to a large extent did. These questions have to do with the kind of being specific to language as a whole:

> In the last resort, philosophical research must resolve to ask what kind of being goes with language in general. Is it a kind of equipment ready-to-hand within-the-world, or has it Dasein's kind of being, or is it neither of these? What kind of being does language have, if there can be such a thing as a 'dead' language?
>
> (SZ 166/209)

It is by focusing on these questions that Heidegger comes to see language no longer as the mere articulation of meaning, no longer as one mode of the disclosedness of Dasein, but as the very disclosedness of being itself.

6   Hw 47–8/59–60

7   EM 122/159

8   EM 8/10.

9   This difficult question of the intimate relation and yet absolute separation between *Denken* (thinking) and *Dichten* (poeticizing), to which Heidegger often adds *Handeln* (doing or acting) – a question that will remain at the very heart of Heidegger's meditation until the very end – finds one of its very first formulations in the following passage from the 1934/5 lecture course:

> Given the singularity of our world-historical situation – and in general – we can neither predict nor plan how Hölderlin's poetry will be put into words and to work in the whole of the actualization of our historical determination. We can only say this: the Western historical Dasein is ineluctably and unsurpassably a *knowing* [Wissen]. ... Since our Dasein is a knowing Dasein – where knowing here cannot be taken to simply mean a calculation of the understanding – there will never be for us a *purely poetic* Dasein, no more than a *purely thinking* or a *purely acting* Dasein. What is required from us is not to set up regular and convenient equivalents between the forces of poetry, of thought and of action, but to take seriously their seclusion in the sheltered summits, and thus to experience the secret of their originary belonging together and to bring them originarily into a new and so far unheard configuration of beyng.
>
> (GA 39, 184–5)

10 GA 39, 214.

11 Friedrich Hölderlin, *Germanien*, v. 17–27. English translation by Michael Hamburger in *Friedrich Hölderlin: Poems and Fragments* (London: Anvil Press, 1994), p. 423.

12 See GA 39, 98.

13 GA 39, 97.

14 Hölderlin coins this word in his famous letter to Casimir Ulrich Böhlendorf, dated 4 December 1801. See Friedrich Hölderlin, *Sämtliche Werke* (Stuttgart: Verlag W. Kohlkammer, 1954), Bd. VI (*Briefe*), ed. Adolf Beck, 425–8. I have already discussed some aspects of this question in Chapter 2 of this book.

15 See GA 65, section 19: "Philosophy (On the Question: Who are We?)."

16 Address to the German students of 3 November 1933. English translation by William S. Lewis in *The Heidegger Controversy* (Cambridge: The MIT Press, 1993), ed. Richard Wolin, 46–7.

17 See GA 39, section 6: "The Determination of the "We" on the Basis of the Horizon of the Question of Time," a) "The Measurable Time of the Individual and the Original Time of the People."

18 See, for example, Karl Löwith's "My Last Meeting with Heidegger in Rome, 1936" in *Mein Leben in Deutschland vor und nach 1933* (Stuttgart: Metzler, 1986), pp. 56–9.

19   On the essential complicity between art and politics in general, and with reference to Heidegger in particular, see Philippe Lacoue-Labarthe, *La fiction du politique* (Paris: Christian Bourgois, 1987) and *L'imitation des Modernes* (Paris: Galilée, 1986).

20   See SZ 385/437.

21   GA 65, 401.

22   GA 39, 104.

23   GA 53, 60.

24   Hölderlin, *Briefe.*

25   See GA 39, 290–4; GA 53, 168–70; EHD, 83–7.

26   There is some strong evidence to support this view, and we have already alluded to some of it at the beginning of this chapter. Heidegger's Greco-German-centrism has come under severe criticism in the last few years. The most systematic and nuanced critique in the Anglo-American academy comes out of Robert Bernasconi's work. See, for example, his "Heidegger and the Invention of the Western Philosophical Tradition" in *The Journal of the British Society for Phenomenology*, vol. XXVI, October 1995, 240–54 and "On Heidegger's Other Sins of Omission: His Exclusion of Asian Thought from the Origins of Occidental Metaphysics and his Denial of the Possibility of Christian Philosophy" in *American Catholic Philosophical Quarterly*, vol. LXIX, 2, 1995, 333–50.

27   GA 39, 293.

28   Friedrich Hölderlin, letter to Casimir Ulrich Böhlendorf dated 12 December 1801, *Briefe.*

Before Politics

1   Yet the virulence and the dismissiveness with which Heidegger refers to both countries, and particularly to the United States, would suggest that more was at stake than just this global diagnosis. What exactly? A feeling of persecution? Heidegger will continue to see Germany as the victim of this historical process, and its fate as that of a third way, whether that of the conservative revolution of Adolf Hitler or the poetry of Hölderlin. This privilege of Germany – indeed an exclusively metaphysical privilege – will never be called into question, and will be largely responsible for Heidegger's own ignorance and blindness with respect to not only Nazi Germany, but also the United States and the Soviet Union. For some of Heidegger's most staggering statements – increasingly aggressive as the Second World War developed – see EM 28–9, 34–8, and GA 53, 68, 79–80, 86.

2   Specifically, *Hölderlins Hymne "Der Ister"* (GA 53), a lecture course from the Summer Semester of 1942, *Parmenides* (GA 54), a lecture course from the Winter Semester of 1942/3, and *Heraklit* (GA 55), a lecture course from the Summer Semester of 1943.

3   The question, however, is to know whether Heidegger, in his perhaps legitimate reinterpretation of the essence and function of myth, does not in turn mythologize myth itself, thus creating a new mythology, one that will forever be suspicious of any type of anthropology. Does this suspicion, already firmly in place in the very way in which the project of fundamental ontology comes to be formulated, not stem from a titanic effort to preserve philosophy, to keep it pure of any anthropology, to affirm its essence and task over and against all other disciplines, to grasp it as the mode of thinking attuned to the discreet voice of the non-foundational foundation of being? And is this not also what rendered Heidegger blind to the social, economic and ideological forces behind the rise of Nazism? Is it not this very thought of essence that allowed him to maintain the "inner truth and greatness" of National Socialism long after the collapse of the "movement"? Must philosophy not let itself be traversed and worked by the forces at work in the world and by the various discourses that try to thematize them? Does philosophy not become philosophy in the very opening to non-philosophy?

4   Is it not this absolute and unquestioned primacy of the visible that underlies the more recent theories of the "spectacle" and the "simulacrum"?

5   By way of comparison, and to indicate the extent to which Heidegger's own translation/interpretation wrests the passage from its ethical, political and religious context so as to reorient it ontologically, this is how a more traditional, and perhaps more "correct" translation would read:

> With some sort of cunning, inventive
> beyond all expectation
> he reaches sometimes evil,
> and sometimes good.
> If he honours the laws of earth,
> and the justice of the gods he has confirmed by oath,
> high is his city; no city
> has he with whom dwells dishonour
> prompted by recklessness.

(Translated by David Grene in *Greek Tragedies* [Chicago: The University of Chicago Press, 1991], eds David Grene and Richmond Lattimore, p. 195)

6   In a remarkable essay devoted to the "shapes" and the "limits" of technological thought in ancient Greece (*"Remarques sur les formes et les limites de la pensée technique chez les Grecs," Mythe et pensée chez les Grecs* [Paris: Maspero, 1974], vol. II, pp. 44–64), J. P. Vernant notes that the Greeks, who invented philosophy, science, ethics, politics and certain forms of art remained utterly non-innovative in the area of technology: their tools and their industrial techniques, inherited from the Orient, were not modified by further discoveries and inventions. They simply perfected, and sometimes innovated within the technological system that was already fixated in the classical epoch, a system that consisted in the application of human or animal force to a wide variety of instruments, and not in the use of the forces of nature through driving machines, such as the windmill, which appeared only

in the third century AD, thus marking the beginning of a new technological age. Vernant expresses his surprise before this "technological stagnation," given the fact that the Greeks, by that time, possessed the "intellectual tools" (sic) that should have enabled them to make some decisive progress in the development of machines and technologies. Specifically, many technical problems, most often mechanical in nature were already resolved mathematically. But these discoveries remained unrealized. They were meant, Vernant argues, to impress the spectator, who would see them as objects of marvel, as *thaumata*. Their practical use as well as their concrete realization was not the principal stake. And Vernant, in a statement that is a direct allusion to Descartes, and that, no doubt, Heidegger would have delighted in, concludes: "Never does the idea appear, according to which, through the help of these machines, man can command the forces of nature, transform it, become its master and possessor" (p. 50). To the interpretation of certain scholars, who attribute this lack of interest in the concrete application of scientific expertise to the availability of slave labor and to the largely depreciated categories of the useful, of labor, of the practical and of the artificial (as opposed to the highly valued domain of theory, contemplation and nature), Vernant wishes to oppose the following metaphysical interpretation: for the Greeks, an insurmountable gap separates the realm of the mathematical from that of the physical, in that the mathematical, and science in general, aims at grasping unmovable essences or the regular movements of the skies, whereas the terrestrial world is the domain of moving substances, and therefore of the approximate (this separation is perhaps most clearly articulated in the Aristotelian corpus). One can only imagine how, from a Heideggerian perspective, although on the right track, that is, on the track of the metaphysical framework within which certain material specificities come to be developed, Vernant's interpretation would simply be not metaphysical enough. One would need to go further and see how, in the Greek context, mathematics, and the technology that might result from it, remained subordinated to metaphysics, not as a constituted science, but as this experience of truth according to which there is more to nature than its sheer visibility, that the extension and the mathematical spatiality of the world does not exhaust its essence. If movement belongs so essentially to the realm of *phusis*, as Aristotle pointed out, it is because *phusis* is the open region in which beings come into being and withdraw into concealment, because *phusis* is not primarily physio-mathematical, but aletheo-poetic.

7   In a footnote of his English translation of *Introduction to Metaphysics*, p. 160.

8   GA 53, 87.

9   GA 53, 88.

10   100 GA 53, 97.

11   GA 53, 98.

12   GA 53, 98. For those who might believe that, in 1942, Heidegger had lost all of his National Socialist illusions, this statement will serve as a reminder.

13   GA 53, 98.

14   GA 53, 100.

15   I am indebted to Marc Froment-Meurice for this ingenious translation of *Umstand* and *Zustand*. See his recent *C'est-à-dire. Poétique de Heidegger* (Paris: Galilée, 1996), p. 128.

16   GA 53, 106.

17   Vernant, *Mythe et pensée*, I, p. 126.

18   *Cratylus*, 401 c-e.

19   Louis Deroy, "Le culte du foyer dans la Grèce mycénienne," *Revue de l'histoire des religions*, 1950, pp. 32, 43.

20   Vernant, *Mythe et pensée*, I, pp. 168–9.

21   See GA 55, 6–10.

22   Aristotle, *De part. anim.* A5. 645 a 17ff.

23   The other story that Heidegger recounts in the Heraclitus volume (GA 55, 10–13) can be seen as the symmetry of the first one, and is perhaps more *directly* political: it is the story told by Diogenes Laertius (IX, 3) according to which, one day, as the Ephesian surprised Heraclitus playing knuckle bones with some children in the temple of Artemis, goddess of *phusis*, the master dismissively replied: "What, you wretched imbeciles, do you find so surprising? Is it not better to do this than to concern myself with the *polis* with you?" The truly political action is perhaps not where one ordinarily expects it to be, and it is perhaps more essentially political to be playing games with children in the temple of Artemis than to be "doing" politics. In playing in such a way in a divine abode, Heraclitus is perhaps asserting the innocence of childhood as a divine activity of nature, and his action is perhaps the revelation of play as the most unfamiliar of all activities. Is there a parallel between Heraclitus in the temple, or by the oven, and Heidegger in the university, or in the *Hütte* after the turn away from politics in the strictest sense?

24   See *Republic*, 616ff; *Phaedrus*, 247a; *Cratylus*, 401 c-e.

25   See GA 53, 130–52, in particular section 18, "The Hearth as Being," and GA 55, 5–27.

26   GA 53, 147.

27   On this question of translation, see GA 53, 74–83.

28   See GA 54, section 6.

29   See Jacques Taminaux, *Le théâtre des philosophes* (Grenoble: Jérôme Millon, 1995), pp. 220–1.

30   In his essay on "The Formation of Positive Thought in Archaic Greece" (*Mythe et pensée chez les Grecs*, II, pp. 95–124), Vernant reveals how the

emergence of the Greek *polis* is not an event of a purely political signification, but is also accompanied by a transformation in the economic sphere.
Specifically, to the increase and the acceleration of the power, the speeches
and the deeds characteristic of the *polis* also corresponds an intensification
of the exchange of goods through the systematic introduction of money. To
be sure, this transformation is one that for the longest time will be considered as counter-natural: whereas an old term such as *tokos* (the interest of
money), derived from the root *tek-* (to give birth, to generate), associated
the product of capital with the increase of the cattle that grows, season after
season, according to the laws of *phusis*, Aristotle describes interest and usury
as an artifice that establishes the appearance of a common measure between
things of entirely different values. Similarly, the term *ousia*, which, in the
philosophical vocabulary, designates being, the substance, the essence or even
phusis, also designates, at the level of economy, the patrimony, wealth, the
most stable and permanent economic substance, generally associated with the
possession of land (*kleros*). This apparent good (*ousia phanera*) is opposed
to the category of the *ousia aphanes*, the inapparent good, which includes
cash, money. In this opposition, money is clearly less valued than land, the
more visible, substantial, permanent, in other words "real" good.
Nonetheless, as the commercial experience grows and the monetary practice
develops, the vocabulary, including the philosophical one, under the influence of certain Sophists, evolves and tends to incorporate money into the
sphere of those things that can be said to be. (This is not simply to say that
the philosophical discourse comes to map itself after the practice of monetary exchange. Far from it. Philosophy – at least that type of philosophy that
begins with Plato, perhaps even with Parmenides, and that came to be designated as metaphysical – will insist on isolating and thematizing a sphere of
being that is absolutely singular, excludes change and division, and is opposed
to the constant becoming of the plurality of beings. The being that is at stake
in such a sphere would seem to escape monetary economy altogether: it is
neither exchangeable nor interchangeable, and is a principle of fixity, not
circularity.) Thus, *ta chremata*, Vernant suggests, designates all things, reality
in general as well as goods in particular, specifically in the form of ready
money. This is confirmed by Aristotle, who writes: "We call goods [*chremata*] all things the value of which is measured by money" (*Nicomachean
Ethics*, IV, 1119 b26)

And into Silence . . .

1 Søren Kierkegaard, *Frygt og Baeven, Samlede Vaerker* (Copenhagen:
   Gyldendal, 1901–6), vol. III, p. 160. English translation by Howard V. Hong
   and Edna V. Hong, *Fear and Trembling, Kierkegaard's Writings* (Princeton:
   Princeton University Press, 1983), vol. VI, edited, with Introduction and
   Notes by Howard V. Hong and Edna V. Hong, p. 114.

2 Ibid., p. 115.

3 Emmanuel Levinas, XXIII Colloque des intellectuels juifs de la langue
   française.

4   Maurice Blanchot, *L'écriture du désastre* (Paris: Gallimard, 1980) p. 107.

5   Edmond Jabès, *La mémoire des mots* (Paris: fourbis, 1990), p. 14.

6   The longest treatment of the passage is to be found in Derrida's "Heidegger's Ear. Philopolemology (*Geschlecht* IV)," trans. John P. Leavey, originally published in *Reading Heidegger*, ed. by John Sallis (Bloomington: Indiana University Press, 1993) and now available in French under the title "L'oreille de Heidegger. Philopolémologie (*Geschlecht* IV)," in *Politiques de l'amitié* (Paris: Galilée, 1994). Other references include Christopher Fynsk's *Heidegger: Thought and Historicity* (Ithaca: Cornell University Press, 1986), pp. 42–4 and Jean-Luc Nancy's "La tentation d'exister" in *"Etre et temps" de Heidegger* ed. Dominique Janicaud (Marseille: Sud, 1989), p. 239.

7   SZ 276/320.

8   "Ackerbau is jetzt motorisierte Ernähungsindustrie, im Wesen das Selbe wie die Fabrikation von Leichen in Gaskammern und Vernichtungslagern, das Selbe wie die Blockade und Aushugerung von Ländern, das Selbe wie die Fabrikation von Wasserstoffbomben." Cited in Wolfgang Schirmacher, *Technik und Gelassenheit* (Freiburg: Alber, 1983), from p. 25 of a typescript of the lecture. The English translation, along with an explanatory footnote, appears in Thomas Sheehan, "Heidegger and the Nazis," *New York Review of Books*, 16 June 1988, pp. 41–2. As Thomas Sheehan rightly points out in his footnote, it is interesting to note that "all but the first five words of the sentence are omitted from the published version of the lecture," "Die Frage nach der Technik," in *Die Technik und die Kehre* (Neske: Pfullingen, 1962), pp. 14–15. English translation by William Lovitt, "The Question Concerning Technology," in *Martin Heidegger. Basic Writings* (New York: Harper and Row, 1977), ed. David Farrell Krell, p. 296. The reference to the gas chambers and the Berlin blockade, as well as to their technological essence does not appear in the published version of "Das Ge-stell." Is it because Heidegger thought these events were no longer relevant, indeed past events of a still ruling essence? Or did he find the comparison inadequate, perhaps too controversial?

9   Letter from Marcuse to Heidegger, dated 28 August 1947. Reproduced and translated by Richard Wolin in *The Heidegger Controversy* (Cambridge: The MIT Press, 1993), ed. Richard Wolin, p. 161.

10   Letter from Heidegger to Marcuse, dated 20 January 1948. Reproduced and translated by Richard Wolin in *The Heidegger Controversy*, op. cit.

11   This is made clear throughout the lecture, and is confirmed in the fact that in the published version of the lecture, the references to the extermination camps and the Berlin blockade are omitted and replaced by other examples (and it is precisely the use of the gas chambers as an "example" that we find most problematic and in need of deconstruction).

12   TK 16/298

13   TK 26/308

14   To locate the "essence" of Nazism in the figure of "evil" and not in the *Gestell* is of course to suspend the possibility of associating technology as the covering up of the withdrawal of being with evil as the "malice of rage," and thus to think against Heidegger himself, who always ran the risk of that association (see in particular the "Letter on Humanism," Wm 189/237). Thus it is also to wrest evil from its Heideggerian delimitation, while reaffirming its ontological and existential nature. For a renewed and sustained discussion of the question of evil in connection with Heidegger, see Jean-Luc Nancy's *L'expérience de la liberté* (Paris: Galilée, 1988), section 12. "Le mal. La décision".

15   Maurice Blanchot, *L'écriture du désastre* (Paris: Gallimard, 1980), p. 80.

Three Concluding Questions

1   Reiner Schürmann, *Les principes de l'anarchie. Heidegger et la question de l'agir* (Paris: Seuil, 1982). English translation by Christine-Marie Gros, in collaboration with the author, *Heidegger on Being and Acting: From Principles to Anarchy* (Bloomington: Indiana University Press, 1987). See Parts II and IV in particular.

2   To my knowledge, Jean-Luc Nancy and Philippe Lacoue-Labarthe are the only ones to have made decisive steps in that direction. See Nancy's *La communauté désœuvrée* (Paris: Christian Bourgois, 1986), Part II, "Le mythe interrompu," as well as Nancy and Lacoue-Labarthe's *Le mythe nazi* (La Tour d'Aigues: Editions de l'aube, 1991), first published in 1980. More recently, John D. Caputo's *Demythologizing Heidegger* (Bloomington: Indiana University Press, 1993) addresses similar issues.

3   G. W. F. Hegel, "Das älteste Systemprogramm des deutschen Idealismus," *Werke* (Frankfurt am Main: Suhrkamp, 1971), Band I, pp. 234–6.

Bibliography

Adorno, Theodor W. *Jargon der Eigentlichkeit. Zur deutschen Ideologie.* Frankfurt: Suhrkamp, 1964.
—— *Musikalische Schriften.* Frankfurt am Main: Suhrkamp, 1976.
Allemann, Beda. *Hölderlin und Heidegger.* Zürich: Atlantis, 1954.
Apollinaire, Guillaume. *Œuvres complètes.* Volume 3. Paris: André Balland et Jacques Lecat, 1966.
Aristotle. *The Basic Works.* Edited by Richard McKeon. New York: Random House, 1941.
Barash, Jeffrey Andrew. *Heidegger et son siècle.* Paris: PUF, 1995.
Bauemler, Alfred. *Nietzsche der Philosoph und Politiker.* Leipzig: Reclam, 1931.
Benjamin, Andrew. "Time and Task: Benjamin and Heidegger Showing the Present." In Andrew Benjamin and Peter Osborne, eds, *Walter Benjamin's Philosophy.* London: Routledge, 1993.
Bernasconi, Robert. "Repetition and Tradition: Heidegger's Destructuring of the Distinction between Essence and Existence in *Basic Problems of Phenomenology.*" In Theodore Kiesel and John Van Buren, eds, *Reading Heidegger from the Start.* Albany: SUNY, 1994.
—— "Heidegger and the Invention of the Western Philosophical Tradition." *The Journal of the British Society for Phenomenology,* volume XXVI, October 1995, pp. 240–54.
—— "On Heidegger's Other Sins of Omission: His Exclusion of Asian Thought from the Origins of Occidental Metaphysics and His Denial of the Possibility of Christian Philosophy." *American Catholic Philosophical Quarterly,* volume LXIX, 2, 1995, pp. 333–50.
Blanchot, Maurice. *L'écriture du désastre.* Paris: Gallimard, 1980.
—— *L'entretien infini.* Paris: Gallimard, 1969.
Bourdieu, Pierre. *L'ontologie politique de Martin Heidegger.* Paris: Editions de Minuit, 1988.
Brainard, Marcus et al. (eds) *The Graduate Faculty Philosophy Journal* (New School for Social Research), vol. 14, no. 2 and vol. 15, no. 1. Published as a double volume in 1991.

Caputo, John D. *Demythologizing Heidegger*. Bloomington: Indiana University Press, 1993.

Dallmayr, Fred. *The Other Heidegger*. Ithaca: Cornell University Press, 1993.

Derrida, Jacques. *De l'esprit. Heidegger et la question*. Paris: Galilée, 1987.

—— *Du droit à la philosophie*. Paris: Galilée, 1990.

—— *Politiques de l'amitié*. Paris: Galilée, 1994.

Deroy, Louis. "Le culte du foyer dans la Grèce mycénienne." *Revue de l'histoire des religions*, 1950.

Farias, Victor. *Heidegger and Nazism*. Edited, with a foreword by Joseph Margolis and Tom Rockmore. Translated by Paul Burrell and Gabriel Ricci. Philadelphia: Temple University Press, 1989.

Faye, Jean-Pierre. *Le Piège. La philosophie heideggerienne et le Nazisme* (Paris: Balland, 1994).

Ferry, Luc, Pesron, Jean-Pierre and Renaut, Alain, eds. *Philosophies de l'université*. Paris: Payot, 1979.

Ferry, Luc and Renaut, Alain. *Heidegger and Modernity*. Translated by Franklin Philip. Chicago: University of Chicago Press.

Fichte, J. G. *Addresses to the German Nation*. Edited by George Armstrong Kelly. New York: Harper and Row, 1968.

—— "Deductive Plan for an Establishment of Higher Learning to be founded in Berlin (Deducierter Plan einer zu Berlin zu errichtenden höheren Lehranstalt)". *Sämtliche Werke*. Volume 8. Berlin: Veit, 1845.

Fóti, Véronique M. *Heidegger and the Poets. Poiésis, Sophia, Techné*. Atlantic Highlands: Humanities Press, 1992.

Franzen, Winfried. "Die Sehnsucht nach Härte und Schwere." In Annemarie Gethmann-Siefert and Otto Pöggeler, eds, *Heidegger und die praktische Philosophie*. Frankfurt: Suhrkamp, 1989.

Froment-Meurice, Marc. *C'est-à-dire. Poétique de Heidegger*. Paris: Galilée, 1996.

Fynsk, Christopher. *Heidegger: Thought and Historicity*. Ithaca: Cornell University Press, 1986.

Gethmann-Siefert, Annemarie and Pöggeler, Otto, eds. *Heidegger und die praktische Philosophie*. Frankfurt: Suhrkamp, 1989.

Habermas, Jünger. "Work and Weltanschaaung: The Heidegger Controversy from a German Perspective," trans. John McCumber. *Critical Inquiry*, 15, Winter 1988, pp. 431–56.

Hegel, G. W. F. "Das älteste Systemprogramm des deutschen Idealismus". *Werke*. Volume 1. Frankfurt: Suhrkamp, 1971.

—— *Über den Vortrag der Philosophie auf Universitäten. Werke*. Volume 4. Frankfurt: Suhrkamp, 1971.

Heidegger, Martin–Kästner, Erhart. *Briefwechsel*. Frankfurt: Insel Verlag.

"Heidegger, la philosophie, et le Nazisme." (Contains texts by Pierre Aubenque, Henri Crétella, Michel Deguy, François Fédier, Gérard Granel, Stéphane Moses, and Alain Renaut.) *Le Débat* 48, 1988, pp. 113–76.

Hölderlin, Friedrich. *Essays and Letters on Theory*. Translated and edited by Thomas Pfau. Albany: SUNY Press, 1988.

—— *Poems and Fragments*. Translated and edited by Michael Hamburger. London: Anvil Press, 1994.

—— *Sämtliche Werke*. Grosse Stuttgarter Ausgabe. Edited by Friedrich Beissner, followed by Adolf Beck. 15 volumes. Stuttgart: Verlag W. Kohlhammer, 1946–57.

Humboldt von, W. "Über die innere und äußere Organisation der höheren wissenschaftlichen Anstalten in Berlin (1810)". *Schriften* München: Wilhem Goldmann Verlag, 1964, pp. 300–9.

Jabès, Edmond. *La mémoire des mots*. Paris: fourbis, 1990.

Janicaud, Dominique. *L'ombre de cette pensée: Heidegger et la question politique*. Grenoble: Jérôme Millon, 1990.

Jonas, Hans. "Heidegger's Resoluteness and Resolve." In Günther Neske and Emil Kettering, eds, *Martin Heidegger and National Socialism. Questions and Answers*. Translated by Lisa Harries. New York: Paragon House, 1990.

Jünger, Ernst. *Der Arbeiter: Herrschaft und Gestalt. Werke*. Volume 6. *Essays II*. Stuttgart: Ernst Klett Verlag, 1960.

—— *The Storm of Steel* (In Stahlgewittern). Translated by Basil Creighton. London: Chatto & Windus, 1929.

—— "Die totale Mobilmachung." *Werke*. Volume 5. *Essays I*. Stuttgart: Ernst Klett Verlag, 1960.

Kant, Immanuel. *Der Streit der Facultäten. Werke*. Volume 7. Berlin: Walter de Gruyter, 1968.

—— *Political Writings*. Ithaca: Cornell University Press, 1991.

Kierkegaard, Søren. *Fear and Trembling*. Translated by Howard V. Hong and Edna H. Hong. Princeton: Princeton University Press, 1983.

Krell, David Farrell. *Daimon Life. Heidegger and Life-Philosophy*. Bloomington: Indiana University Press, 1992.

Lacoue-Labarthe, Philippe. *La fiction du politique*. Paris: Christian Bourgois éditeur, 1987.

—— "La transcendance finie/t dans la politique" and "Poétique et politique." *L'imitation des Modernes*. Paris: Galilée, 1986.

—— and Nancy, Jean-Luc. *Le mythe nazi*. La Tour d'Aigues: Editions de l'aube, 1991.

Löwith, Karl. *Heidegger: Denker in dürftiger Zeit. Sämtliche Schriften*. Volume 8. Stuttgart: J. B. Metzler, 1984.

—— "Les implications politiques de la philosophie de l'existence chez Heidegger." *Les Temps Modernes*, volume 2, 1946, pp. 346–60.

—— *Mein Leben in Deutschland vor und nach 1933*. New York: Columbia University Press, 1984.

Mallarmé, Stéphane. *Œuvres complètes*. Volume 1. Paris: Flammarion, 1983.

Müller, Max. "A Philosopher and Politics: A Conversation." In Günther Neske and Emil Kettering, eds, *Martin Heidegger and National Socialism. Questions and Answers*. Translated by Lisa Harries. New York: Paragon House, 1990.

Nancy, Jean-Luc. *La communauté désœuvrée*. Paris: Christian Bourgois, 1986.

—— *L'expérience de la liberté*. Paris: Galilée, 1988.

—— "La tentation d'exister." In Dominique Janicaud, ed., *"Etre et temps" de Heidegger*. Marseille: Sud, 1989.

Neske, Günther and Kettering, Emil, eds. *Martin Heidegger and National Socialism. Questions and Answers*. Translated by Lisa Harries. New York: Paragon House, 1990.

Ott, Hugo. *Martin Heidegger: Unterwegs zu seiner Biographie*. Frankfurt: Campus, 1988.

Plato. *The Collected Dialogues*. Edited by Edith Hamilton and Huntington Cairns. Princeton: Princeton University Press, 1963.

Pöggeler, Otto. "Heideggers politisches Selbstverständnis." In Annemarie Gethmann-Siefert and Otto Pöggeler, eds, *Heidegger und die praktische Philosophie*. Frankfurt: Suhrkamp, 1988.

Ricœur, Paul. *Temps et récit*. Paris: Editions du Seuil, 1985.

Rockmore, Tom. *On Heidegger's Nazism and Philosophy* (Berkeley: University of California Press, 1992).

Sallis, John. *Being and Logos. The Way of Platonic Dialogue*. Atlantic Highlands: Humanities Press, 1975.

Scheler, Max. *Der Formalismus in der Ethik und die materiale Wertethik*. Bern: Franke, 1963.

Schelling, W. J. *Werke*. Band III. Edited by Manfred Schröter. München: Beck, 1927.

Schirmacher, Wolfgang. *Technik und Gelassenheit*. Freiburg: Alber, 1983.

Schleiermacher, F. "Occasional Thoughts on Universities in the German Sense (Gelegentliche Gedanken über Universitäten in deutschem Sinn)". *Sämtliche Werke*. Volume 1.

Schürmann, Reiner. *Les principes de l'anarchie: Heidegger et la question de l'agir*. Paris: Editions du Seuil, 1982.

Schwann, Alexander. *Politische Philosophie im Denken Martin Heideggers*. Köln/Opladen: Westdeutscher Verlag, 1965.

Sheehan, Thomas. "Heidegger and the Nazis." *New York Review of Books*, June 16, 1988, pp. 38–47.

Sluga, Hans. *Heidegger's Crisis. Philosophy and Politics in Nazi Germany*. Cambridge: Harvard University Press, 1993.

Sophocles. *Antigone*. Translated by David Grene. In David Grene and Richmond Lattimore, eds, *Greek Tragedies*. Volume 1. Chicago: Chicago University Press, 1991.

Spanos, William V. *Heidegger and Criticism. Retrieving the Cultural Politics of Destruction*. (Minneapolis: The University of Minnesota Press, 1993.

Spengler, Oswald. *Der Mensch und die Technik*. München: C. H. Beck'sche Verlag, 1931.

—— *Jahre der Entscheidung*. München: Deutscher Taschenbuch Verlag, 1961.

—— *Der Untergang des Abendlandes*. München: Beck, 1920.

Taminaux, Jacques. *Le théâtre des philosophes*. Grenoble: Jérôme Millon, 1995.

Tertulian, Nicolas. "Histoire de l'être et révolution politique," *Les Temps Modernes*, 523, February 1990, pp. 109–36.

Tönnies, Ferdinand. *Gemeinschaft und Gesellschaft. Grundbegriffe der reinen Psychologie*. Darmstadt: Wissenschaftliche Buchgesellschaft, 1963.

Vernant, Jean-Pierre. *Mythe et pensée chez les Grecs*. Paris: Maspero, 1974.

Weber, Max. *Wirtschaft und Gesellschaft. Grundrisse der verstehenden Soziologie*. Tübingen: J. C. B. Mohr (Paul Siebeck), 1956.

Wolin, Richard, ed. *The Heidegger Controversy*. Cambridge: The MIT Press, 1993.

—— *The Politics of Being: The Political Thought of Martin Heidegger* (New York: Columbia University Press, 1990).

Zimmerman, Michael. *Heidegger's Confrontation with Modernity. Technology, Politics, Art*. Bloomington: Indiana University Press, 1990.

Index

198   Index